I'm a Catholic in the Modern World, What Do I Do After My Confirmation?

Practical Spiritual Tools to Bring You Closer to Jesus of Nazareth, The Christ Consciousness and The Holy Trinity for a Fulfilling, Meaningful, and Joyous Life!

"Very truly I tell you, whoever believes in me will do the works I have been doing, and they will do even greater things than these, because I am going to the Father". - John 14:12
Holy Bible, New International Version (NIV)

Rev. ORESTE J. DAVERSA
Interfaith Minister

PUBLISHER'S NOTE

This book is designed to provide accurate and authoritative information. information in regard to the subject matter covered. It is sold with the understanding that neither the author nor publisher is engaged in rendering psychological, legal, or other professional service. If psychological, legal, professional advice or other expert assistance is required, the services of a professional in that field should be sought. The principles and concepts presented in this book are the opinions of the author and are based on his interpretations of the aforementioned principles. Neither the author nor publisher is liable or responsible to any person or entity for any errors contained on this book, or website, or for any special, incidental, or consequential damage caused or alleged to be caused directly or indirectly by the information contained on this book or website. Any application of the techniques, ideas, and suggestions in this book is at the reader's sole discretion and risk.

No part of this publication may be reproduced, redistributed, taught, stored in a retrieval system, or transmitted, in any form, or by any means, electronic, mechanical, photocopy, recording, or otherwise, without the prior written permission of the publisher.

Disclosure Statement: This book contains both AI-assisted and AI-generated content. The AI-assisted content was developed using tools to aid in brainstorming, editing, and refining the text, while the AI-generated content includes sections of the book created entirely by artificial intelligence. All AI-generated content has been reviewed and edited to ensure it meets the high standards of quality and originality.

FIRST EDITION

ISBN: 978-1-952294-45-7

Library of Congress Control Number: 2024919714

Published by: Cutting Edge Technology Publishing

Copyright © Oreste J. D'Aversa, 2024. All rights reserved.

TABLE OF CONTENTS

About the Author	7
Disclaimer	11
Dedication	13
Preface	15
Introduction	23

Part I: Basic Spiritual Tools

Chapter 01: Gifts from GOD – Free Will, Discernment, Wisdom	27
Chapter 02: Prayer and Meditation	37
Chapter 03: Communing with Nature	47
Chapter 04: Your Spiritual Companions – Guardian Angels, Spirit Guides, and Archangels	57
Chapter 05: Sacred Catholic Texts	67
Chapter 06: Sacred Music	77
Chapter 07: Spiritual Journaling	87
Chapter 08: The Human Energy Field	95
Chapter 09: Energy Healing Basics and The Chakras	103

Part II: Jesus the Boy, the Man, the Messiah

Chapter 10: The Early Years of Jesus — 111

Chapter 11: The Lost Years of Jesus — 119

Chapter 12: Books about Jesus — 127

Part III: Advanced Teachings of Jesus

Chapter 13: Becoming a Disciple of Jesus the Christ — 137

Chapter 14: Jesus the Mystic and Mystical Teacher — 145

Chapter 15: Jesus the Healer and You the Healer — 155

Chapter 16: Jesus and the Teachings of "A Course in Miracles" — 165

Part IV: Foundations of the Catholic Faith

Chapter 17: The Holy Trinity – GOD, Jesus and The Holy Spirit — 175

Chapter 18: The Core Beliefs of Catholicism — 185

Chapter 19: Understanding the Sacraments — 195

Chapter 20: The Nicene Creed – the Profession of Faith — 205

Chapter 21: Core Prayers of Catholic Devotional Practice — 215

Chapter 22: The Liturgical Calendar — 225

Part V: Being Catholic is More than Going to Church

Chapter 23: What Does it Mean to Be Catholic? 235

Chapter 24: Learning, Reading and Contemplating Sacred Texts (The Holy Bible, The New Testament, etc.) 245

Chapter 25: Going to Mass 255

Chapter 26: Volunteering at Church 265

Chapter 27: Fellowship with Others – Locally, Nationally, Worldwide 275

Chapter 28: Service to Others – Elderly, Single Parents, Children, etc. 285

Chapter 29: Church Ministries – Prayer Ministry, Sick Ministry, Youth Ministry, Food Pantry, etc. 295

Part VI: Suggestions for Growth in The Catholic Faith

Chapter 30: Catholic Classes, Workshops and Seminars 305

Chapter 31: Catholic Spiritual Direction and Mentoring 317

Chapter 32: Catholic Church Elders 329

Chapter 33: Catholicism and The Future 341

Conclusion 351

Footnotes 355

Bibliography	363
Glossary of Terms	383
Prayers and Other Resources	395
Suggestion Reading List	411

About The Author

Reverend Oreste J. DAversa (O-rest-ee DA-versa),
is an Inter-Faith (All-Faiths) Minister
(www.GODLovesYouAndMe.org)
ordained by *The New Seminary* in New York City, New York.
He is an Interfaith Minister, a spiritual guide who honors the diverse tapestry of world religions and spiritual traditions.
He has studied the following world religions:
Buddhism, Christianity, Confucianism, Hinduism, Islam, Jainism, Judaism, Shinto, Sikhism, Taoism and Zoroastrianism.as well as the spiritual traditions of indigenous people such as the Native Americans, African Spiritual Traditions and World-wide Shamanism.
He fosters understanding and unity among faith communities, offering inclusive ceremonies, counseling, and guidance rooted in universal values of love, compassion, and peace.
He is also a **Certified Professional Coach** (CPC)
as a Life Coach, Career/Job Search Coach, and College Major Coach
(www.CollegeMajorCoaching.com).
He is the owner of Metropolitan Small Business Coaching LLC
(www.MetroSmallBusinessCoaching.com)
as a Business Coach, Consultant, and Trainer.
He appears on podcasts, radio, and television discussing his expertise in personal growth and business-related subjects.

He is the author of the following books:

- *Hey World! Why do I Feel All Alone in a Planet Full of People*

- *Gen STOP IT! Uniting Generations*

- *UNPLUGGED! A Practical Guide to Managing Teenage Stress in the Digital Age*

- *AI, Robots and Humans: Our Servants or Masters?*

- *Life Beyond the Pandemic: A Practical New Journey Handbook*

- *The Resume and Cover Letter Writing Toolkit for the Successful Job Seeker*

- *Power Interviewing: Proven Job Interview Techniques That Get You Results!*

- *The Step-by-Step Business Networking Kit: The Ultimate Business Networking System that Delivers Superior Results!*

- *SELL More Technology NOW!*

- *Selling for Non-Selling Professionals©*

- *Baby Boomer Entrepreneur: Implementing the Boomer Business Success System ®*

- *Discovering Your Life Purpose: The Journey Within*

- *The Seven Simple Principles of Prosperity: Practical Exercises to Achieve a Rich, Happy and Joyous Life*

- *I Didn't Get a Chance to Say Good-bye ... Now What Can I Do?*

- *Write Your Own Funeral Service*

- *Healing the Holes in My Soul!: How I Saved My Own Life, Became Whole to Lead a Happy, Fulfilling and Joyous Life!*

THIS

PAGE

INTENTIONALLY

LEFT

BLANK

DISCLAIMERS

As the author of this book I would like to make the following disclaimers:

1. I am not or have ever been a member of The Catholic Church clergy (priesthood), an employee of or have any type of professional connection or affiliation directly with The Catholic Church other than being a member of The Catholic Church laity.

2. This book is designed to provide accurate and authoritative information. information in regard to the subject matter covered. It is sold with the understanding that neither the author nor publisher is engaged in rendering religious, medical, psychological, legal, or other professional service. If religious, medical, psychological, legal, professional advice or other expert assistance is required, the services of a professional in that field should be sought. The principles and concepts presented in this book are the opinions of the author and are based on his interpretations of the aforementioned principles. Neither the author nor publisher is liable or responsible to any person or entity for any errors contained on this book, or website, or for any special, incidental, or consequential damage caused or alleged to be caused directly or indirectly by the information contained on this book or website. Any application of the techniques, ideas, and suggestions in this book is at the reader's sole discretion and risk.

THIS

PAGE

INTENTIONALLY

LEFT

BLANK

DEDICATIONS

This book is dedicated to the man known to the world by many names: Jesus, Jesus Christ, Jesus the Christ, Jesus of Nazareth, Jesus Son of Joseph, Yeshua (Jesus in Hebrew) and Ascend Master Jesus.

To The Creator of all things known and unknown to humankind, GOD the Father/GOD the Mother, whose love transcends all space and time for us, GOD's beloved children.

To the supernatural, mystical and the instrument of GOD, known as The Holy Spirit that sends love, guidance and strength to all that request it.

To all the readers of this book, may you get know Jesus the Christ better, understand who he was and is, even to this day, and understand that his teachings, guidance and love have and will withstand the test of time. May you develop a personal relationship with Jesus that transforms your life in a positive, loving and beneficial manner. Know that you are never alone as long as you have Jesus in your life.

THIS PAGE INTENTIONALLY LEFT BLANK

PREFACE

Part One

Being a member of the catholic faith, though not a church going member, nor following The Liturgical Calendar, or active practicing catholic, I have received the Sacraments of: **Baptism**, **Holy Communion** and have been **Confirmed** after completing the Catholic Catechism that was a requirement for receiving Confirmation from The Catholic Church. I attend Mass on occasion, be it in person or on television, as well as pray in churches when I am moved to do so. I continue to enjoy the holiness, sacredness, and comfort that being in a church brings me, especially being surrounded by the statues of Jesus, the Saints, Archangels and the Angels.

As for my personal stance of The Catholic Church as I have told and continue to tell people in my travels, there are two parts to the modern day catholic church – One part is the church which consists of an organization of people (predominately men) and the other part of the church that are the teachings of Jesus the Christ.

Unfortunately, many times when people get "upset" with and leave the church (by voting with their feet) they throw "the baby out with bath water" meaning they walk away from both the organization of the church and the teachings of Jesus.

While the organization of the church has its issues, dysfunctions and interpersonal transgressions. The teachings of Jesus have been, are and always will be consistent and withstand the test of time in a positive manner.

As the author of this book, I am not here to pass judgment on the church – being in the manner it is being managed, the behavior of its members or the manner it deals with the issues of modern day society – all of which are the jurisdiction of GOD Almighty (Judge not, that ye be not judged. Mathew 7:1). The facts speak for themselves, over the past 25 years, based on surveys and studies, it is estimated that around 20 million people have left the Catholic Church in the United States alone during this period. This estimation comes from the fact that about 52% of U.S. adults who were raised Catholic have left the church at some point, with 41% not returning to the faith at all **((Pew Research Center) (Smithsonian Magazine))**. And more people continue to leave the catholic church daily…

It is the sincere hope of the author that this book offers practical tools to the followers, believers and disciples of Jesus the Christ and that The Catholic Church consider incorporating these tools in its current teachings to the modern day catholic laity so that the catholic church can be seen as a contemporary, modern day, and life-long resource to all people of the catholic faith that want to follow Jesus the Christ.

With the above said, this book and the information contained herein has been written to be used *"in addition to and not instead of"* the current teachings of the catholic church.

In loving service to the beloved *The Holy Trinity* – (Mother/Father GOD, Jesus the Christ and The Holy Spirit)
Rev. Oreste J. D'Aversa – Interfaith (All Faiths) Minister

Part Two

Being born into an immigrant Italian family **_NOT_** going to catholic church was not an option in my family life. From the time I was enrolled into catholic school at the age of 5, to the age of 18, I went to church, rain or shine, every Sunday morning. Though I was only enrolled in catholic school for 3 years in New York City then moving to the suburbs of Long island where going to catholic was much more sizeable financial investment, being a "Good Catholic" was engraved in my DNA. Though I was born in the United States, I was still Italian and the words "Italian" and "Church" were part of the same sentence in my world. I received the Sacrament of Baptism after birth, the Sacrament of Holy Communion at the age of 7 and the Sacrament of Confirmation at age 13, completing my initiation into The Catholic Church.

As the years went by I attended church until the age of 18. After 18 I started to attend church only at Christmas and Easter. Now I occasionally watch The Daily Mass on television and go to church when I want to be with the solace of my thoughts, get away from the modern hustle and bustle of modern day life, to pray and enjoy the sacred energy that a catholic church provides.

To this day, having never been taught by the church, still do not know, understand or truly appreciate all of the "equipment" (for lack of a better word) used on the altar. From, what is the purpose of the candles and their placements, the Communal Wafers, to the Monstrance (a friend told me and taught me that word), to the Tabernacle. If someone were to ask me the "why" of all of the sacred objects, rituals and tools of Celebrating Mass I am hard pressed to give them an intelligent, faith-based answer. And why is called "Celebrating Mass"? I never have witnessed a party, dancing or catering after a church service.

Let me not digress…

As the years past and I was in my twenties, I required surgery which necessitated full anesthesia. As most people are aware, full anesthesia, is a medical procedure that may be risky (as all medical procedures are) and rarely people do not come out of this procedure and may die. I went to my local parish priest to request and receive a blessing before my surgery only to be asked when the last time was I attended Confession (for people who are not of the catholic faith – Confession, also known as the Sacrament of Reconciliation or Penance, is a sacrament in which a penitent confesses their sins to a priest, expresses contrition, and receives absolution.)

I told him it was about 7 years ago. He informed me that I have been "away from the church too long" and he was **NOT** going to give me a blessing before my surgery. Needless to say, in my mind, I was shocked! How can a priest deny a person requesting a blessing? I walked away , hurt, dejected and sad. I thought to myself, a priest would give a convicted murderer on death row a blessing but not a member of the catholic faith in their own parish before an medical procedure.

SIDE BAR: Let a priest not give me or any other person in my presence a requested blessing, I'll make the movie *"The Exorcist"* look like a comedy! How dare a priest, a man supposedly representing GOD on earth (hence why they are called Father) and The Catholic Church, deny one of GOD's children a blessing? Would Jesus deny a blessing to any person that would ask him?

As time continued to march on, I had more questions than The Catholic Church had answers. So I decided to learn for myself who Jesus the Christ really was/is, what is the real meaning being a follower of Jesus and how it all works in my life.

My religious and spiritual journey started in the late 1990's as I started learning about the "True Jesus". Back then the internet was not as prevalent or powerful as in current times so all my learning came from books, classes and television documentaries.

One thing led to another and I enrolled in a two year seminary program administered by *The New Seminary* in New York City where I learned about all of the major religions of the world as well as my own religion of Catholicism. Once I completed the seminary program I was ordained as an Interfaith (All-Faiths Minister) in a spectator ceremony in The Cathedral of Saint John the Divine in New York City. I learned about the life of Jesus the Christ in a manner that the catholic faith does not make mention. I have also learned about and have worked with other spiritual traditions like Shamanism in the years to follow.

SIDE BAR: For government reporting purposes I was born a catholic and on my death certificate it will say a died a catholic, but in between I am a "visiting catholic".

This book represents my continued learning about the man I call Jesus the Christ, who has brought with him the "Christ Consciousness" from the heavens to be shared with all of humankind to experience heaven on earth.

Whether he is called Jesus, Jesus Christ, Jesus the Christ, Jesus of Nazareth, Jesus Son of Joseph, Ascended Master Jesus or Yeshua (his Hebrew name), his teaching, healings and presence are just as important today as it was over 2,000 years ago and his is needed now more than ever in our world.

I have been and continue to be blessed by his teachings, presence and his love in my life. I do my best, on a daily basis, to emulate the man he is and the man I strive to become.

Rev. Oreste J. D'Aversa, Interfaith Minister
www.GODLovesYouAndMe.org

Introduction

In the journey of faith, Confirmation is a significant milestone—a sacred moment where you receive the gifts of The Holy Spirit and are fully initiated into the Catholic Church. It's a powerful experience, a rite of passage that marks the transition from spiritual adolescence to a more mature, adult faith. Yet, for many, the question arises: What do I do after my Confirmation? How do I continue to grow in my relationship with GOD, Jesus, and The Holy Spirit? How do I live out the fullness of my Catholic faith in a world that is increasingly complex, complicated and often challenging to navigate spiritually?

This book is designed to be your guide in answering these questions. Whether you are newly Confirmed catholic or have been living out your Catholic faith for years, the goal here is to offer practical, spiritual tools that will help you deepen your connection with Jesus of Nazareth, The Christ Consciousness, and The Holy Trinity. The path to a fulfilling, meaningful, and joyous life is not always straightforward, but with the right tools and guidance, it can be navigated with grace and purpose.

Understanding the Importance of Spiritual Tools

Before we dive into the various practices and teachings that will be explored in this book, it's important to understand the concept of spiritual tools. Just as a carpenter needs the right instruments to build a sturdy house, a Catholic needs the appropriate spiritual tools to build a strong and resilient faith. These tools are not physical objects but practices, disciplines, and beliefs that shape and strengthen your spiritual life. They include prayer, meditation, the sacraments, study of sacred texts, and the cultivation of virtues like love, patience, and humility.

Spiritual tools are essential because they help you stay connected to GOD in your daily life. In the hustle and bustle of modern living, it's easy to lose sight of your spiritual goals and become overwhelmed by worldly concerns. The tools provided in this book are designed to help you maintain that connection, to ground yourself in your faith, and to grow in your relationship with the Divine.

The Journey Beyond Confirmation

Confirmation is not an end, but a beginning - a doorway to a deeper and more personal relationship with GOD. After Confirmation, you are called to actively participate in the life of the Church, to engage with your community, and to be a witness of Christ's love in the world. This can be both exhilarating and daunting. The responsibilities of being a Confirmed Catholic can feel overwhelming, especially in a world that often seems indifferent or even hostile to religious beliefs.

This book will guide you through the process of integrating your faith into every aspect of your life. It's about moving from simply being a member of the Church to becoming a true disciple of Christ. This involves not just understanding the teachings of the Church but living them out in your everyday actions and decisions. It's about embodying the love, compassion, and mercy of Jesus in all that you do.

Embracing the Christ Consciousness

One of the central themes of this book is the idea of the Christ Consciousness - a term that refers to the awareness of the divine presence within you and within all of creation. This concept goes beyond the historical person of Jesus of Nazareth and speaks to the universal truth that Jesus taught that <u>we are all connected to GOD</u> and to each other through love. The Christ Consciousness is about awakening to this truth and allowing it to guide your thoughts, words, and actions.

As Catholics, we are called to be more than just followers of Christ; we are called to embody Christ's love in the world. This means cultivating a deep inner awareness of GOD's presence in your life and striving to reflect that presence in all that you do. The spiritual tools in this book are designed to help you cultivate this awareness and live in alignment with the Christ Consciousness.

Navigating the Challenges of Modern Life

Living as a Catholic in the modern world comes with its own set of challenges. We are constantly bombarded with messages that are contrary to our faith, and it can be difficult to stay grounded in our beliefs. The fast pace of life, the pressure to conform to secular standards, and the distractions of technology can all pull us away from our spiritual path.

This book acknowledges these challenges and offers practical solutions for overcoming them. Whether it's finding time for prayer in a busy schedule, dealing with doubts and questions about your faith, or staying true to your values in a world that often promotes the opposite, you will find guidance and support here.

A Roadmap for Spiritual Growth

The chapters that follow will provide you with a roadmap for spiritual growth. Each chapter will introduce a specific spiritual tool or concept, explain its importance in the Catholic tradition, and offer practical advice on how to incorporate it into your daily life. You will learn how to deepen your prayer life, engage with sacred texts, understand the mysteries of the sacraments, and much more.

As you embark on this journey, remember that spiritual growth is a lifelong process. There will be times of great joy and times of struggle, but with perseverance and the right spiritual tools, you can build a faith that is strong, resilient, and deeply fulfilling.

Welcome to the journey. Let us begin…

Chapter 01: Gifts from GOD – Free Will, Discernment, Wisdom

The Divine Gifts That Guide Our Spiritual Journey

The essence of this chapter revolves around three foundational gifts from GOD: Free Will, Discernment, and Wisdom. These gifts are not merely abstract concepts but are vital spiritual tools that enable Catholics to navigate the complexities of modern life while staying true to their faith. In the journey of spiritual growth, understanding and utilizing these gifts is crucial for a fulfilling and meaningful life. They form the bedrock upon which we build our relationship with GOD, Jesus, and The Holy Spirit, guiding us in making decisions that align with the divine will and leading us closer to The Christ Consciousness.

Theological Insights

Free Will: A Divine Endowment

Free Will is a profound gift from GOD that allows us to choose our paths in life. It is the ability to make choices that are not predetermined by external forces, giving us the power to shape our destiny in accordance with GOD's will or, conversely, to turn away from it. Theologically, free will is closely linked to the concept of human dignity, as it reflects the image of GOD in which we are created (Genesis 1:27) . This divine endowment is what makes love, morality, and spiritual growth possible, as these can only occur when actions are freely chosen.

Free will, however, comes with responsibility. The choices we make can either lead us closer to GOD or away from Him. As the Catechism of the Catholic Church states, "Freedom makes man responsible for his acts to the extent that they are voluntary"[1]. Therefore, understanding and exercising our free will in a way that aligns with divine teachings is essential for spiritual growth.

Discernment: The Spiritual Compass

Discernment is the spiritual tool that helps us make decisions aligned with GOD's will. It is the process of distinguishing between good and evil, right and wrong, and ultimately, discerning the path that leads us closer to GOD. In the New Testament, St. Paul emphasizes the importance of discernment when he advises the Thessalonians to "test everything; hold fast what is good" (1 Thessalonians 5:21)[2].

In the context of modern Catholic life, discernment involves more than just moral decision-making. It encompasses the ability to recognize the movements of The Holy Spirit within our lives and to respond accordingly. This requires a deep connection with GOD, cultivated through prayer, meditation, and study of the scriptures. As Pope Francis has said, "Discernment is a gift of GOD, which must be sought and cultivated in prayer"[3]. In a world filled with distractions and conflicting values, discernment helps Catholics stay true to their faith and make decisions that reflect the teachings of Christ.

Wisdom: The Fruit of Spiritual Maturity

Wisdom is the gift that allows us to see the world through GOD's eyes. It is the ability to judge correctly and to follow the best course of action, based on knowledge and understanding of GOD's principles. In the Bible, wisdom is often personified and praised as a divine attribute. Proverbs 2:6 tells us, "For the Lord gives wisdom; from his mouth come knowledge and understanding"[4].

Wisdom is not merely intellectual knowledge but a deep, intuitive understanding of GOD's will. It enables us to live in harmony with GOD's plan, making choices that lead to peace, joy, and fulfillment. In contemporary terms, wisdom is what helps Catholics navigate the complexities of modern life, balancing spiritual commitments with secular responsibilities. It is through wisdom that we learn to apply the teachings of Christ in our everyday lives, making decisions that are not only beneficial to ourselves but also to the broader community.

Application in Modern Life

Integrating Spiritual Gifts into Daily Living

In today's fast-paced world, it can be challenging to live out the spiritual gifts of free will, discernment, and wisdom. However, these gifts are not meant to be confined to Sunday Mass or moments of quiet reflection; they are tools to be used in every aspect of our lives. Whether it's making decisions at work, managing relationships, or raising a family, these gifts are essential for living a life that is both spiritually fulfilling and practically successful.

For instance, in the workplace, free will allows us to choose ethical actions even when they may not be the easiest or most profitable. Discernment helps us navigate complex moral dilemmas, such as balancing the demands of a job with the need to maintain personal integrity and fairness. Wisdom, meanwhile, guides us in making decisions that consider not only immediate outcomes but also long-term impacts on ourselves, others, and our relationship with GOD.

In personal relationships, these gifts help us to love more deeply and authentically. Free will enables us to choose love and forgiveness over anger and resentment. Discernment allows us to understand the needs and motivations of others, fostering empathy and compassion. Wisdom helps us to maintain healthy boundaries and to cultivate relationships that are nurturing and supportive.

Real-Life Example: Balancing Career and Faith

Consider the example of Maria, a Catholic professional working in a demanding corporate environment. Maria faces the daily challenge of balancing her career ambitions with her commitment to her faith. By applying the spiritual gifts of free will, discernment, and wisdom, she navigates her workplace with integrity and grace. When faced with a promotion that would require her to compromise her values, Maria uses discernment to weigh the pros and cons, ultimately deciding to decline the offer in favor of a role that aligns better with her spiritual principles. Her choice, guided by wisdom, leads not only to personal fulfillment but also earns her the respect of her colleagues, who admire her integrity.

Practical Spiritual Tools

Prayer for Discernment

One practical tool for cultivating discernment is the "Prayer for Discernment." This prayer, which can be said daily, asks for GOD's guidance in making decisions:

> "Lord, help me to discern your will in my life. Grant me the wisdom to choose what is right, the courage to follow your path, and the grace to trust in your plan for me. Amen."

This prayer can be incorporated into your morning routine, setting the tone for a day guided by GOD's wisdom and grace.

Meditation on the Gifts of The Holy Spirit

Another tool is a guided meditation focused on the Gifts of The Holy Spirit, particularly wisdom and discernment. Begin by finding a quiet space where you won't be disturbed. Close your eyes and take several deep breaths, centering yourself in the present moment. Visualize The Holy Spirit filling you with light, bringing clarity to your mind and peace to your heart. As you meditate, reflect on the decisions you need to make and ask

The Holy Spirit to guide you towards choices that align with GOD's will.

Journaling for Wisdom

Journaling is a powerful practice for cultivating wisdom. Set aside time each day to write about your experiences, decisions, and the outcomes of those decisions. Reflect on how you used your free will, how discernment played a role, and what wisdom you gained from the experience. Over time, this practice will help you to see patterns in your decision-making process and to grow in spiritual maturity.

The gifts of Free Will, Discernment, and Wisdom are essential tools for navigating the journey of faith. By understanding and applying these gifts in our daily lives, we can live in closer alignment with GOD's will and grow in our relationship with Him. These gifts not only help us make better decisions but also lead us to a life that is more fulfilling, meaningful, and joyous—a life that reflects the love and teachings of Jesus Christ.

Exercise: Applying Free Will, Discernment, and Wisdom in Daily Life

Objective: To deepen the reader's understanding and practical application of the gifts of Free Will, Discernment, and Wisdom in their daily life.

Instructions:

Step 1: Reflective Journaling (15-20 minutes)

- **Objective:** Identify and reflect on a recent decision or challenge you faced.
- **Action:**
    - ✓ Choose a situation from the past week where you had to make a decision. It could be related to work, relationships, or a personal goal.
    - ✓ In your journal, describe the situation in detail. What were the options available to you? How did you feel about each option?
    - ✓ Reflect on how you used your free will in this situation. Were you aware of making a choice, or did you act out of habit or pressure?

Step 2: Discernment Practice (10-15 minutes)

- **Objective:** Strengthen your ability to discern GOD's will in decision-making.
- **Action:**
    - ✓ Find a quiet space where you can meditate or pray without interruption.
    - ✓ Bring to mind a current decision you need to make. Close your eyes and take a few deep breaths to center yourself.

- ✓ Ask GOD for guidance. You might say, *"Lord, help me to see this situation through your eyes. Grant me the wisdom to choose the path that aligns with your will."*
- ✓ Spend a few minutes in silence, allowing any thoughts, feelings, or insights to arise. Note them down afterward in your journal.

Step 3: Wisdom Application (Daily Practice)

- **Objective:** Integrate wisdom into your daily decisions.
- **Action:**
  - ✓ Each morning, set an intention to apply wisdom in your decisions throughout the day.
  - ✓ At the end of the day, reflect on how you applied wisdom. Did you consider long-term consequences? Did you seek a balance between your own needs and those of others?
  - ✓ Write down one area where you felt you applied wisdom well and one area where you could improve. Make a note of any adjustments you would like to make moving forward.

Step 4: Group Discussion or Personal Reflection (Optional)

- **Objective:** Share and learn from others or deepen personal insights.
- **Action:**
  - ✓ If you have a spiritual mentor or are part of a Catholic study group, discuss your experiences with them. How did they approach similar situations?
  - ✓ Alternatively, you can reflect on your own: What have you learned about your use of Free Will, Discernment, and Wisdom? How can you continue to grow in these areas?

Outcome: By completing this exercise, you will gain practical experience in applying the gifts of Free Will, Discernment, and Wisdom to real-life situations. This will help you to make decisions that are more aligned with GOD's will, leading to a more fulfilling and spiritually enriched life.

NOTES:

Chapter 02: Prayer and Meditation

The Power of Connection with the Divine

Prayer and Meditation are two fundamental practices that connect us with GOD, deepen our faith, and anchor us in the spiritual life. In this chapter, we explore how these practices serve as vital spiritual tools that not only nurture our relationship with GOD but also guide us through the complexities of modern life. By understanding the theological foundations of prayer and meditation, and integrating these practices into our daily routines, we can achieve a more profound sense of peace, purpose, and spiritual fulfillment.

Theological Insights

The Nature of Prayer: A Divine Conversation

Prayer is often described as a conversation with GOD, a way for believers to communicate their thoughts, desires, and needs to the Divine. Theologically, prayer is more than just speaking to GOD; it is a sacred act that opens the heart to the presence of The Holy Spirit, allowing us to align our will with GOD's will. In the New Testament, Jesus teaches the importance of prayer, saying, "But when you pray, go into your room, close the door and pray to your Father, who is unseen. Then your Father, who sees what is done in secret, will reward you" (Matthew 6:6)[1].

Prayer is not just a ritualistic activity; it is an intimate encounter with GOD that brings us closer to the Christ Consciousness -

the awareness of GOD's love and presence within us. Through prayer, we acknowledge our dependence on GOD and open ourselves to His guidance and grace. This understanding of prayer as a divine conversation underscores its importance in the life of every Catholic, serving as both a source of strength and a means of maintaining a personal relationship with GOD.

Meditation: The Practice of Divine Presence

While prayer is often vocal or mental, meditation is a practice that involves focused contemplation, typically on a specific scripture, aspect of GOD, or divine truth. Meditation in the Catholic tradition is deeply rooted in the desire to experience GOD's presence in a profound and transformative way. St. Teresa of Ávila, a Doctor of the Church, emphasized the importance of meditation as a way to foster a deeper union with GOD, describing it as "an intimate sharing between friends" [2].

Meditation helps Catholics cultivate the Christ Consciousness by quieting the mind and focusing the heart on GOD. This practice enables believers to go beyond words and enter into a state of receptivity where they can listen to GOD's voice and feel His presence. In contemporary contexts, meditation offers modern-day Catholics a powerful tool for navigating the challenges of daily life, providing a spiritual anchor in a world that often feels chaotic and disconnected from the sacred.

The Holy Trinity and Contemplative Prayer

Contemplative prayer, a form of meditation, involves resting in GOD's presence and is closely associated with The Holy Trinity. In contemplative prayer, believers are invited to experience the indwelling of The Holy Trinity within their souls. The Catechism of the Catholic Church describes contemplative prayer as "a communion of love, bearing life for the multitude", highlighting its role in deepening our connection with the Father, Son, and Holy Spirit[3].

For modern Catholics, understanding the role of the Holy Trinity in contemplative prayer is crucial. It reminds us that prayer is not just an individual activity but a communal experience with the Triune GOD. This awareness can transform how we approach prayer, encouraging us to see it as an opportunity to engage with the fullness of GOD's presence in our lives.

Application in Modern Life

Integrating Prayer and Meditation into Daily Living

In the fast-paced world we live in, finding time for prayer and meditation can be challenging. However, these practices are essential for maintaining spiritual balance and staying connected to GOD's guidance. By integrating prayer and meditation into our daily routines, we can create a spiritual foundation that supports all aspects of our lives.

One practical approach is to designate specific times of the day for prayer, such as morning and evening. This practice helps to establish a rhythm of prayer that anchors the day in GOD's presence. For instance, starting the day with a prayer of gratitude and ending it with a prayer of reflection allows us to begin and conclude each day in communion with GOD.

Meditation can be integrated into daily life by setting aside time for quiet contemplation, even if it's just a few minutes. During these moments, focus on a scripture passage or a specific aspect of GOD's nature, allowing your heart and mind to dwell in GOD's presence. This practice can be particularly helpful in managing stress and finding peace amidst the demands of modern life.

Real-Life Example: A Balanced Approach to Work and Faith

Consider the example of John, a busy executive who struggled to balance his demanding career with his spiritual commitments. By incorporating prayer and meditation into his daily routine, John was able to create a sense of balance and clarity in his life. Each morning, he began with a short prayer, asking for GOD's guidance in his work. Throughout the day, he took brief moments to meditate, focusing on GOD's presence and seeking wisdom for the decisions he needed to make. This approach not only improved his professional performance but also deepened his relationship with GOD, bringing a sense of peace and purpose to his life.

Practical Spiritual Tools

The Jesus Prayer

The Jesus Prayer is a simple yet powerful prayer that can be used throughout the day to keep one's focus on Christ. It involves repeating the phrase, *"Lord Jesus Christ, Son of GOD, have mercy on me,"* either silently or aloud. This prayer can be integrated into daily activities, serving as a constant reminder of Christ's presence and mercy.

Instructions:

- Begin by finding a quiet place where you can focus without distractions.
- Repeat the Jesus Prayer slowly and rhythmically, aligning your breathing with the words.
- Continue this practice for several minutes, allowing the prayer to deepen your awareness of GOD's presence.

Scriptural Meditation

Another practical tool is scriptural meditation, which involves selecting a passage from the Bible and meditating on its meaning and relevance to your life.

Instructions:

- Choose a scripture passage that resonates with you. For example, Psalm 23 or Matthew 11:28-30.

- Read the passage slowly and reflect on each word or phrase, considering what GOD might be saying to you through the text.

- Spend a few minutes in silence, allowing the message of the scripture to sink deeply into your heart.

- Conclude with a prayer, asking GOD to help you live out the insights gained from your meditation.

Prayer Journaling

Prayer journaling is a powerful way to deepen your prayer life by recording your thoughts, prayers, and experiences with GOD.

Instructions:

- Set aside a specific time each day for journaling.

- Begin by writing down your prayers, expressing your thoughts and emotions to GOD.

- Record any insights or answers you receive during prayer or meditation.

- Over time, review your journal entries to see how GOD has been at work in your life.

Prayer and meditation are indispensable spiritual tools that connect us with GOD and provide a foundation for a fulfilling and meaningful life. By understanding the theological significance of these practices and incorporating them into our daily routines, we can deepen our relationship with GOD, navigate the challenges of modern life with greater ease, and experience the peace and joy that come from living in communion with the Divine.

Exercise: Deepening Your Connection with GOD Through Prayer and Meditation

Objective: To enhance the reader's understanding and practical application of prayer and meditation as tools for deepening their connection with GOD.

Instructions:

Step 1: Establishing a Daily Prayer Routine (10-15 minutes daily)

- **Objective:** Create a consistent prayer practice that integrates into your daily life.
- **Action:**
    - ✓ Set a specific time each day for prayer, such as first thing in the morning or before bed.
    - ✓ Begin with the *Lord's Prayer* or the *Jesus Prayer* ("Lord Jesus Christ, Son of GOD, have mercy on me.").
    - ✓ Spend a few minutes in silent prayer, listening for GOD's guidance or simply resting in His presence.
    - ✓ Conclude your prayer by expressing gratitude for the day's blessings and asking for strength for the challenges ahead.

Step 2: Practicing Scriptural Meditation (15-20 minutes, 2-3 times a week)

- **Objective:** Deepen your understanding of scripture and its relevance to your life.

- **Action:**
    - ✓ Choose a passage from the Bible that resonates with you. For example, you might meditate on Psalm 23 or the Beatitudes in Matthew 5:1-12.
    - ✓ Find a quiet space where you won't be disturbed. Read the passage slowly, reflecting on its meaning.
    - ✓ Spend a few minutes in silence, allowing the words to resonate deeply within you. Ask GOD to reveal any specific messages or insights through the scripture.
    - ✓ Conclude by journaling your thoughts and any insights gained during the meditation.

Step 3: Reflective Prayer Journaling (10 minutes daily)

- **Objective:** Foster a deeper awareness of GOD's presence and activity in your life.
- **Action:**
    - ✓ At the end of each day, take a few moments to reflect on your experiences. Write down any moments where you felt GOD's presence or where prayer helped guide your actions.
    - ✓ Consider any challenges you faced and how prayer or meditation might have influenced your response.
    - ✓ Write a short prayer of thanks for the day and ask for GOD's continued guidance.

Step 4: Weekly Contemplative Practice (20-30 minutes weekly)

- **Objective:** Cultivate a deeper sense of communion with The Holy Trinity.
- **Action:**
  - ✓ Set aside 20-30 minutes each week for contemplative prayer. Begin by finding a comfortable, quiet place to sit.
  - ✓ Focus on your breathing, allowing yourself to relax and center your mind on GOD's presence.
  - ✓ As you sit in silence, invite The Holy Trinity to dwell within you. Focus on the indwelling presence of the Father, Son, and Holy Spirit.
  - ✓ If your mind wanders, gently return your focus to GOD's presence, using a simple phrase like "Come, Holy Spirit" to help maintain your focus.
  - ✓ Afterward, spend a few moments in silent gratitude before concluding with a prayer.

Outcome: By completing this exercise, you will establish a regular practice of prayer and meditation that deepens your connection with GOD and enhances your spiritual life. This structured approach will help you integrate these practices into your daily routine, providing spiritual strength and guidance in all aspects of life. As you continue with these practices, you should notice an increased sense of peace, purpose, and a closer relationship with GOD.

NOTES:

Chapter 03: Communing with Nature

Discovering GOD Through His Creation

Nature has always been a profound means of connecting with the Divine. This chapter explores how communing with nature can be a powerful spiritual tool for modern-day Catholics, enabling them to deepen their relationship with GOD. By recognizing the divine presence in the natural world, believers can cultivate a greater sense of peace, balance, and spiritual awareness. This chapter will delve into the theological underpinnings of this practice, its relevance in today's world, and offer practical guidance on how to integrate this form of communion into daily life.

Theological Insights

Nature as a Reflection of the Divine

The natural world is a testament to GOD's creative power and glory. Throughout scripture, nature is depicted as a reflection of GOD's majesty, a means through which His presence is made manifest to humanity. Psalm 19:1 beautifully encapsulates this idea: "The heavens declare the glory of GOD; the skies proclaim the work of his hands"[1]. This verse highlights how creation itself serves as a witness to GOD's existence and grandeur.

Theologically, this concept is rooted in the belief that all of creation is imbued with GOD's presence. The Christ Consciousness, which is the awareness of GOD's presence within and around us, is often heightened when we engage with the natural world. Jesus Himself frequently used elements of nature in His teachings, such as the parables of the mustard seed (Matthew 13:31-32)[2] and the vine and branches (John 15:1-8)[2], to illustrate spiritual truths. These references emphasize the interconnectedness of all creation and the ways in which nature can reveal divine wisdom.

For modern-day Catholics, this understanding can transform the way they experience the world. Recognizing that nature is a reflection of GOD's glory invites believers to approach the natural world with reverence and mindfulness. It encourages them to see beyond the physical and to perceive the spiritual significance of their surroundings.

The Holy Trinity and the Sanctity of Creation

The doctrine of The Holy Trinity - Father, Son, and Holy Spirit - further deepens our understanding of the sanctity of nature. As the Creator, GOD the Father brought the world into being through the Son, Jesus Christ, all things were made; and The Holy Spirit sustains and renews creation. This Trinitarian view affirms that all of creation is interconnected and that GOD's presence permeates every aspect of the natural world.

The Church teaches that humans, as stewards of creation, have a responsibility to care for the environment. Pope Francis, in his encyclical *Laudato Si'*, calls on all people to acknowledge the interconnectedness of creation and to take action to protect it. He writes, "The entire material universe speaks of GOD's love, his boundless affection for us. Soil, water, mountains: everything is, as it were, a caress of GOD"[3] . This perspective invites Catholics to see their relationship with nature as an integral part of their spiritual life, one that reflects their commitment to living out the teachings of the Gospel.

Application in Modern Life

Integrating Nature into Daily Spiritual Practice

In today's fast-paced world, it can be challenging to find time to connect with nature. However, making space for this practice can significantly enhance one's spiritual life. By intentionally engaging with the natural world, Catholics can find a sense of peace and clarity that helps them navigate the complexities of modern life.

One way to incorporate nature into daily spiritual practice is through mindful walks. This involves taking time to walk in a natural setting - whether it's a park, forest, or garden - while being fully present and aware of GOD's creation. As you walk, take note of the sights, sounds, and smells around you. Reflect on how each element of nature reveals something about GOD's character - His creativity, His power, His beauty.

Another practical approach is to create a sacred space at home that includes natural elements. This could be a small altar with flowers, stones, or plants that serve as reminders of GOD's presence in creation. Spending time in this space for prayer or meditation can help deepen your connection with GOD and bring a sense of the natural world into your everyday life.

Balancing Spiritual and Secular Responsibilities

For many, balancing spiritual commitments with the demands of daily life can be a struggle. However, integrating nature into your spiritual practices can help maintain this balance. Nature has a way of grounding us, reminding us of the simplicity and beauty of GOD's creation, even amidst the busyness of life.

Consider the example of Sarah, a working mother who often feels overwhelmed by her responsibilities. By setting aside time each week for a nature walk with her family, Sarah not only finds a way to connect with GOD but also strengthens her family bonds. These walks provide an opportunity for her to reflect on GOD's goodness and to teach her children about the importance of caring for creation. This practice helps Sarah maintain a sense of balance between her spiritual life and her role as a mother and professional.

Practical Spiritual Tools

Nature-Based Meditation

Nature-based meditation is a simple yet effective way to deepen your connection with GOD through His creation.

Instructions:

- Find a quiet outdoor location where you can sit comfortably.

- Begin by taking a few deep breaths, centering yourself in the present moment.

- As you sit in silence, focus on the natural elements around you— the rustling of leaves, the warmth of the sun, the scent of flowers.

- Reflect on how these elements reveal GOD's presence and love. Allow yourself to be fully immersed in the experience of GOD's creation.

- Conclude with a prayer of gratitude, thanking GOD for the gift of nature and for the ways it nurtures your spirit.

Creation-Focused Scripture Study

Another practical tool is to incorporate nature themes into your scripture study.

Instructions:

- Choose scripture passages that highlight the beauty and significance of creation, such as Psalm 104, Genesis 1, or Matthew 6:25-34.

- As you read, reflect on how these passages relate to your own experiences with nature.

- Consider how the scripture invites you to see the natural world as a reflection of GOD's glory and a means of deepening your relationship with Him.

- Journaling your reflections can help reinforce the insights gained during this study.

Community Activities

Engaging in community activities that focus on environmental stewardship can also be a powerful way to live out your faith.

Suggestions:

- Participate in a local cleanup event, tree planting, or conservation project.

- Join or start a church group focused on caring for creation, where members can share experiences, resources, and support each other in integrating nature into their spiritual practices.

- Use these activities as opportunities to reflect on the ways in which caring for creation is a form of worship and service to GOD.

Communing with nature is not just a passive experience but an active form of spiritual engagement that can profoundly deepen your relationship with GOD. By recognizing the divine presence in creation and integrating nature into your daily spiritual practices, you can cultivate a greater sense of peace, balance, and connection with the Divine. Whether through mindful walks, nature-based meditation, or community activities, these practices offer practical ways to incorporate the beauty and wisdom of GOD's creation into your spiritual journey.

Exercise: Deepening Your Spiritual Connection Through Nature

Objective: To enhance the reader's understanding of how communing with nature can deepen their spiritual life and to provide practical steps for integrating this practice into daily routines.

Instructions:

Step 1: Mindful Nature Walk (20-30 minutes)

- **Objective:** Cultivate awareness of GOD's presence in nature.
- **Action:**
    - ✓ Choose a natural setting where you can walk undisturbed, such as a park, forest, or garden.
    - ✓ As you begin your walk, take a few deep breaths to center yourself. Focus on being fully present in the moment.
    - ✓ As you walk, observe the details around you - the colors, textures, sounds, and smells. Reflect on how each element reveals something about GOD's character.
    - ✓ Spend time in silent reflection or pray as you walk, asking GOD to open your heart to His presence in creation.

- ✓ After your walk, take a moment to journal your thoughts and any insights or feelings that emerged during the experience.

Step 2: Creating a Nature-Inspired Sacred Space at Home (15-20 minutes)

- **Objective:** Establish a daily practice of connecting with GOD through nature, even indoors.

- **Action:**

    - ✓ Identify a space in your home where you can create a small altar or sacred space. It could be a windowsill, a corner of a room, or a shelf.
    - ✓ Gather natural elements that resonate with you, such as flowers, stones, leaves, or small plants.
    - ✓ Arrange these items in your chosen space, creating a peaceful and inspiring area for prayer or meditation.
    - ✓ Spend a few minutes each day in this space, using it as a focal point for prayer, meditation, or quiet reflection.
    - ✓ Reflect on how this connection with nature enhances your sense of GOD's presence in your daily life.

Step 3: Nature-Based Meditation (10-15 minutes daily)

- **Objective:** Use nature as a tool for deepening meditation and spiritual awareness.

- **Action:**

    - ✓ Find a quiet outdoor space or sit near a window with a view of nature.
    - ✓ Begin by closing your eyes and taking deep breaths, focusing on the natural sounds around

you - birds chirping, wind rustling through trees, etc.
- ✓ Visualize GOD's presence in each element of nature, and let your thoughts dwell on His creativity and power.
- ✓ Spend 10-15 minutes in silent meditation, allowing yourself to feel connected to GOD through the beauty of creation.
- ✓ After your meditation, journal any insights, emotions, or messages you felt during this time.

Step 4: Environmental Stewardship Activity (1-2 hours weekly)

- **Objective:** Put your faith into action by caring for GOD's creation.
- **Action:**
    - ✓ Choose an environmental stewardship activity that aligns with your interests, such as participating in a community cleanup, planting trees, or conserving resources.
    - ✓ As you engage in this activity, reflect on how caring for creation is a form of worship and service to GOD.
    - ✓ Use this time to pray or meditate on your role as a steward of the earth, and how you can continue to integrate these practices into your life.
    - ✓ After completing the activity, spend time reflecting or journaling about the experience, considering how it deepened your connection to GOD and nature.

Outcome: By completing this exercise, you will develop a deeper understanding and appreciation for GOD's presence in nature and learn practical ways to integrate this connection into your daily spiritual practices. This exercise aims to enhance your spiritual awareness, reduce stress, and foster a greater sense of peace and purpose in your life.

Chapter 04: Your Spiritual Companions – Guardian Angels, Spirit Guides, and Archangels

Embracing the Presence of Spiritual Companions in Our Lives

The theme of this chapter centers on the profound and often overlooked companionship offered by spiritual beings such as Guardian Angels, Spirit Guides, and Archangels. These spiritual companions play vital roles in the lives of Catholics, guiding, protecting, and supporting us in our journey toward spiritual growth and deeper communion with GOD. Understanding their presence and learning how to engage with them can significantly enrich our spiritual lives, offering both comfort and divine assistance in navigating the challenges of modern life.

Theological Insights

The Nature of Guardian Angels

The concept of Guardian Angels is deeply rooted in Catholic theology, with these beings seen as personal protectors assigned by GOD to watch over each individual. The Catechism of the Catholic Church states, "From infancy to death, human life is surrounded by their watchful care and intercession" (CCC 336)[1]. This belief is supported by scripture, particularly in Matthew 18:10, where Jesus emphasizes the protective role of angels: "See that you do not despise one of these little ones. For I tell you that their angels in heaven always see the face of my Father in heaven" (Matthew 18:10)[2].

Guardian Angels are considered messengers of GOD, guiding us through life's challenges and helping us stay on the path that leads to Him. They serve as reminders of GOD's omnipresent care and His desire for our well-being. For modern Catholics, recognizing the presence of Guardian Angels can provide a sense of comfort and security, knowing that divine protection and guidance are always near.

Spirit Guides: A Broader Understanding

While Guardian Angels are explicitly mentioned in Catholic doctrine, the concept of Spirit Guides often requires a broader interpretation. Spirit Guides can be understood as spiritual beings or souls who assist individuals in their spiritual journey. Though not officially recognized within Catholic teachings, the idea of spiritual guidance aligns with the broader Christian understanding of GOD's providence and the communion of saints. Hebrews 12:1 speaks of being "surrounded by such a great cloud of witnesses[3]," which can be interpreted as the spiritual presence and influence of those who have gone before us .

For Catholics, Spirit Guides might be seen as saints, departed loved ones, or other spiritual beings who, under GOD's direction, provide insight, encouragement, and inspiration.

Engaging with Spirit Guides can help Catholics feel more connected to the broader spiritual community, reinforcing the belief that we are never alone in our faith journey.

Archangels: Powerful Protectors and Messengers

Archangels hold a significant place in Catholic tradition, with figures like Michael, Gabriel, and Raphael playing prominent roles in scripture. Archangels are seen as powerful protectors and messengers of GOD's will, tasked with significant responsibilities in both the spiritual and earthly realms. The Archangel Michael, for instance, is revered as the leader of GOD's army, a defender against evil, as depicted in Revelation 12:7-9. Gabriel is known as the messenger who announced the birth of Jesus to the Virgin Mary (Luke 1:26-38), and Raphael is recognized for his role in healing and guidance, particularly in the Book of Tobit.

Understanding the roles of Archangels can deepen our appreciation for the divine assistance available to us. These beings exemplify GOD's power and love, acting as intermediaries who bring His messages to us and help us combat spiritual challenges.

Application in Modern Life

Integrating Spiritual Companions into Daily Living

In the hustle and bustle of modern life, it can be easy to overlook the presence of our spiritual companions. However, by cultivating an awareness of these beings, we can draw strength, guidance, and protection from them daily. One practical way to integrate this awareness is through regular prayer and reflection on the presence of your Guardian Angel or a particular Archangel who resonates with you.

For instance, starting or ending your day with a simple prayer of gratitude to your Guardian Angel can help reinforce the sense of divine presence in your life. Prayers like the "Angel of GOD" prayer can be a daily reminder of your Guardian Angel's constant watchfulness:

> *"Angel of GOD, my guardian dear,*
> *To whom GOD's love commits me here,*
> *Ever this day, be at my side,*
> *To light and guard, to rule and guide. Amen."*

Balancing Spiritual Awareness with Secular Responsibilities

While the awareness of spiritual companions can enhance our faith life, it is essential to maintain a balance between this spiritual focus and our secular responsibilities. Engaging with your spiritual companions should not become an escape from the realities of daily life but rather a way to infuse your everyday activities with spiritual purpose.

Consider the example of Michael, a Catholic father and business owner. Michael begins each day with a prayer to the Archangel Michael, asking for protection and guidance as he navigates the challenges of work and family life. By invoking the

Archangel's assistance, Michael feels more confident and grounded in his decisions, knowing that he is not facing these challenges alone. This practice helps him maintain a spiritual perspective while fulfilling his worldly duties.

Practical Spiritual Tools

Daily Angelic Invocation

A practical tool for deepening your connection with your spiritual companions is a daily angelic invocation. This practice involves setting aside a few minutes each day to consciously invite the presence and guidance of your Guardian Angel or a specific Archangel into your life.

Instructions:

- Find a quiet place where you can sit or kneel comfortably.

- Close your eyes and take a few deep breaths to center yourself.

- Mentally or verbally invite your Guardian Angel or a specific Archangel (such as Michael, Gabriel, or Raphael) to be with you, guiding and protecting you throughout the day.

- You might say something like, "Archangel Michael, please be with me today. Protect me from harm and guide my thoughts, words, and actions to align with GOD's will."

- Spend a few moments in silence, feeling the presence of your spiritual companion.

Meditation on Spiritual Companions

Meditating on the presence and role of your spiritual companions can deepen your awareness of their guidance in your life.

Instructions:

- Sit comfortably in a quiet space and close your eyes.
- Focus on your breathing, allowing your mind to settle.
- Visualize your Guardian Angel or an Archangel standing beside you, radiating light and love.
- Reflect on any challenges or decisions you are facing and ask for their guidance.
- Spend 10-15 minutes in this meditative state, allowing insights or feelings of peace to arise.

Creating an Angelic Altar

Creating a small altar dedicated to your spiritual companions can serve as a visual reminder of their presence in your life.

Instructions:

- Choose a space in your home where you can set up a small altar.

- Place items that symbolize your connection with your spiritual companions, such as candles, angel figurines, or images of Archangels.

- Use this space for prayer, meditation, or simply as a reminder of the divine assistance available to you.

Your spiritual companions - Guardian Angels, Spirit Guides, and Archangels - offer invaluable support and guidance as you navigate your spiritual journey. By recognizing their presence and actively engaging with them through prayer, meditation, and daily invocation, you can deepen your relationship with GOD and find comfort in knowing that you are never alone. These spiritual tools provide practical ways to integrate the divine into your daily life, helping you balance your spiritual commitments with your secular responsibilities and enriching your overall faith experience.

Exercise: Strengthening Your Connection with Spiritual Companions

Objective: To enhance the reader's awareness of and connection with their spiritual companions - Guardian Angels, Spirit Guides, and Archangels - by integrating these relationships into daily life.

Instructions:

Step 1: Morning Angelic Invocation (5-10 minutes daily)

- **Objective:** Start each day with a focused connection to your Guardian Angel or a specific Archangel.

- **Action:**
    - ✓ Each morning, set aside 5-10 minutes in a quiet space.
    - ✓ Begin with a prayer or invocation, such as: *"Guardian Angel [or Archangel Michael], guide and protect me today. Help me to align my actions with GOD's will."*
    - ✓ Visualize your chosen spiritual companion standing beside you, offering guidance and protection.
    - ✓ Spend a few moments in silence, feeling their presence and setting an intention for the day.

Step 2: Midday Check-In (3-5 minutes daily)

- **Objective:** Maintain awareness of your spiritual companions throughout the day.
- **Action:**
    - ✓ During a break at work or home, pause for a few minutes to reconnect with your Guardian Angel or Archangel.
    - ✓ Reflect on how your day has unfolded so far and ask for continued guidance.
    - ✓ Say a simple prayer or affirmation, such as: *"Thank you, [Guardian Angel/Archangel], for being with me. Continue to guide me in making decisions aligned with GOD's love and wisdom."*

Step 3: Evening Reflection and Gratitude (10 minutes daily)

- **Objective:** End the day by acknowledging the presence and assistance of your spiritual companions.
- **Action:**

- ✓ Before bed, find a quiet place to reflect on your day.
- ✓ Think about moments when you felt the presence or guidance of your spiritual companions. How did they help you navigate challenges or decisions?
- ✓ Write a brief entry in a journal, expressing gratitude for their support and noting any insights or experiences you had.
- ✓ Conclude with a prayer of thanks, such as: *"Thank you, Guardian Angel [or Archangel], for guiding me today. I am grateful for your presence in my life."*

Step 4: Creating a Personal Angelic Ritual (Weekly Practice)

- **Objective:** Develop a personalized ritual to strengthen your connection with your spiritual companions.
- **Action:**
  - ✓ Choose a time each week to engage in a special ritual dedicated to your spiritual companions.
  - ✓ This could involve lighting a candle on your angelic altar, saying specific prayers, or meditating on the presence of your Guardian Angel or Archangels.
  - ✓ Focus on any areas of your life where you need particular guidance or protection and ask for their assistance.
  - ✓ Use this time to deepen your relationship with your spiritual companions and reflect on the ways they have supported you throughout the week.

Outcome: By completing this exercise, you will develop a stronger and more conscious connection with your spiritual companions. This will help you feel more supported, guided, and protected in your daily life, enhancing your overall spiritual journey. Through consistent practice, you will cultivate a deeper awareness of the divine presence in your life and learn to rely on your spiritual companions as trusted allies in your walk with GOD.

Chapter 05: Sacred Catholic Texts

The Foundation of Faith in Sacred Texts

The sacred texts of The Catholic Church serve as the cornerstone of the faith, providing guidance, wisdom, and spiritual nourishment for believers. These texts not only offer a historical account of the life and teachings of Jesus Christ but also reveal the profound mysteries of The Holy Trinity and the path to spiritual growth. In this chapter, we will explore the significance of sacred Catholic texts, delve into key theological concepts, and discuss practical ways to integrate these teachings into daily life. By engaging deeply with these texts, modern Catholics can strengthen their relationship with GOD, navigate the complexities of contemporary life, and find peace and purpose in their spiritual journey.

Theological Insights

The Nature of Jesus and the Christ Consciousness

Central to the sacred texts of the Catholic Church is the figure of Jesus Christ, whose life, death, and resurrection form the bedrock of Christian faith. The Gospels - Matthew, Mark, Luke, and John - are the primary sources that chronicle the life of Jesus, presenting Him as both fully human and fully divine. This dual nature of Christ is a fundamental theological concept, emphasizing that Jesus is the incarnate Word of GOD (John 1:14)[1] and the ultimate revelation of GOD's love for humanity.

The concept of the Christ Consciousness, while not explicitly mentioned in traditional Catholic doctrine, can be understood as the awareness of Christ's presence within and the embodiment of His teachings in one's life. This consciousness is nurtured through regular engagement with sacred texts, where believers encounter the living Word of GOD and are invited to internalize Christ's message of love, compassion, and redemption.

The Gospels, along with other New Testament writings, provide a framework for understanding Jesus' role in the divine plan of salvation. They invite believers to reflect on the mysteries of Christ's incarnation, crucifixion, and resurrection, and to consider how these events continue to influence their lives today. For modern Catholics, these texts are not merely historical documents but living words that speak to the heart and soul, guiding them on their spiritual journey.

The Holy Trinity in Sacred Texts

The doctrine of The Holy Trinity - one GOD in three persons: Father, Son, and Holy Spirit - is another central theme in Catholic sacred texts. The Catechism of the Catholic Church describes the Trinity as "the central mystery of Christian faith and life" (CCC 234)[2]. This mystery is woven throughout the scriptures, from the creation narrative in Genesis, where the Spirit of GOD hovers over the waters (Genesis 1:2)[3], to the Great Commission in Matthew 28:19[4], where Jesus commands His disciples to baptize in the name of the Father, the Son, and The Holy Spirit.

Understanding The Trinity through sacred texts allows believers to grasp the relational nature of GOD and the interconnectedness of the divine persons. This understanding is crucial for modern Catholics, as it shapes their approach to prayer, worship, and community life. By reflecting on the scriptural foundations of the Trinity, believers can deepen their relationship with each person of The Trinity and experience the fullness of GOD's presence in their lives.

Application in Modern Life

Integrating Sacred Texts into Daily Living

For many Catholics, finding time to engage with sacred texts amidst the demands of daily life can be challenging. However, integrating these texts into everyday routines is essential for spiritual growth and maintaining a strong connection with GOD. One practical approach is to set aside a specific time each day for scripture reading and reflection. This could be in the morning, as a way to start the day with GOD's Word, or in the evening, as a time of reflection and prayer.

Another effective method is to incorporate scripture into daily prayer. The Liturgy of the Hours, also known as the Divine Office, is a powerful tool that allows Catholics to pray with the Church through the recitation of psalms, readings, and prayers at set times throughout the day. By participating in this ancient tradition, believers can immerse themselves in the rhythm of the Church's prayer life and stay connected to the sacred texts that form the foundation of their faith.

In addition to personal scripture reading and prayer, Catholics can benefit from engaging in group Bible studies or faith-sharing groups. These gatherings provide an opportunity to explore sacred texts in a communal setting, where insights and experiences can be shared, and the Word of GOD can be discussed and applied to contemporary life challenges.

Balancing Spiritual and Secular Responsibilities

Balancing spiritual commitments with secular responsibilities is a common challenge for modern Catholics. However, sacred texts offer guidance on how to integrate faith into all aspects of life. For example, the teachings of Jesus in the Sermon on the Mount (Matthew 5-7)[5] provide practical advice on how to live out the values of the Kingdom of GOD in everyday situations, such as work, relationships, and social interactions.

Consider the example of Maria, a working mother who struggles to find time for prayer and scripture reading amidst her busy schedule. By incorporating short scripture passages into her daily routine - such as reading a psalm during her lunch break or reflecting on a Gospel passage before bed - Maria can stay connected to GOD's Word and draw strength and inspiration from it. Additionally, by discussing these passages with her family, Maria can foster a spiritual environment in her home, where the teachings of Christ are lived out in daily life.

Practical Spiritual Tools

Lectio Divina: A Method for Sacred Reading

Lectio Divina, or "divine reading," is a traditional Catholic practice that involves reading and meditating on scripture in a prayerful and contemplative manner. This method allows believers to engage deeply with the Word of GOD and to listen for His voice speaking through the text.

Instructions:

- Begin by selecting a passage of scripture. This could be a reading from the day's liturgy or a passage that speaks to you personally.

- Read the passage slowly and attentively, allowing the words to resonate in your heart.

- Reflect on the passage, considering what GOD might be saying to you through these words.

- Respond to GOD in prayer, sharing your thoughts, feelings, and desires with Him.

- Rest in GOD's presence, allowing His Word to take root in your heart.

Scripture Journaling

Another effective tool for deepening your engagement with sacred texts is scripture journaling. This practice involves writing down reflections, prayers, and insights that arise from your reading of scripture.

Instructions:

- After reading a passage of scripture, take a few minutes to write down your thoughts and reflections.
- Consider how the passage applies to your life and what GOD might be calling you to do in response.
- Use your journal as a place to record your spiritual journey, noting moments of growth, challenges, and answered prayers.

Incorporating Scripture into Prayer

Integrating scripture into your daily prayer life can help you stay connected to GOD's Word and draw strength from it throughout the day.

Instructions:

- Choose a scripture passage to focus on during your prayer time. This could be a Psalm, a verse from the Gospels, or a passage from the Epistles.
- Meditate on the passage, allowing it to guide your prayer and reflection.

- Use the passage as a basis for your petitions, praises, and intercessions, asking GOD to help you live out His Word in your daily life.

Sacred Catholic texts are a rich source of spiritual nourishment and guidance, offering insights into the nature of Jesus, The Holy Trinity, and the path to spiritual growth. By engaging deeply with these texts, modern Catholics can strengthen their relationship with GOD, navigate the complexities of contemporary life, and find peace and purpose in their spiritual journey. Whether through daily scripture reading, prayer, or communal study, the Word of GOD is a powerful tool that can transform lives and draw believers closer to the heart of Christ.

Exercise: Deepening Your Engagement with Sacred Catholic Texts

Objective: To enhance the reader's understanding and practical application of sacred Catholic texts, fostering a deeper relationship with GOD and integrating spiritual insights into daily life.

Instructions:

Step 1: Daily Scripture Reading (10-15 minutes daily)

- **Objective:** Establish a consistent habit of engaging with sacred texts.
- **Action:**
    - ✓ Choose a specific time each day to read a passage from the Bible, such as the Gospels, Psalms, or the daily readings from the Catholic liturgical calendar.

- ✓ As you read, focus on understanding the message and its relevance to your life.
- ✓ After reading, spend a few minutes in quiet reflection, asking yourself:
    - What is GOD saying to me through this passage?
    - How can I apply this teaching to my daily life?
- ✓ Write down any insights or thoughts in a journal.

Step 2: Lectio Divina Practice (15-20 minutes, 2-3 times a week)

- **Objective:** Engage deeply with scripture through contemplative prayer.
- **Action:**
    - ✓ Select a scripture passage that resonates with you or relates to a current situation in your life.
    - ✓ Follow the steps of Lectio Divina:
        1. **Lectio (Reading):** Slowly read the passage, paying attention to any words or phrases that stand out.
        2. **Meditatio (Meditation):** Reflect on the meaning of these words and what GOD might be saying to you.
        3. **Oratio (Prayer):** Respond to GOD in prayer, sharing your thoughts, feelings, and desires.
        4. **Contemplatio (Contemplation):** Rest in GOD's presence, allowing His Word to transform you.

- ✓ Record your experience and any insights in your journal.

Step 3: Scripture Journaling (10 minutes daily)

- **Objective:** Reflect on and internalize scripture through journaling.
- **Action:**
    - ✓ After your daily scripture reading or Lectio Divina session, write about your reflections in a dedicated journal.
    - ✓ Consider the following prompts:
        - How did the passage resonate with you?
        - What challenges or encouragements did you receive from the text?
        - How can you live out this scripture in your daily interactions and decisions?
    - ✓ Review your journal entries weekly to track your spiritual growth and insights.

Step 4: Group Bible Study or Faith-Sharing (Weekly)

- **Objective:** Enhance understanding and application of scripture through community engagement.
- **Action:**
    - ✓ Join a Bible study group or form a small faith-sharing group with friends or family members.
    - ✓ Choose a book of the Bible or a thematic study based on the readings from the liturgical calendar.
    - ✓ Discuss the selected passages together, sharing personal reflections, questions, and applications.
    - ✓ Encourage each participant to share how they are integrating the teachings into their daily lives.

- ✓ Use the group as a source of accountability and support in your spiritual journey.

Step 5: Integrating Scripture into Daily Prayer (Ongoing Practice)

- **Objective:** Incorporate scripture into your regular prayer routine to deepen your spiritual life.
- **Action:**
    - ✓ Start your prayer time with a scripture verse that aligns with your intentions or spiritual needs.
    - ✓ Reflect on the verse as you pray, allowing it to guide your thoughts and petitions.
    - ✓ Conclude your prayer by asking GOD to help you live out the scripture in your interactions, decisions, and challenges throughout the day.

Outcome: By completing this exercise, you will develop a stronger connection to sacred Catholic texts, making them an integral part of your spiritual practice. This consistent engagement with scripture will deepen your understanding of GOD's Word, enrich your prayer life, and provide guidance for navigating the challenges of modern life. As you internalize these teachings, you will find greater peace, purpose, and direction in your spiritual journey.

Chapter 06: Sacred Music

The Transformative Power of Sacred Music

Sacred music holds a unique place in the spiritual life of Catholics, serving as both a medium for worship and a vehicle for deepening one's relationship with GOD. This chapter explores the significance of sacred music within the Catholic tradition, delving into its theological underpinnings, its role in the liturgy, and its impact on the spiritual growth of believers. By engaging with sacred music, Catholics can experience the divine in a profound and intimate way, allowing the melodies and lyrics to elevate their hearts and minds toward GOD.

Theological Insights

The Role of Music in Worship

Music has been an integral part of worship since the earliest days of the Church. Theologically, music is seen as a means of expressing the inexpressible, a way to communicate with GOD that transcends words alone. The Psalms, often referred to as the Church's first hymnbook, are filled with references to singing and music as forms of worship. Psalm 95:1, for instance, calls believers to "come, let us sing for joy to the Lord; let us shout aloud to the Rock of our salvation" (Psalm 95:1)[1]. This invitation to sing reflects the belief that music is a powerful tool for praising GOD and expressing the joy of faith.

In the context of the Catholic Mass, sacred music serves several key functions. It enhances the liturgical action, helps the faithful to pray, and fosters a sense of unity among the congregation. The Second Vatican Council's *Sacrosanctum Concilium* emphasizes the importance of music in the liturgy, stating that "the musical tradition of the universal Church is a treasure of inestimable value, greater even than that of any other art" (SC 112)[2]. This underscores the belief that music is not merely an accessory to worship but an essential element that enriches the liturgical experience and draws the faithful closer to the mystery of The Holy Trinity.

Christ Consciousness Through Music

The concept of Christ Consciousness refers to the awareness of Christ's presence within and the embodiment of His teachings in one's life. Sacred music plays a vital role in cultivating this awareness, as it provides a way for believers to meditate on the mysteries of Christ's life, death, and resurrection. Hymns and chants that focus on the life of Jesus help to internalize His teachings and bring the listener into a deeper communion with Him.

For example, the hymn "*Ave Verum Corpus*," which reflects on the true presence of Christ in the Eucharist, allows believers to meditate on the profound mystery of the Incarnation and the sacrificial love of Jesus. Through such hymns, Catholics can enter into the spirit of Christ's love and mercy, allowing the music to transform their hearts and minds.

Application in Modern Life

Integrating Sacred Music into Daily Life

In the busy world of modern life, finding time for spiritual practices can be challenging. However, sacred music offers a unique opportunity to integrate spirituality into daily routines. Whether listening to hymns during a commute, playing sacred music at home, or participating in a choir, Catholics can use music to stay connected with their faith throughout the day.

One practical approach is to create a playlist of favorite hymns and sacred songs that can be played during moments of quiet reflection, such as early in the morning or before bed. This practice not only fosters a sense of peace but also helps to set a spiritual tone for the day. Additionally, listening to sacred music while performing routine tasks can transform those moments into opportunities for prayer and meditation.

For those involved in parish life, joining a church choir or participating in the music ministry can be a powerful way to engage with sacred music more deeply. Singing in a choir not only enhances the liturgical experience for the congregation but also provides personal spiritual benefits, such as increased awareness of GOD's presence and a greater sense of community.

Balancing Spiritual and Secular Responsibilities

Maintaining a balance between spiritual commitments and secular responsibilities is a common challenge for many

Catholics. Sacred music can serve as a bridge between these two aspects of life, allowing believers to carry their faith into their daily activities. For example, playing sacred music in the background while working or studying can create a peaceful environment that keeps the mind focused on GOD. This practice can also help reduce stress and anxiety, providing a sense of calm in the midst of a busy day.

Consider the example of John, a young professional who struggles to find time for prayer amidst his demanding work schedule. By incorporating sacred music into his daily routine - playing hymns during his morning commute and listening to chant while working - John is able to maintain a spiritual connection throughout the day. This practice not only helps him stay grounded in his faith but also provides a source of comfort and inspiration during challenging times.

Practical Spiritual Tools

Creating a Sacred Music Playlist

A simple yet effective spiritual tool is creating a personal playlist of sacred music that resonates with your spiritual journey.

Instructions:

- Begin by selecting a variety of hymns, chants, and sacred songs that hold personal significance or reflect important aspects of your faith.

- Include pieces that evoke different moods, such as praise, reflection, or consolation.
- Dedicate specific times of the day to listen to your playlist, such as during your morning routine, while commuting, or before prayer.
- Use the music as a means of entering into a deeper state of prayer and reflection, allowing the melodies and lyrics to guide your thoughts toward GOD.

Participating in a Church Choir

Joining a church choir is another powerful way to engage with sacred music while contributing to the worship experience of your parish community.

Instructions:

- Contact your parish's music director to express your interest in joining the choir. No previous experience is necessary, just a willingness to learn and participate.
- Attend regular rehearsals and practice the hymns and chants at home to become more familiar with the music.
- Reflect on the meaning of the hymns you sing, considering how they relate to the liturgy and your own spiritual journey.

- Use your participation in the choir as an opportunity to offer your voice in praise and to deepen your relationship with GOD through music.

Using Sacred Music for Meditation

Sacred music can be a powerful aid in meditation, helping to focus the mind and create a conducive atmosphere for prayer.

Instructions:

- Choose a piece of sacred music that you find particularly moving or spiritually significant.

- Find a quiet place where you can sit comfortably and listen without distraction.

- As the music plays, close your eyes and allow the sounds to envelop you, guiding your thoughts toward GOD.

- Reflect on the emotions and images that the music evokes, using them as a starting point for prayer or contemplation.

- Spend a few moments in silence after the music ends, resting in the presence of GOD.

Sacred music is a profound spiritual tool that has the power to elevate the soul and deepen one's relationship with GOD. By incorporating sacred music into daily life, Catholics can maintain a constant connection with their faith, whether at home, at work, or in the community. Whether through personal playlists, participation in a church choir, or using music for meditation, the melodies and harmonies of sacred music can transform ordinary moments into opportunities for prayer and reflection. As a vital part of the Catholic tradition, sacred music continues to inspire and uplift the faithful, guiding them ever closer to the heart of GOD.

Exercise: Integrating Sacred Music into Your Spiritual Practice

Objective: To deepen the reader's understanding and experience of sacred music by incorporating it into their daily spiritual practices, enhancing their connection with GOD and enriching their prayer life.

Instructions:

Step 1: Sacred Music Listening Routine (15-20 minutes daily)

- **Objective:** Establish a daily habit of engaging with sacred music as a form of prayer and reflection.
- **Action:**
    - ✓ Choose a specific time each day to listen to a piece of sacred music. This could be in the morning to start your day with a spiritual focus, during a lunch break, or in the evening as a form of winding down.
    - ✓ Select a piece of sacred music that resonates with you, such as a hymn, chant, or instrumental piece.
    - ✓ As you listen, close your eyes and focus on the music, allowing it to guide your thoughts and emotions toward GOD.

- ✓ Reflect on how the music makes you feel and how it deepens your awareness of GOD's presence.
- ✓ Conclude by offering a brief prayer of gratitude or by meditating silently on the experience.

Step 2: Creating a Personal Sacred Music Playlist (30 minutes)

- **Objective:** Curate a collection of sacred music that you can use to enhance your spiritual practices.
- **Action:**
  - ✓ Spend some time selecting sacred music that has personal significance or that you find spiritually uplifting.
  - ✓ Include a variety of pieces that evoke different emotions and spiritual reflections, such as hymns of praise, contemplative chants, and instrumental sacred music.
  - ✓ Create a playlist on your preferred music platform or burn a CD that you can easily access during your daily routines.
  - ✓ Use this playlist during moments of prayer, meditation, or as background music while you go about your day.

Step 3: Reflective Journaling with Sacred Music (10-15 minutes, 3 times a week)

- **Objective:** Use sacred music as a tool for deeper reflection and journaling on your spiritual journey.
- **Action:**
  - ✓ Choose a quiet space where you can listen to sacred music without distractions.

- ✓ Select a piece of music that speaks to your current spiritual state or that aligns with your prayer intentions.
- ✓ As the music plays, allow your thoughts and feelings to flow freely, reflecting on what the music evokes in you.
- ✓ After listening, take a few minutes to write down your reflections in a journal. Consider the following prompts:
    - How did the music influence your thoughts and emotions?
    - Did it bring to mind any particular scripture, prayer, or spiritual insight?
    - How can you apply this reflection to your spiritual life or daily actions?

Step 4: Participating in a Church Choir or Music Ministry (Ongoing)

- **Objective:** Deepen your connection to sacred music and the liturgy by actively participating in your parish's music ministry.
- **Action:**
    - ✓ Contact your parish's music director or choir leader to express your interest in joining the choir or music ministry.
    - ✓ Attend rehearsals regularly and practice the hymns and music at home.
    - ✓ Reflect on the meaning of the hymns you sing and how they enhance the liturgical experience for the congregation.
    - ✓ Use your participation as an opportunity to offer your voice in worship and to deepen your personal connection with GOD through music.

Step 5: Sacred Music Meditation Practice (Weekly)

- **Objective:** Use sacred music as a meditative practice to deepen your spiritual awareness.

- **Action:**
    - ✓ Set aside time each week for a sacred music meditation session.
    - ✓ Choose a piece of music that is slow, contemplative, and conducive to meditation, such as Gregorian chant or a sacred instrumental piece.
    - ✓ Find a comfortable, quiet place where you won't be disturbed. Close your eyes and focus on your breathing as you begin the meditation.
    - ✓ As the music plays, allow your mind to quiet and your heart to open to GOD's presence. Let the music guide your meditation, focusing on any thoughts, images, or feelings that arise.
    - ✓ After the music ends, spend a few minutes in silent prayer or reflection, resting in the presence of GOD.

Outcome: By completing this exercise, you will develop a deeper appreciation for sacred music and its role in your spiritual life. You'll find that integrating sacred music into your daily routine can enhance your prayer life, reduce stress, and foster a stronger connection with GOD. Whether through personal listening, active participation in a choir, or reflective meditation, sacred music offers a powerful way to enrich your spiritual journey and bring a sense of peace and sacredness to your everyday life.

Chapter 07: Spiritual Journaling

The practice of spiritual journaling serves as a profound tool for deepening one's relationship with GOD, fostering introspection, and nurturing spiritual growth. This chapter explores the significance of spiritual journaling within the Catholic faith, highlighting its theological foundations, practical applications, and relevance in the modern world. As we delve into this practice, we will uncover how spiritual journaling can serve as a bridge between the sacred and the secular, helping Catholics navigate the complexities of contemporary life while staying rooted in their faith.

Theological Insights

Spiritual journaling is more than a simple record of thoughts and experiences; it is a sacred dialogue with GOD. Within the Catholic tradition, this practice finds its roots in the understanding of GOD as a personal and relational being, as revealed through Jesus Christ and The Holy Trinity. The act of journaling can be seen as an extension of prayer, where the written word becomes a medium through which we communicate with GOD and reflect on His presence in our lives.

Theologically, this practice is grounded in the concept of the *Imago Dei* - the belief that humans are created in the image and likeness of GOD (Genesis 1:27)[1]. This divine imprint within us calls for a continuous, conscious engagement with our Creator. Journaling provides a space for such engagement, allowing us to articulate our spiritual journeys, wrestle with doubts, and celebrate moments of grace.

In the Gospels, Jesus frequently withdrew to solitary places to pray and commune with the Father (Luke 5:16)[2]. While the scriptures do not explicitly mention Jesus journaling, His practices of solitude and reflection offer a model for Christians today. Through spiritual journaling, modern-day Catholics can emulate this aspect of Christ's life, creating a private space to listen for GOD's voice and discern His will.

The concept of The Christ Consciousness, which refers to the awareness of Christ's presence within us and the transformative power of His love, also plays a crucial role in spiritual journaling. As we write, we invite The Holy Spirit to illuminate our hearts and minds, guiding our thoughts and words. This practice aligns with the Catholic understanding of The Holy Trinity, where the Father, Son, and Holy Spirit work in unity to draw us closer to GOD.

Spiritual journaling, therefore, becomes a tool for cultivating this Christ Consciousness, allowing us to reflect on our experiences through the lens of Christ's teachings and to discern how GOD is working in our lives today.

Application in Modern Life

In the fast-paced, technology-driven world we live in, finding time for spiritual practices can be challenging. Many Catholics struggle to balance their spiritual commitments with the demands of work, family, and social obligations. However, spiritual journaling offers a flexible and accessible way to integrate faith into daily life.

For example, setting aside just ten minutes each morning or evening for journaling can create a meaningful ritual that anchors the day in prayer and reflection. This practice can be as simple as writing a few lines about a scripture passage that resonates with you, or as elaborate as chronicling your spiritual journey over time. The key is consistency and intentionality.

One real-life example of the power of spiritual journaling comes from the life of St. Thérèse of Lisieux, also known as The Little Flower. St. Thérèse kept a journal, which later became her autobiography, *The Story of a Soul.* In her writings, she documented her deep love for Jesus and her "little way" of seeking holiness in everyday life. Her journal became a source of inspiration for countless Catholics, demonstrating how personal reflections can contribute to the broader spiritual community[3].

For modern Catholics, spiritual journaling can serve a similar purpose. It can be a space to process life's challenges, from career decisions to personal relationships, in light of faith. Writing about these experiences helps to identify patterns, recognize GOD's guidance, and cultivate gratitude. It also provides a tangible record of spiritual growth, which can be revisited in times of doubt or difficulty.

Furthermore, spiritual journaling can be integrated into other aspects of life. For instance, a Catholic professional might use their journal to reflect on ethical dilemmas at work, seeking GOD's wisdom in making decisions that align with their values. A parent might journal about the joys and struggles of raising children in the faith, using the practice as a way to pray for their family's spiritual well-being.

Creating Practical Spiritual Tools

To help readers deepen their practice of spiritual journaling, here are some practical tools and techniques:

1. **Daily Reflection Prompts:** Start each journaling session with a prompt to guide your thoughts. Examples include:

    - "Where did I see GOD's presence today?"

    - "What challenges did I face, and how did I respond with faith?"

    - "What scripture passage speaks to my current situation?"

2. **Scripture Journaling:** Choose a passage from The Bible and write about its relevance to your life. Consider how the passage challenges, comforts, or guides you. Reflect on how it relates to the broader themes of the Christ Consciousness and The Holy Trinity.

3. **Prayer Journaling:** Transform your journal into a written prayer, addressing GOD directly. This can include prayers of thanksgiving, confession, or petition. Over time, you'll notice how your prayers evolve and how GOD answers them.

4. **Gratitude Journaling:** Dedicate a section of your journal to recording daily blessings. This practice fosters a spirit of gratitude and helps you focus on the positive aspects of life, even during challenging times.

5. **Discernment Journaling:** Use your journal as a tool for discernment, especially when facing significant decisions. Write about the pros and cons, pray for guidance, and document any insights you receive during the process.

By incorporating these tools into your daily routine, spiritual journaling can become a powerful practice for nurturing your relationship with GOD. It provides a structured yet flexible approach to deepen your faith, offering a sanctuary of peace and reflection amidst the busyness of life.

Exercise: *Spiritual Journaling Practice*

Objective: To deepen your understanding of spiritual journaling and integrate it into your daily routine for enhanced spiritual growth and connection with GOD.

Step 1: Set Your Intention

Before you begin journaling, take a moment to pray and set an intention for your practice. This could be a desire to deepen your relationship with GOD, seek clarity on a specific issue, or simply to express gratitude. Write down your intention at the top of your journal entry.

Step 2: Scripture Reflection

Choose a scripture passage that resonates with you. Read it slowly and mindfully, allowing the words to sink in. Spend a few minutes in silence, reflecting on how the passage speaks to your current life situation. Write down your reflections, focusing on the following questions:

- What message do I believe GOD is communicating to me through this passage?
- How does this scripture challenge or comfort me?
- How can I apply this teaching in my daily life?

Step 3: Daily Gratitude Journal

At the end of each day, take five minutes to write down three things you are grateful for. These can be simple or profound but focus on recognizing GOD's presence in your life throughout the day. This practice will help you develop a habit of seeing GOD's grace in the everyday moments.

Step 4: Prayer Journal

Transform your journaling into a written prayer. Address GOD directly, sharing your thoughts, concerns, and gratitude as you would in spoken prayer. Be honest and open, knowing that your journal is a private space for your spiritual dialogue with GOD.

Conclude your prayer with a request for guidance or strength in your spiritual journey.

Step 5: Weekly Review and Reflection

At the end of each week, review your journal entries. Look for patterns in your thoughts, prayers, and reflections. Ask yourself:

- What have I learned about my spiritual journey this week?
- How has my understanding of GOD's presence in my life evolved?
- Are there areas where I need to focus more attention or seek further guidance?

Write a brief summary of your reflections, noting any insights or areas where you feel called to grow.

Step 6: Share Your Experience

(Optional) If you feel comfortable, share your journaling experience with a trusted friend, spiritual director, or small group. Discuss how the practice has impacted your spiritual life and explore how you might support each other in your faith journeys.

Results: By consistently engaging in this exercise, you will develop a deeper, more personal relationship with GOD. You will also create a tangible record of your spiritual growth, which you can revisit and reflect upon over time. This practice will help you integrate the teachings of this chapter into your daily life, making your faith an active and vibrant part of who you are.

NOTES:

Chapter 08: The Human Energy Field

The human energy field is a concept that bridges the physical and spiritual realms, reflecting the interconnectedness of body, mind, and spirit. This chapter explores the theological significance of the human energy field, offering insights into how it aligns with the teachings of the Catholic faith. We will also examine practical ways to understand and nurture this energy field to deepen our relationship with GOD and enhance our spiritual well-being.

Theological Insights

The concept of the human energy field may seem foreign to some Catholics, yet it is deeply intertwined with the theological understanding of the human person as created in the image of GOD (*Imago Dei*). This concept suggests that just as GOD is a spiritual being, humans too possess a spiritual dimension that transcends the physical body. The human energy field can be understood as a manifestation of this spiritual dimension, where the body, mind, and soul intersect and interact with the divine.

In the context of Catholic theology, the human energy field is not explicitly mentioned, but its elements can be found in various teachings of the Church. The Holy Spirit, the third person of The Holy Trinity, plays a crucial role in energizing and sustaining the spiritual life of believers. As St. Paul writes in his first letter to the Corinthians, *"Do you not know that your bodies are temples of The Holy Spirit, who is in you, whom you have received from GOD?"* (1 Corinthians 6:19, NIV)[1]. This passage highlights the sacredness of the human body and, by extension, the energy that animates it.

The Christ Consciousness, which refers to the awareness of Christ's presence within us, also aligns with the concept of the human energy field. When we live in accordance with Christ's teachings, we allow His energy - His love, peace, and grace - to flow through us, influencing our thoughts, actions, and interactions with others. This divine energy not only sustains our spiritual life but also has the power to heal and transform us.

In modern times, the understanding of the human energy field can be harmonized with the Catholic belief in the sanctity of the human person and the indwelling of The Holy Spirit. Catholics are called to be stewards of their bodies and souls, recognizing that the energy within them is a gift from GOD, meant to be nurtured and used for His glory[2].

Application in Modern Life

Integrating the concept of the human energy field into everyday life can provide Catholics with a deeper understanding of their spiritual and physical well-being. In a world that often emphasizes the material and the tangible, recognizing the existence of the human energy field can help individuals maintain a balanced perspective, where both the spiritual and physical aspects of life are valued and nurtured.

One common challenge faced by modern Catholics is the constant stress and demands of daily life. These pressures can lead to spiritual fatigue and a sense of disconnection from GOD. Understanding the human energy field can offer practical tools for managing stress and maintaining spiritual vitality. For example, regular prayer, meditation, and participation in the sacraments can help recharge one's spiritual energy, creating a sense of peace and centeredness amidst the chaos of everyday life[3].

Consider the example of a working professional who struggles to balance career responsibilities with spiritual commitments. By recognizing the importance of their human energy field, they can incorporate practices like mindfulness, deep breathing, and reflective prayer into their daily routine. These practices not only help to reduce stress but also open channels for The Holy Spirit to work within them, providing clarity and guidance in their decisions.

Another practical application of this concept can be found in relationships. When we understand that each person has their own energy field, influenced by their spiritual state, we can approach interactions with greater compassion and empathy. This perspective encourages us to see others not just as physical beings but as spiritual entities created in GOD's image. This understanding can transform how we relate to others, fostering deeper, more meaningful connections rooted in Christ's love.

Creating Practical Spiritual Tools

To help readers deepen their understanding and nurture their human energy field, here are some practical spiritual tools and practices:

1. **Daily Prayer and Meditation:**

- Begin and end each day with a few minutes of prayer and meditation. Focus on inviting The Holy Spirit into your life, asking for guidance, peace, and protection. Visualize the energy of GOD's love flowing through you, filling you with light and strength.

2. **Scripture Reflection:**

- Choose a passage from The Bible that speaks to you about the sacredness of the body and the presence of The Holy Spirit. Reflect on how this passage relates to your own life and energy field. Consider journaling your thoughts to deepen your understanding.

3. **Breathing Exercises:**

- Practice deep breathing exercises to calm the mind and rejuvenate your energy field. As you inhale, imagine breathing in GOD's love and grace; as you exhale, release any tension or negativity. This simple practice can be done anywhere, providing a quick way to reconnect with GOD throughout the day.

4. **Mindful Movement:**

   - Engage in physical activities like walking, stretching, or yoga with a mindful focus on GOD's presence within you. As you move, be aware of how your body feels and how your energy shifts. Offer each movement as a prayer, thanking GOD for the gift of your body and the energy that sustains it.

5. **Sacramental Participation:**

   - Regularly participate in the sacraments, especially the Eucharist and Reconciliation. These sacraments are powerful means of spiritual renewal, cleansing your energy field and filling you with divine grace. Approach each sacrament with the intention of deepening your connection with GOD and revitalizing your spiritual energy.

6. **Spiritual Journaling:**

   - Keep a journal to document your experiences with these practices. Reflect on how your energy field feels before and after prayer, meditation, or sacramental participation. Use your journal to track your spiritual growth and identify areas where you may need to focus more attention.

The concept of the human energy field offers Catholics a profound way to understand the integration of body, mind, and spirit. By nurturing this energy field through prayer, meditation, and sacramental participation, we can deepen our relationship with GOD and live more fully in His presence. These practices not only enhance our spiritual well-being but also empower us to carry Christ's energy into the world, touching the lives of others with His love and grace.

Exercise: *Nurturing Your Human Energy Field*

Objective: To help you understand and integrate the concept of the human energy field into your daily life, enhancing your spiritual, mental, and physical well-being through practical exercises.

Step 1: Daily Energy Check-In

Begin each day with a brief energy check-in. Find a quiet space where you can sit comfortably. Close your eyes, take a few deep breaths, and ask yourself:

- How do I feel physically, emotionally, and spiritually right now?
- Do I sense any areas of tension, discomfort, or imbalance in my body?
- Where do I feel most at peace or energized?

Spend about five minutes reflecting on these questions. Write down your observations in a journal, noting any patterns or changes over time.

Step 2: Intentional Prayer and Meditation

Dedicate at least 10 minutes each day to prayer and meditation focused on your energy field. Begin with a prayer inviting the Holy Spirit to fill you with divine energy. Then, practice the following meditation:

- Sit comfortably and close your eyes.

- Imagine a warm, bright light at the top of your head, representing GOD's presence.
- Visualize this light slowly moving down through your body, filling every part of you with healing energy.
- As the light moves, focus on areas where you felt tension or discomfort during your check-in. Imagine the light dissolving these tensions and restoring balance.
- End the meditation by expressing gratitude to GOD for His healing presence.

Step 3: Mindful Movement Practice

Incorporate mindful movement into your day, such as stretching, walking, or simple yoga. As you move, focus on the connection between your body and spirit. Pay attention to how your movements affect your energy levels. For example:

- During a walk, sync your breath with your steps, imagining each breath drawing in divine energy and each step grounding you in GOD's creation.
- While stretching, focus on the release of tension and the flow of energy through your body. Offer each stretch as a prayer of thanks for the gift of your body.

Step 4: Sacramental Preparation and Reflection

Before participating in the sacraments, especially the Eucharist or Reconciliation, take time to prepare by reflecting on your energy field. Ask yourself:

- What spiritual or emotional burdens am I carrying that I need to release?
- How can I open myself more fully to receive GOD's grace through this sacrament?

After participating in the sacrament, reflect on how you feel. Write in your journal about any changes in your energy levels, emotions, or spiritual state. Note how the sacrament impacted your sense of connection with GOD.

Step 5: Weekly Review and Adjustment

At the end of each week, review your journal entries. Reflect on how your practices have affected your overall energy field and spiritual well-being. Ask yourself:

- What practices made the most significant impact on my energy and spiritual connection?
- Are there areas where I still feel imbalanced or disconnected?
- How can I adjust my daily routine to better nurture my energy field?

Make any necessary adjustments to your practices based on these reflections. Consider sharing your experiences with a trusted spiritual director or friend to gain additional insights.

Results: By consistently engaging in these exercises, you will develop a heightened awareness of your human energy field and its connection to your spiritual life. Over time, you will experience a greater sense of balance, peace, and divine presence in your daily activities. This exercise will also help you identify and address areas of spiritual or emotional imbalance, leading to a more integrated and fulfilling spiritual journey.

Chapter 09: Energy Healing Basics and The Chakras

The exploration of energy healing and the chakras provides a unique intersection of spirituality and holistic well-being. This chapter aims to explain the basics of energy healing within a Christian context and how the concept of chakras can be understood through the lens of Catholic theology. By integrating these concepts into daily life, Catholics can deepen their connection with GOD and enhance their spiritual, emotional, and physical health.

Theological Insights

Energy healing, though often associated with Eastern traditions, can be approached from a Christian perspective that respects the sanctity of the human body as the temple of the Holy Spirit (1 Corinthians 6:19)[1]. The idea that our physical bodies are imbued with divine energy aligns with the Christian understanding of GOD's immanence - His presence within creation and within us. This divine presence is reflected in The Christ Consciousness, the awareness of Christ's indwelling presence that empowers us to live according to GOD's will.

The concept of chakras, which refers to the energy centers within the body, can be reconciled with Christian theology by viewing them as facets of the soul's interaction with the physical body. Just as the sacraments provide spiritual nourishment and healing, understanding and balancing the chakras can be seen as a way of cooperating with GOD's grace to maintain the health of both body and soul. The Holy Trinity - Father, Son, and Holy Spirit - can be understood as the ultimate source of the energy that flows through these chakras, sustaining and sanctifying our entire being.

In this context, each chakra can be viewed as a center where divine energy manifests in different aspects of our lives. For example, the Heart Chakra, often associated with love and compassion, can be linked to the Christian commandment to love one another as Christ has loved us (John 13:34)[2]. By focusing on the spiritual significance of each chakra, Catholics can use this understanding to draw closer to GOD and live more fully in His presence.

Application in Modern Life

In the modern world, where stress, anxiety, and physical ailments are commonplace, energy healing offers practical tools for Catholics to maintain spiritual and physical balance. By understanding and working with their chakras, individuals can address not only their physical well-being but also their emotional and spiritual health. This holistic approach to healing aligns with the Christian call to care for the whole person - body, mind, and spirit.

One of the common challenges faced by modern Catholics is the disconnection between their spiritual practices and their daily lives. The constant demands of work, family, and social obligations can lead to a compartmentalization of faith, where spiritual practices are reserved for specific times and places, rather than being integrated into every aspect of life. By incorporating energy healing and chakra work into daily routines, Catholics can create a continuous awareness of GOD's presence, allowing their faith to permeate all areas of life.

Consider the example of a Catholic who struggles with anxiety and stress due to work pressures. By understanding the role of the Solar Plexus chakra, which is associated with personal power and self-esteem, they can use prayer and meditation to invite GOD's healing presence into this energy center. This might involve focusing on scripture passages that emphasize GOD's strength and protection, such as Philippians 4:13: *"I can do all things through Christ who strengthens me[3]."* By regularly meditating on this verse while visualizing divine light filling the Solar Plexus chakra, the individual can experience a sense of peace and empowerment that carries over into their work life.

Another practical application is in relationships. The Heart chakra, which governs love and relationships, can be nurtured through acts of compassion and forgiveness. When faced with conflicts or emotional pain, Catholics can turn to the example of Jesus' unconditional love and forgiveness. By meditating on the Heart chakra and asking for GOD's grace to heal and open their hearts, they can approach difficult relationships with a renewed sense of compassion and understanding.

Creating Practical Spiritual Tools

To help readers integrate energy healing and chakra work into their spiritual practice, here are some practical tools and exercises:

1. **Chakra Meditation with Scripture:**

- Begin by choosing a chakra to focus on, such as the Heart chakra. Sit in a quiet space, close your eyes, and take a few deep breaths. As you breathe in, visualize a warm, healing light filling the chakra, and as you exhale, release any tension or negativity.
- Pair this visualization with a relevant scripture passage. For the Heart chakra, you might meditate on 1 Corinthians 13:4-7[4], which describes the qualities of love. Repeat the passage slowly in your mind as you focus on the chakra, inviting GOD's love to fill and heal your heart.

2. **Chakra Alignment Prayer:**

- Develop a prayer routine that includes specific intentions for each chakra. For example, when praying for the Throat chakra (associated with communication and truth), ask GOD to help you speak with honesty and kindness in all your interactions.
- This prayer can be incorporated into your morning or evening routine, allowing you to start or end your day with a balanced energy field aligned with GOD's will.

3. **Healing Touch:**

- If you are comfortable with physical touch as part of your spiritual practice, you can incorporate gentle self-massage or placing your hands over different chakras while praying. This can enhance your awareness of these energy centers and help you feel more connected to GOD's healing presence.
- For example, while praying for healing in your relationships, you might place your hands over your Heart chakra and ask GOD to fill your heart with His love and peace.

4. **Daily Chakra Check-In:**

- At the beginning or end of each day, take a few minutes to check in with your chakras. Reflect on how each one feels - are there any areas where you feel blocked, tense, or depleted? Use this awareness to guide your prayers and spiritual practices for the day.
- This can also be a time to express gratitude for any areas where you feel strong and balanced, thanking GOD for His continuous presence and support.

Understanding and working with the chakras within a Christian context offers Catholics a valuable tool for maintaining spiritual, emotional, and physical health. By integrating these practices into daily life, Catholics can foster a deeper connection with GOD, allowing His grace to flow more freely through their entire being. This holistic approach to healing and well-being not only enhances personal spiritual growth but also empowers individuals to live out their faith more fully in every aspect of life.

Exercise: *Balancing Your Chakras with Christian Meditation*

Objective: To help you understand and integrate the concepts of energy healing and chakras into your spiritual practice, enhancing your physical, emotional, and spiritual well-being through Christian meditation and prayer.

Step 1: Chakra Identification and Prayer Intention

Begin by identifying the chakra you wish to focus on. Here's a brief overview of the seven main chakras:

- **Root Chakra (Base of the spine):** Associated with stability and grounding.
- **Sacral Chakra (Lower abdomen):** Linked to creativity and emotions.
- **Solar Plexus Chakra (Upper abdomen):** Related to personal power and self-esteem.
- **Heart Chakra (Center of the chest):** Governs love and compassion.
- **Throat Chakra (Throat):** Involves communication and truth.
- **Third Eye Chakra (Forehead):** Connected to intuition and insight.
- **Crown Chakra (Top of the head):** Associated with spiritual connection and enlightenment.

Choose one chakra that resonates with your current spiritual or emotional needs. Set a clear prayer intention for this exercise, such as seeking GOD's guidance in communication (Throat Chakra) or deepening your capacity for love and forgiveness (Heart Chakra).

Step 2: Scripture-Based Meditation

Find a quiet place where you can sit comfortably. Close your eyes and take a few deep breaths to center yourself. Select a scripture passage that aligns with the chakra you are focusing on. Here are some examples:

- **Root Chakra:** *"The Lord is my rock, my fortress, and my deliverer"* (Psalm 18:2).

- **Heart Chakra:** *"Love one another as I have loved you"* (John 13:34).

- **Throat Chakra:** *"Let your speech always be gracious, seasoned with salt"* (Colossians 4:6).

Read the passage slowly, allowing its meaning to sink into your mind and heart. As you meditate on the scripture, visualize the corresponding chakra filling with light and energy, infused with the power of GOD's Word.

Step 3: Chakra Healing Prayer

After your meditation, begin a prayer focused on healing and balancing the chakra. For example, if you are focusing on the Heart Chakra, your prayer might be:

"Lord, fill my heart with Your love and compassion. Help me to forgive those who have hurt me and to love others as You have loved me. Let Your divine love flow through my heart, healing any wounds and opening me to greater empathy and kindness."

Place your hand over the chakra area as you pray, imagining GOD's healing energy flowing into that part of your body.

Step 4: Daily Chakra Check-In

Incorporate a quick chakra check-in into your daily routine, either in the morning or before bed. Spend a few moments in prayer, asking GOD to reveal any imbalances or areas where you need His healing touch. Use this time to reflect on your chosen chakra and how it has influenced your day. Consider journaling your thoughts, noting any changes in your emotional, physical, or spiritual state.

Step 5: Weekly Reflection and Adjustment

At the end of each week, review your chakra check-ins and meditation experiences. Ask yourself:

- Which chakra felt most balanced, and which needed more attention?
- How did focusing on this chakra impact your relationship with GOD and others?
- Are there other chakras you feel called to work on?

Based on your reflections, choose a new chakra to focus on for the next week or continue deepening your work with the same chakra.

Results: By consistently practicing these exercises, you will gain a deeper understanding of how your chakras interact with your spiritual life. You will learn to recognize imbalances and address them through prayer, scripture, and meditation, leading to a more harmonious and integrated state of being. This practice will help you maintain a balanced energy field, fostering a stronger connection with GOD and enhancing your ability to live out your faith in everyday life.

Chapter 10: The Early Years of Jesus

The early years of Jesus, often referred to as His "hidden years," provide a profound foundation for understanding His human and divine nature. This chapter delves into the significance of these formative years, exploring how they shaped Jesus' mission and offering insights into how modern Catholics can draw from His example to navigate their own spiritual journeys.

Theological Insights

The early years of Jesus are primarily recorded in the Gospels of Matthew and Luke, with key events such as the Nativity, the Presentation in the Temple, the Flight into Egypt, and the finding of Jesus in the Temple at age twelve. These events highlight the mystery of the Incarnation - GOD becoming man in the person of Jesus Christ (John 1:14)[1]. The concept of the Incarnation is central to Christian theology, emphasizing that Jesus is both fully divine and fully human, possessing the nature of GOD while also experiencing the realities of human life.

Theologically, these early years are significant because they demonstrate Jesus' full immersion into human existence. He was born into a humble family, lived in a small village, and was obedient to His earthly parents, Mary and Joseph. This reflects the humility of GOD, who chose to enter the world not as a powerful ruler but as a vulnerable child. The Christ Consciousness - an awareness of Christ's divine nature within us - can be fostered by reflecting on how Jesus embraced every aspect of human life, including its challenges and obscurities.

The Holy Trinity also plays a role in understanding the early years of Jesus. Though Jesus was a child, He was still the Son of GOD, eternally begotten of the Father, and filled with the Holy Spirit. His early life was a preparation for His public ministry, where the full revelation of The Trinity would become more apparent, especially at His baptism (Matthew 3:16-17)[2].

For modern Catholics, the early years of Jesus are a reminder that every stage of life, no matter how ordinary, is filled with divine purpose. Jesus' hidden years invite us to value the quiet, unnoticed moments of our own lives, recognizing that GOD's work often unfolds in the background, away from public view.

Application in Modern Life

The early years of Jesus offer several insights that can be applied to the lives of modern Catholics. One key lesson is the importance of patience and trust in GOD's timing. Jesus lived thirty years in relative obscurity before beginning His public ministry. This teaches us that periods of waiting or apparent inactivity are not wasted but are times of preparation and growth.

In our fast-paced world, it is easy to feel pressured to achieve immediate results or public recognition. However, the example of Jesus' early years encourages us to embrace the hidden, quiet seasons of life. These are the times when GOD often does His deepest work in us, forming our character and strengthening our faith.

For example, consider a Catholic professional who is frustrated with a lack of visible progress in their career. By reflecting on the hidden years of Jesus, they can find peace in knowing that GOD is working in their life even when the results are not immediately apparent. They can use this time to deepen their relationship with GOD, trusting that He is preparing them for future opportunities.

Another application is the importance of family life and obedience. Jesus' submission to Mary and Joseph (Luke 2:51) underscores the value of honoring family responsibilities and living in harmony with those around us. In modern life, balancing spiritual commitments with family obligations can be challenging, but Jesus' example shows that family life is not separate from our spiritual journey - it is a vital part of it.

For instance, a parent who is struggling to balance work, spiritual life, and family duties can look to Jesus' early years as a model for integrating faith into everyday life. By prioritizing time with family and seeing these interactions as opportunities to live out their faith, they can create a harmonious balance that honors GOD.

Creating Practical Spiritual Tools

To help readers integrate the lessons from Jesus' early years into their daily lives, here are some practical spiritual tools:

1. **Meditation on the Hidden Years:**

    - Set aside time each week to meditate on the hidden years of Jesus. Reflect on the humility and patience of Jesus during this period and how these virtues can be applied to your own life. Use passages like Luke 2:39-52[3] as a starting point for your meditation.

2. **Daily Offering:**

    - Begin each day with a prayer of offering, dedicating all your actions, both seen and unseen, to GOD. This practice helps to sanctify the ordinary moments of your day, reminding you that every task, no matter how small, has spiritual significance.
    - Example prayer: *"Lord, I offer You this day, with all its tasks, challenges, and joys. May everything I do be for Your glory and in accordance with Your will."*

3. **Family Prayer Time:**

    - Incorporate regular family prayer into your routine, such as saying the Rosary together or reading a Bible passage before meals. This practice strengthens family bonds and aligns your household with the example of the Holy Family.

4. **Patience Journal:**
   - Keep a journal where you reflect on areas of your life where you are called to patience and trust in GOD's timing. Write about your struggles and victories in these areas and note how reflecting on the hidden years of Jesus has helped you grow in patience.

5. **Acts of Humility:**
   - Consciously choose acts of humility each day, whether it's taking on a simple task without seeking recognition or offering a word of encouragement to someone in need. These acts mirror the hidden, humble life of Jesus and help cultivate a Christ-like character.

The early years of Jesus provide a rich source of spiritual insights for modern Catholics. By reflecting on His hidden life, we can learn to value the quiet, unseen moments in our own lives, trusting that GOD is at work even when we cannot see it. By applying these lessons to our daily routines, we deepen our relationship with GOD and grow in the virtues of patience, humility, and trust. These practices not only enhance our spiritual life but also help us to live more fully in accordance with GOD's will, just as Jesus did during His early years.

Exercise: *Embracing the Hidden Years of Your Life*

Objective: To help you reflect on and embrace the "hidden years" of your life, where growth and preparation take place away from public view, and to apply the virtues of patience, humility, and trust as modeled by Jesus during His early years.

Step 1: Reflective Meditation on Jesus' Hidden Years

Find a quiet space where you can sit comfortably. Begin by reading Luke 2:39-52, which describes the early years of Jesus, particularly the event of finding Him in the Temple. As you read, imagine what Jesus' daily life might have been like during these years - His time with Mary and Joseph, His learning, and His work as a carpenter.

Spend 10-15 minutes in silent meditation, reflecting on how these hidden years were a time of preparation and growth for Jesus. Consider the parallels in your own life where you might feel "hidden" or unnoticed. What lessons might GOD be teaching you during these times?

Step 2: Journaling Your Own Hidden Years

After your meditation, take out a journal and write about a period in your life that felt like a "hidden" time - perhaps a season where you were working diligently without recognition, waiting for an opportunity, or simply going through daily routines without any apparent progress.

Ask yourself:
- How did I feel during this time?

- What did I learn about myself and my relationship with GOD?
- How can I see GOD's hand at work, even in the small, unnoticed details?

Write freely for about 15-20 minutes, allowing your thoughts and reflections to flow naturally.

Step 3: Identify Areas for Growth

Now, think about your current life situation. Identify areas where you might need to practice the virtues of patience, humility, or trust, as Jesus did during His hidden years.

Create a list of specific situations where these virtues can be applied. For example:

- Waiting for a promotion or recognition at work.
- Managing family responsibilities without immediate appreciation.
- Trusting in GOD's timing for personal or spiritual growth.

For each situation, write down one concrete action you can take to practice the corresponding virtue.

Step 4: Daily Practice of Humility and Patience

Choose one action from your list each day and consciously practice it. This could be as simple as completing a task at work without seeking praise, or patiently listening to a family member without rushing to give advice.

At the end of the day, reflect on your experience:

- How did practicing this virtue affect your attitude and interactions?
- Did you feel closer to GOD through this practice?
- What insights did you gain about yourself and your spiritual journey?

Step 5: Weekly Family Reflection

If you have a family, set aside time once a week to reflect together on the hidden years of Jesus and how His example can inspire your daily lives. You might read a short scripture passage together and discuss how everyone can apply the lessons of humility, patience, and trust in their own lives.

Encourage each family member to share their experiences of practicing these virtues throughout the week, and close with a prayer asking for the grace to continue growing in these areas.

Results: By engaging in this exercise, you will develop a deeper appreciation for the hidden seasons of your life and recognize them as opportunities for spiritual growth. You will also cultivate the virtues of patience, humility, and trust, allowing you to navigate life's challenges with a Christ-like attitude. This practice will help you integrate your faith into everyday activities, making even the most mundane tasks a meaningful part of your spiritual journey.

Chapter 11: The Lost Years of Jesus

The "Lost Years of Jesus" refers to the period between Jesus' childhood and the beginning of His public ministry at around 30 years of age, a time largely unrecorded in the Gospels. This chapter explores the significance of these years, offering theological insights and practical applications for modern Catholics. By reflecting on this period, readers can gain a deeper understanding of Jesus' humanity and divinity and learn how to integrate faith into the seemingly ordinary aspects of life.

Theological Insights

The "Lost Years" of Jesus, though not detailed in the scriptures, are rich in theological significance. This period, often seen as a time of preparation, underscores the mystery of the Incarnation - the belief that Jesus is fully GOD and fully man. The Gospels tell us little about these years, except for the account of Jesus being found in the Temple at the age of twelve (Luke 2:41-52)[1]. This episode, however, provides a glimpse into Jesus' growing awareness of His divine mission.

Theologically, the silence of the Gospels about these years can be understood as emphasizing the ordinariness of Jesus' life, which is itself a profound statement about the sanctity of everyday human existence. Jesus, who is the Christ, spent many years living a simple life in Nazareth, working as a carpenter, and fulfilling His duties as a son. This hidden life is a testament to the value GOD places on the ordinary and the mundane. **The Christ Consciousness - an awareness of the divine presence within us** - can be deepened by recognizing that Jesus' divinity was not diminished by His participation in ordinary human life; rather, it was expressed through it.

The Holy Trinity is also relevant to understanding these lost years. Even in His hidden life, Jesus was in perfect communion with the Father and the Holy Spirit. This period of quiet preparation was integral to His public ministry, as it allowed for the human development necessary for His role as the Savior. For modern-day Catholics, this period encourages us to trust in GOD's timing and to recognize that periods of waiting or apparent inactivity can be spiritually fruitful[2].

Application in Modern Life

The concept of the "Lost Years" resonates with many modern Catholics who experience seasons of life that seem uneventful or unremarkable. In a world that often glorifies busyness and achievement, the hidden years of Jesus offer a countercultural message: that our worth is not measured by visible accomplishments, but by our faithfulness in the small, daily tasks of life.

One common challenge for modern Catholics is the tension between spiritual commitments and secular responsibilities. It can be difficult to see the spiritual significance of routine tasks such as work, household chores, or even the quiet moments of solitude. However, the example of Jesus' lost years reminds us that these ordinary moments are sacred. They are opportunities to grow in virtue, to deepen our relationship with GOD, and to prepare for the mission He has for us.

For example, consider a Catholic who is currently working in a job that feels monotonous and unfulfilling. By reflecting on the lost years of Jesus, they can find meaning in their work, knowing that Jesus too lived an ordinary life for many years. This perspective can transform their approach to work, helping them to see it as a way to serve GOD and others, rather than merely a means to an end[3].

Another application is in the area of personal development and spiritual growth. The lost years of Jesus were likely a time of learning, both in His trade as a carpenter and in His spiritual life. This teaches us the importance of continuous learning and growth, even when it seems like nothing significant is happening. For Catholics, this might mean committing to regular prayer, scripture study, or learning new skills, trusting that these efforts will bear fruit in GOD's time.

Creating Practical Spiritual Tools

To help readers integrate the lessons from the lost years of Jesus into their daily lives, here are some practical spiritual tools:

1. **Daily Reflection on Hidden Blessings:**

- At the end of each day, take a few moments to reflect on the hidden blessings in your life. These might be small moments of peace, unnoticed acts of kindness, or quiet achievements. Write them down in a journal, offering thanks to GOD for His presence in these ordinary moments.

2. **Sanctifying Ordinary Tasks:**

- Choose one routine task each day - whether it's doing the dishes, driving to work, or folding laundry - and consciously offer it to GOD as a prayer. As you perform the task, repeat a simple prayer like, *"Lord, I offer this to You," and focus on doing it with love and attention.*

3. **Scripture Meditation:**

- Meditate on the account of Jesus in the Temple (Luke 2:41-52). Imagine yourself as one of the onlookers, witnessing this moment of divine revelation. Reflect on how Jesus, even at a young age, was preparing for His mission. Consider how GOD might be preparing you during your own "hidden years."

4. **Patience and Trust Practice:**

- If you are in a season of waiting or feel stuck in a routine, practice patience and trust by setting aside a few minutes each day for silent prayer. In this silence, ask GOD to help you trust in His timing and to open your heart to the growth that is happening beneath the surface.

5. **Spiritual Growth Plan:**

   - Create a simple spiritual growth plan for yourself. Identify one area where you want to grow - such as in prayer, scripture reading, or a particular virtue - and set small, achievable goals. Review your progress regularly, knowing that even slow growth is valuable in GOD's eyes.

The lost years of Jesus offer a profound lesson for modern Catholics: that the ordinary, hidden moments of life are deeply valuable in the eyes of GOD. By embracing these times with faithfulness and trust, we can grow in our relationship with GOD and prepare for the mission He has for us. The practical spiritual tools provided in this chapter are designed to help you integrate these insights into your daily life, transforming the mundane into a sacred space where GOD's presence is felt and His work is accomplished.

Exercise: *Embracing the Hidden Seasons of Life*

Objective: To help you recognize the value of "hidden" periods in your life - times of growth, learning, and preparation that may seem uneventful on the surface - and to integrate the lessons from the lost years of Jesus into your daily spiritual practice.

Step 1: Reflect on a Hidden Season

Begin by identifying a period in your life that felt "hidden" or unremarkable. This could be a time when you were waiting for something significant to happen, or when you were engaged in routine tasks that seemed to lack spiritual significance.

- Take 10-15 minutes to write about this period in a journal. Reflect on the following questions:
    - ✓ What did you learn during this time?
    - ✓ How did this period prepare you for something later in life?
    - ✓ Can you see GOD's hand at work during this season, even if it was not immediately obvious?

Step 2: Daily Offerings for Ordinary Tasks

Choose a routine task you perform daily—such as cooking, cleaning, or commuting—and turn it into a spiritual offering. Before beginning the task, say a simple prayer: *"Lord, I offer this task to You. May it be a part of my preparation for the mission You have for me."*

- As you complete the task, focus on doing it with care and attention, seeing it as an act of service to GOD.
- Afterward, take a moment to thank GOD for the opportunity to serve Him in small ways.

Step 3: Scripture Meditation on the Lost Years

Set aside time each day for a week to meditate on

Luke 2:41-52, the story of Jesus being found in the Temple.

Use the following method:

- Read the passage slowly and prayerfully, imagining yourself in the scene.

- Reflect on Jesus' early life, His time of preparation, and the importance of His hidden years.
- Ask GOD to reveal how He is preparing you during your own hidden seasons.
- Journal your thoughts and any insights you receive during this meditation.

Step 4: Practice Patience in Waiting

If you are currently in a season of waiting - whether for a job, a relationship, or spiritual growth - practice patience by setting aside time each day to silently wait on GOD. During this time, avoid asking for specific outcomes. Instead, focus on surrendering your timeline to GOD and trusting in His perfect timing.

- As you practice this, write down any frustrations, fears, or hopes you have in your journal. Reflect on how these feelings might be opportunities for growth in trust and patience.

Step 5: Weekly Review and Reflection

At the end of each week, review your journal entries and reflections from the exercises above. Consider the following:

- How has your perspective on your "hidden" seasons changed?
- What spiritual growth or insights have emerged from embracing these periods?
- Are there specific ways you can continue to integrate these lessons into your daily life?

Write a summary of your reflections and set a goal for how you will carry these lessons forward into the next week.

Results: By engaging in this exercise, you will develop a deeper understanding of the value of hidden seasons in your life. You will learn to embrace these times as opportunities for spiritual growth and preparation, just as Jesus' lost years were a time of divine preparation for His public ministry. This practice will help you cultivate patience, trust in GOD's timing, and a greater appreciation for the ordinary moments that contribute to your spiritual journey.

Chapter 12: Books about Jesus:
- The Gospel of Thomas
- The Gospel of John
- Aquarian Gospel of Jesus Christ
- The Nag Hammadi Scriptures,
- The Unknown Life of Jesus Christ
- The Mystical Theology of Dionysius and Areopagite,
- The Untold Story of Jesus: A Modern Biography from The Urantia Book

The core theme of this chapter is to explore various non-canonical and lesser-known texts about Jesus, shedding light on alternative perspectives and deeper spiritual insights that contribute to a richer understanding of Christ. This exploration is not merely academic; it serves the larger purpose of this book by providing practical spiritual tools and theological insights that modern Catholics can integrate into their daily lives. By examining these texts, we aim to bridge the gap between traditional Catholic teachings and the broader spiritual quest that many believers embark on in today's complex world.

Theological Insights

At the heart of this chapter is the exploration of the nature of Jesus, not just as a historical figure, but as a profound spiritual presence that transcends time and space. The texts we examine offer diverse interpretations and insights into Jesus' nature, his teachings, and his role in the broader context of the Christ Consciousness and The Holy Trinity.

The Gospel of Thomas offers a collection of sayings attributed to Jesus, emphasizing a more mystical understanding of his teachings. This text, discovered near Nag Hammadi in 1945, presents Jesus as a revealer of divine knowledge rather than solely a savior through atonement. It challenges readers to seek the Kingdom of GOD within themselves, resonating with the idea that Jesus' message was one of self-realization and inner enlightenment. This aligns with the concept of the Christ Consciousness - a universal, divine essence accessible to all believers, calling them to embody the same consciousness that Jesus demonstrated in his life.

The Gospel of John, one of the four canonical gospels, offers a distinct theological perspective that emphasizes Jesus' divinity. This gospel is central to traditional Christian teachings on The Holy Trinity, particularly in its portrayal of Jesus as the Logos - the Word made flesh[1]. The Gospel of John underscores the unity of Jesus with GOD the Father and The Holy Spirit, a foundational concept for understanding the Holy Trinity. For modern Catholics, this gospel offers a profound insight into the mystery of Christ, urging believers to see Jesus not only as a teacher but as the embodiment of GOD's Word in the world.

The Aquarian Gospel of Jesus the Christ, written by Levi H. Dowling, is a New Age text that presents a narrative of

Jesus' life, including his "lost years" and travels through various cultures[2]. While not considered authoritative by the Church, this text can inspire a broader view of Jesus as a universal teacher whose wisdom transcends cultural and religious boundaries. It supports the idea that Jesus' teachings are relevant to all of humanity, not just to those within the Christian tradition, thereby encouraging Catholics to explore a more inclusive and universal approach to spirituality.

The Nag Hammadi Scriptures, which include a variety of Gnostic texts, offer alternative Christian perspectives that were often suppressed by early Church authorities. These texts, such as the *Gospel of Philip* and *The Secret Book of John*, present a complex view of Jesus as a revealer of secret knowledge and a guide to spiritual liberation. While these ideas are not in line with orthodox Catholic doctrine, they can provoke thoughtful reflection on the nature of divine revelation and the ways in which Jesus' message has been understood across different spiritual traditions.

The Unknown Life of Jesus Christ, attributed to the Russian journalist Nicolas Notovitch, claims to document Jesus' travels and teachings in India during his "lost years." Although its authenticity is highly debated, the text offers a fascinating perspective on the universality of Jesus' message and his potential connections with other religious traditions, such as Hinduism and Buddhism. This idea can resonate with modern Catholics who are interested in interfaith dialogue and the universal aspects of Jesus' teachings[3].

The Mystical Theology of Dionysius the Areopagite is a key text in the Christian mystical tradition, attributed to a fifth-century Christian theologian. This work explores the nature of GOD as an incomprehensible, transcendent being and emphasizes the importance of negative theology - the idea that GOD is beyond all human concepts and language[4]. For Catholics, this text can deepen their understanding of the mystery of The Holy Trinity and encourage a more contemplative approach to their faith, where the focus is on experiencing GOD's presence rather than solely on intellectual understanding.

The Untold Story of Jesus: A Modern Biography from The Urantia Book presents an expansive narrative of Jesus' life, claiming to offer a cosmic perspective on his mission. This text, which is part of the larger *Urantia Book*, blends science fiction with theology and offers a highly speculative account of Jesus' life and teachings. While its theological basis is outside mainstream Christianity, it can inspire readers to think about the cosmic significance of Jesus' life and his role in the broader spiritual evolution of humanity.

Application in Modern Life

Incorporating the insights from these diverse texts into daily life requires a thoughtful balance between traditional Catholic practices and an openness to new spiritual perspectives. Modern Catholics often face challenges in maintaining their faith amidst secular pressures and the complexities of contemporary life. These texts, while not all aligned with Church teachings, offer unique perspectives that can enrich a Catholic's spiritual journey.

For instance, the emphasis on inner knowledge found in the *Gospel of Thomas* can encourage believers to engage in deeper meditation and self-reflection as part of their spiritual routine. Similarly, the mystical aspects of Dionysius the Areopagite's theology can be integrated into prayer practices, fostering a sense of awe and mystery in one's relationship with GOD.

Real-life examples include Catholics who have successfully integrated meditation inspired by Eastern traditions, as hinted at in *The Unknown Life of Jesus Christ*, into their daily prayer life, finding it enhances their connection with GOD. Others might find inspiration in the *Aquarian Gospel of Jesus the Christ* to engage in acts of compassion and service, seeing every person as a reflection of the divine.

Creating Practical Spiritual Tools

To deepen their faith and connection with GOD, readers can adopt the following spiritual tools based on the insights from these texts:

1. **Contemplative Prayer**: Inspired by *The Mystical Theology of Dionysius the Areopagite*, engage in silent, contemplative prayer focusing on the mystery of GOD's presence. Set aside 10-15 minutes each day to sit in silence, inviting the Holy Spirit to guide your thoughts.

2. **Meditation on the Inner Light**: Drawing from the *Gospel of Thomas*, practice a simple meditation where you visualize the light of Christ within your heart, growing brighter with each breath. This can be done for 5-10 minutes each morning to start the day with a sense of divine presence.

3. **Interfaith Reflection**: Inspired by *The Unknown Life of Jesus Christ*, spend time reading sacred texts from other religious traditions and reflect on their similarities with the teachings of Jesus. This practice can deepen your appreciation of the universal truths in Jesus' message and foster a spirit of inclusivity.

By incorporating these tools into daily routines, modern Catholics can nurture their spiritual growth, drawing from the rich and diverse perspectives offered by these texts to enhance their faith journey.

Exercise: Integrating Diverse Spiritual Insights into Daily Practice

Objective: This exercise aims to help you deepen your understanding of the various perspectives on Jesus presented in this chapter and to incorporate these insights into your daily spiritual practice. By engaging with these different texts, you will explore how they resonate with your personal faith journey and how you can apply their teachings to enhance your relationship with GOD.

Duration: 7 Days

Day 1: Reflect on the Gospel of Thomas

1. **Read**: Choose a few sayings from *The Gospel of Thomas* (available in many online sources or books).

2. **Reflect**: Spend 10-15 minutes reflecting on how these sayings challenge or expand your current understanding of Jesus' teachings.

3. **Journal**: Write a short entry on what these sayings mean to you and how they can be applied to your daily life.

Day 2: Contemplate the Divinity of Jesus in the Gospel of John

1. **Read**: Select a passage from the *Gospel of John* that highlights the divinity of Jesus, such as John 1:1-14.

2. **Meditate**: Spend 10 minutes in silent meditation, focusing on the concept of Jesus as the Logos (the Word) and how this shapes your understanding of the Holy Trinity.

3. **Journal**: Write about how this perspective influences your view of Jesus as both fully divine and fully human.

Day 3: Explore the Universal Teachings in the Aquarian Gospel

1. **Read**: Read an excerpt from *The Aquarian Gospel of Jesus the Christ*.

2. **Reflect**: Consider how Jesus' teachings, as presented in this text, can be applied universally across different cultures and religions.

3. **Journal**: Note how these teachings might inspire you to engage more openly in interfaith dialogue or to see Christ's presence in people from all walks of life.

Day 4: Delve into the Mystical Aspects of the Nag Hammadi Scriptures

1. **Read**: Explore a passage from *The Nag Hammadi Scriptures*, focusing on the mystical dimensions of Jesus' teachings.

2. **Meditate**: Spend 10 minutes in contemplation, focusing on the concept of hidden or mystical knowledge and how it applies to your spiritual journey.

3. **Journal**: Reflect on how embracing the mystical side of Christianity could deepen your faith.

Day 5: Investigate the Lost Years of Jesus

1. **Read**: Review the claims made in *The Unknown Life of Jesus Christ*.

2. **Reflect**: Think about how the idea of Jesus traveling and learning from other traditions might influence your view of his wisdom and universal teachings.

3. **Journal**: Write about how this broader perspective on Jesus' life might impact your daily spiritual practices.

Day 6: Engage with the Mystical Theology of Dionysius

1. **Read**: Read a passage from *The Mystical Theology* by Dionysius the Areopagite.

2. **Contemplate**: Spend 15 minutes in contemplative prayer, focusing on the transcendence and mystery of GOD.

3. **Journal**: Reflect on how this mystical approach to GOD can be integrated into your prayer life and overall spiritual practice.

Day 7: Synthesize Your Learnings from The Urantia Book

1. **Read**: Explore a chapter from *The Untold Story of Jesus: A Modern Biography from The Urantia Book*.

2. **Reflect**: Consider how this cosmic perspective on Jesus might influence your understanding of his role in the universe.

3. **Journal**: Summarize the key insights you've gained throughout the week and how they can be practically implemented in your spiritual life.

Final Reflection: After completing the 7-day exercise, take some time to review your journal entries. Identify the most impactful insights and consider how you can continue to integrate these diverse perspectives into your ongoing spiritual practice. Share these insights with a spiritual mentor or in a faith-based discussion group to deepen your understanding and commitment to your spiritual journey.

NOTES:

Chapter 13: Becoming a Disciple of Jesus the Christ

Defining Discipleship in the Modern World

In the journey of faith, becoming a disciple of Jesus the Christ is a profound commitment that goes beyond mere belief - it involves an active, ongoing relationship with Jesus, marked by a life of service, love, and spiritual growth. This chapter explores the essence of discipleship, its theological foundations, and practical applications for Catholics in the contemporary world.

Theological Insights

Discipleship is deeply rooted in understanding the nature of Jesus and the concept of the Christ Consciousness. Jesus of Nazareth, both fully human and fully divine, embodies the perfect union of GOD and man. The term "Christ" refers not merely to a title but to the anointed one, the Messiah, who brings the divine presence into human history. This Christ Consciousness is a state of awareness of our inherent connection to GOD, inviting us to live out this divine truth in our daily lives.

The Holy Trinity - Father, Son, and Holy Spirit - is central to understanding Jesus as the Christ. In the Gospel of John, Jesus declares, *"I am the way, the truth, and the life. No one comes to the Father except through me"* (John 14:6)[1]. This statement encapsulates the role of Jesus as the mediator between humanity and GOD, inviting believers to follow Him not only in word but in deed, embodying His teachings in their lives.

The call to discipleship is also echoed in the Great Commission, where Jesus instructs His followers: *"Go therefore and make disciples of all nations, baptizing them in the name of the Father and of the Son and of The Holy Spirit, teaching them to observe all that I have commanded you"* (Matthew 28:19-20)[2]. This passage underscores the active nature of discipleship - it is a mission that involves teaching, spreading the faith, and living according to the commandments of Jesus.

For modern Catholics, these theological concepts are not just historical doctrines but living truths that call for reflection and action. Understanding Jesus as the Christ is essential to comprehending our role as His disciples. In a world where distractions abound and secular values often conflict with spiritual truths, the call to discipleship invites us to ground our lives in the eternal truths of the Gospel, fostering a deeper relationship with GOD through Jesus Christ.

Application in Modern Life

In today's fast-paced world, balancing spiritual commitments with secular responsibilities can be challenging. However, discipleship requires integrating faith into every aspect of life. This means allowing the teachings of Jesus to influence our decisions, relationships, and personal development.

One common challenge is finding time for prayer and reflection amidst the demands of work, family, and social obligations. Yet, Jesus Himself often withdrew to solitary places to pray, even amid His busy ministry (Luke 5:16)[3]. Following His example, modern disciples can create intentional spaces for spiritual practices, ensuring that their connection with GOD remains strong.

For instance, consider the example of a working parent who, despite a hectic schedule, dedicates the first 15 minutes of the day to prayer and scripture reading. This practice sets a spiritual tone for the day, reminding them of their higher purpose and helping them approach their responsibilities with grace and patience. Another example is a professional who incorporates the teachings of Jesus into their workplace, striving to treat colleagues with kindness, integrity, and respect, thus living out their discipleship in a practical, everyday context.

Discipleship also calls for involvement in community life. The early Christian communities were marked by their shared faith, mutual support, and collective worship (Acts 2:42-47)[4]. Modern Catholics can follow this example by participating in parish activities, engaging in service projects, and fostering relationships with fellow believers. These communal aspects of faith provide support and encouragement, helping individuals to live out their discipleship more fully.

Practical Spiritual Tools

To deepen their relationship with GOD and live out their discipleship, Catholics can adopt specific spiritual practices. Here are some practical tools that can be incorporated into daily routines:

1. **Daily Prayer and Meditation:** Begin and end each day with prayer, offering thanks for blessings and seeking guidance for challenges. Meditation on scripture, especially the words of Jesus, can help internalize His teachings and apply them to daily life. An example of this could be meditating on the Beatitudes (Matthew 5:3-12)[5] and reflecting on how to embody these values in daily interactions.

2. **Spiritual Journaling:** Keeping a journal of spiritual reflections, prayers, and insights can help track spiritual growth and deepen one's understanding of discipleship. This practice encourages ongoing reflection on one's relationship with Christ and the application of His teachings.

3. **Community Involvement:** Engage in parish life by joining a ministry, participating in small groups, or volunteering for service projects. These activities provide opportunities to live out discipleship in a communal context, fostering spiritual growth through service and fellowship.

4. **Acts of Service:** Following Jesus' example of serving others, commit to regular acts of service, whether through helping a neighbor, volunteering at a local charity, or supporting church ministries. Service is a tangible expression of discipleship, reflecting Jesus' teaching that "the Son of Man came not to be served but to serve" (Mark 10:45)[6].

5. **Sacramental Life:** Regular participation in the sacraments, especially the Eucharist and Reconciliation, is essential for maintaining a strong spiritual life. These sacraments offer grace and spiritual nourishment, helping disciples to stay connected to the divine life offered by Jesus.

By incorporating these practices into daily life, modern Catholics can deepen their discipleship and grow in their relationship with Jesus Christ. Discipleship is not a one-time event but a lifelong journey of following Jesus, learning from His teachings, and embodying His love and truth in every aspect of life.

Exercise: Living as a Disciple of Jesus Christ in Daily Life

Objective: To help you internalize and implement the principles of discipleship in your daily life, fostering a deeper relationship with Jesus Christ through practical application.

Instructions:

1. **Reflection on Discipleship:**
    - Spend 10 minutes reflecting on what being a disciple of Jesus means to you personally. Consider the

teachings from this chapter, including the nature of Jesus, the Christ Consciousness, and the call to integrate faith into everyday life.

- Write down your thoughts in a journal. Focus on what aspects of discipleship resonate most with you and where you feel challenged.

2. **Identify a Key Area for Growth:**

    - Choose one area of your life where you feel called to grow as a disciple. This could be in your prayer life, your relationships, your work, or your involvement in the community.

    - Write down specific ways in which you can apply the teachings of Jesus in this area. For example, if you choose your workplace, consider how you can exhibit kindness, integrity, and service to others in your interactions.

3. **Set a Discipleship Goal:**

    - Set a clear, measurable goal related to the area you identified. For instance, if you chose to grow in prayer, your goal might be to dedicate 15 minutes each morning to prayer and scripture meditation.

    - Make sure your goal is specific, attainable, and time-bound. Write it down and place it somewhere you will see it daily.

4. **Daily Practice and Accountability:**

    - Commit to practicing your discipleship goal daily for the next two weeks. Use the spiritual tools discussed in this chapter, such as prayer, meditation, or acts of service, to support your commitment.

    - Keep a daily journal of your progress. Each day, note what you did to work toward your goal, any challenges you encountered, and any spiritual insights you gained.

5. **Weekly Reflection:**

    - At the end of each week, take 20 minutes to reflect on your progress. Consider the following questions:
        - ✓ How well did I integrate discipleship into my daily life this week?
        - ✓ What successes did I experience?
        - ✓ What challenges or obstacles did I face?
        - ✓ How did I see GOD working in my life through this exercise?
    - Write your reflections in your journal.

6. **Adjust and Continue:**

    - After two weeks, review your journal and assess your overall progress. Consider whether your goal needs adjusting or if you're ready to set a new goal in another area of your life.
    - Continue this practice, setting new discipleship goals as you grow in your faith journey.

7. **Community Sharing (Optional):**

    - If you feel comfortable, share your experience with a trusted friend, family member, or faith community.
    - Discuss how the exercise has impacted your spiritual life and what you've learned about being a disciple of Jesus.
    - Engaging with others can provide support, encouragement, and additional insights that enhance your growth.

Outcome: By the end of this exercise, you should have a deeper understanding of what it means to be a disciple of Jesus Christ and practical experience integrating His teachings into your daily life. This exercise is designed to help you build a sustainable practice of discipleship, fostering continuous spiritual growth and a closer relationship with GOD.

Chapter 14: Jesus the Mystic and Mystical Teacher

Unveiling the Mystical Nature of Jesus

Jesus of Nazareth is not only the central figure of Christianity but also one of history's most profound mystics. As a mystical teacher, Jesus embodied and taught a spiritual path that invites believers into a deeper, more intimate relationship with GOD. This chapter explores the mystical dimensions of Jesus' life and teachings, offering theological insights and practical tools for modern-day Catholics seeking to integrate these truths into their everyday lives.

Theological Insights

At the heart of understanding Jesus as a mystic lies the recognition of His unique union with GOD. This union is most clearly articulated in the doctrine of The Holy Trinity, where Jesus is understood as the Son, consubstantial with the Father and The Holy Spirit. In John 10:30, Jesus declares, "*I and the Father are one.*" This profound statement encapsulates the mystical nature of Jesus, who, in His divine humanity, reveals the intimate and inseparable relationship between GOD and creation.

The concept of Christ Consciousness is also central to understanding Jesus as a mystical teacher. Christ Consciousness refers to the awareness of the divine presence within all beings, a state of enlightenment that Jesus not only exemplified but also invited His followers to realize within themselves. In John 14:20, Jesus says, *"On that day you will realize that I am in my Father, and you are in me, and I am in you."* This passage emphasizes the mystical unity that believers are called to experience - a union with Christ and, through Him, with the Father.

The teachings of Jesus are filled with mystical elements, from His parables to His direct instructions on prayer and contemplation. For instance, in the Sermon on the Mount, Jesus teaches about the inward, spiritual nature of the Kingdom of GOD, urging His followers to seek it within their own hearts (Luke 17:21). This inward focus is the hallmark of mysticism, which prioritizes the inner spiritual journey over external religious observances.

For modern Catholics, these theological concepts are not merely abstract doctrines but living truths that can transform everyday life. The mystical teachings of Jesus invite believers to move beyond a surface-level understanding of faith and enter into a profound, personal communion with GOD. This shift from external to internal, from head knowledge to heart experience, is crucial for those seeking to deepen their spiritual lives in today's complex world.

Application in Modern Life

Integrating the mystical teachings of Jesus into modern life presents both opportunities and challenges. In a world dominated by noise, distractions, and material concerns, the quiet, inward journey of mysticism can seem elusive. However, it is precisely in this modern context that the mystical path of Jesus becomes even more relevant and necessary.

One of the primary challenges for modern Catholics is maintaining a balance between spiritual commitments and secular responsibilities. Jesus understood the pressures of the world but consistently modeled a life centered on GOD. He often retreated to solitary places to pray, demonstrating the importance of silence and solitude in nurturing a mystical relationship with GOD (Mark 1:35). Following His example, Catholics today can create sacred spaces in their homes or workplaces where they can withdraw, even briefly, to reconnect with GOD.

Consider the example of a busy professional who incorporates short periods of silence into their daily routine. By taking just five minutes at the beginning and end of each day to sit quietly, breathe deeply, and focus on GOD's presence, they can cultivate an inner peace that sustains them through the demands of their day. This practice, though simple, can be a powerful tool for deepening one's spiritual life.

Another challenge is integrating mystical insights into relationships and personal development. Jesus' teachings on love, compassion, and forgiveness are not just ethical guidelines but mystical principles that reveal the divine nature within every person. When a Catholic consciously applies these teachings in their interactions - whether by forgiving a coworker, showing compassion to a stranger, or loving their family unconditionally - they are living out the mystical union with Christ that He invites them to experience.

Real-life examples of integrating mystical teachings into daily life abound. For instance, a married couple might choose to begin each day with a joint meditation on a passage of scripture, allowing the peace and wisdom of GOD's word to guide their relationship. Over time, this practice can transform their marriage into a spiritual partnership rooted in the mystical love of Christ.

Practical Spiritual Tools

To help readers deepen their understanding of Jesus as a mystic and integrate His teachings into their lives, here are some practical spiritual tools:

1. **Lectio Divina (Sacred Reading):**

   - *Instructions:* Begin by selecting a passage of scripture, preferably from the Gospels. Read the passage slowly and reflectively, allowing the words to resonate in your heart. Spend a few minutes in silence, contemplating what GOD is saying to you through the passage. Conclude with a prayer, asking GOD to help you live out the insights you have received.

- *Application:* Practice Lectio Divina daily, perhaps in the morning, to set a spiritual tone for your day. Over time, this practice will deepen your relationship with GOD and help you internalize the mystical teachings of Jesus.

2. **Centering Prayer:**

    - *Instructions:* Choose a sacred word or phrase, such as "Jesus" or "Peace," as the focus of your prayer. Sit comfortably, close your eyes, and silently repeat your chosen word. Whenever you become distracted, gently return to your word. The goal is not to achieve anything but to rest in GOD's presence.
    - *Application:* Centering Prayer can be practiced for 10-20 minutes, once or twice a day. It is a powerful tool for cultivating inner stillness and awareness of GOD's presence within you.

3. **Meditation on the Life of Jesus:**

    - *Instructions:* Spend time meditating on specific events from Jesus' life, such as His baptism, transfiguration, or resurrection. Visualize these events in your mind, imagining yourself as a participant. Reflect on what these events reveal about Jesus' mystical nature and how they invite you into deeper communion with Him.
    - *Application:* Use this meditation to connect more intimately with Jesus as a mystical teacher. Consider

journaling your reflections to track your spiritual growth.

4. **Sacred Space Creation:**

    - *Instructions:* Designate a specific area in your home or workplace as a sacred space for prayer and meditation. Include elements such as a crucifix, candles, icons, or a Bible. Use this space regularly to retreat from the busyness of life and reconnect with GOD.
    - *Application:* Make visiting your sacred space a daily habit, even if only for a few minutes. This practice will help you maintain a continuous awareness of GOD's presence in your life.

By incorporating these spiritual tools into daily routines, readers can cultivate a deeper, more mystical relationship with Jesus Christ. The path of mysticism is not reserved for a select few but is accessible to all who seek to follow Jesus with an open heart and a willing spirit.

Exercise: Embracing the Mystical Path of Jesus

Objective: To help you understand and integrate the mystical teachings of Jesus into your daily life, fostering a deeper connection with GOD and a more profound experience of your faith.

Instructions:

1. **Reflect on Jesus as a Mystic:**

    - Spend 10-15 minutes in silent contemplation, reflecting on the idea of Jesus as a mystic. Consider His deep union with GOD, His teachings on the Kingdom of GOD within, and His practice of withdrawing to solitary places for prayer.

    - Journal your thoughts and feelings about Jesus as a mystical teacher. How does this perspective change or deepen your understanding of Him? What aspects of His mystical teachings resonate most with you?

2. **Practice Lectio Divina:**

    - Choose a passage from the Gospels that highlights Jesus' mystical teachings (e.g., John 14:20, Luke 17:21, or Mark 1:35). Follow these steps:

        - ✓ **Reading (Lectio):** Slowly read the passage, paying attention to any words or phrases that stand out.

        - ✓ **Meditation (Meditatio):** Reflect on the meaning of these words or phrases. What is GOD saying to you through this passage?

        - ✓ **Prayer (Oratio):** Respond to the passage with a prayer, asking GOD to help you internalize and live out the insights you've received.

- ✓ **Contemplation (Contemplatio):** Spend a few moments in silent rest, simply being in GOD's presence without any specific thoughts or words.
- Repeat this practice daily for one week, journaling your reflections after each session.

3. **Create and Use a Sacred Space:**

    - Designate a specific area in your home as a sacred space for prayer and meditation. Include elements that help you feel connected to GOD, such as a crucifix, candles, or a Bible.

    - Commit to spending at least 10 minutes each day in your sacred space, practicing silent prayer or meditation. Use this time to reconnect with GOD and reflect on Jesus' mystical teachings.

    - At the end of each week, reflect on how this practice has impacted your spiritual life. Has it deepened your sense of GOD's presence? Has it helped you better understand Jesus' role as a mystical teacher?

4. **Integrate Mystical Teachings into Daily Life:**

    - Choose one of Jesus' mystical teachings (e.g., "The Kingdom of GOD is within you") and focus on integrating it into your daily activities.

    - Throughout your day, remind yourself of this teaching. For example, when you encounter a challenging situation, pause and recall that the Kingdom of GOD is within you, bringing peace and wisdom.

    - Journal your experiences at the end of each day. How did this teaching influence your thoughts, actions, and interactions with others? Did it help you feel more connected to GOD and others?

5. **Participate in a Community of Practice:**

    - Join or form a small group with others interested in exploring the mystical teachings of Jesus. Meet weekly to discuss your experiences with the exercises, share insights, and support one another in your spiritual journeys.

    - Engage in communal practices such as group Lectio Divina, shared silence, or discussions on mystical theology. This community involvement can provide encouragement and deepen your understanding of Jesus as a mystical teacher.

Outcome: By completing this exercise, you should gain a deeper understanding of Jesus' mystical nature and how His teachings can be integrated into your daily life. The practices of Lectio Divina, sacred space creation, and mindful reflection will help you cultivate a more intimate relationship with GOD, bringing the mystical teachings of Jesus to life in your personal and communal spiritual journey.

NOTES:

Chapter 15: Jesus the Healer and You the Healer

Embracing the Healing Ministry of Jesus in Our Lives

The healing ministry of Jesus is one of the most profound aspects of His earthly mission, reflecting His compassion, power, and the divine desire to restore wholeness to humanity. This chapter explores how Jesus' role as a healer is not just a historical account but an invitation for each of us to participate in healing, both for ourselves and others. By understanding the theological foundations of healing and applying them in modern life, we can become instruments of GOD's healing grace in a world in desperate need of restoration.

Theological Insights

Jesus' identity as the healer is intrinsically linked to His nature as both fully divine and fully human. This dual nature allowed Him to bridge the gap between GOD and humanity, bringing divine healing into the human experience. The Gospels are filled with accounts of Jesus healing the sick, restoring sight to the blind, and even raising the dead. These miracles were not only signs of His divine authority but also expressions of His deep compassion for those suffering. In Matthew 9:35[1], it is written, *"Jesus went through all the towns and villages, teaching in their synagogues, proclaiming the good news of the kingdom and healing every disease and sickness."* This passage encapsulates Jesus' mission of holistic restoration - physical, spiritual, and emotional healing.

The concept of Christ Consciousness also plays a critical role in understanding Jesus as a healer. Christ Consciousness refers to the awareness of the divine presence within each of us, which allows us to participate in the same healing power that Jesus demonstrated. In John 14:12[2], Jesus makes a remarkable statement: *"Very truly I tell you, whoever believes in me will do the works I have been doing, and they will do even greater things than these, because I am going to the Father."* This promise indicates that the healing ministry of Jesus is not confined to the past but is meant to continue through His followers.

The Holy Trinity is also central to understanding healing in the Christian context. The Father, as the source of all life, wills our healing and wholeness. The Son, Jesus, embodies this will through His life and ministry, demonstrating GOD's power to heal. The Holy Spirit continues this work in and through the Church, empowering believers to act as vessels of GOD's healing grace in the world today.

For modern-day Catholics, these theological insights offer profound implications. Healing is not just a miraculous event but an ongoing process of restoration that we are all called to participate in. Whether through prayer, acts of kindness, or simply being present with those who suffer, we are invited to join Jesus in His healing ministry, bringing hope and wholeness to our communities.

Application in Modern Life

Integrating the healing ministry of Jesus into everyday life can be both challenging and rewarding. In a world filled with physical ailments, emotional wounds, and spiritual brokenness, the call to be a healer like Jesus is more relevant than ever. However, modern Catholics often struggle to balance this spiritual calling with the demands of daily life.

One common challenge is the perception that healing is an extraordinary gift reserved for a select few. However, Jesus' life and teachings suggest that healing is a fundamental aspect of Christian discipleship, accessible to all who believe. In today's context, this might involve offering a listening ear to a friend in distress, volunteering at a local charity, or simply praying for those in need. Each of these acts, though seemingly small, participates in the broader mission of healing that Jesus exemplified.

Consider the example of a busy parent who, despite their hectic schedule, takes time each night to pray with their children, asking for GOD's healing presence in their lives. This simple practice not only fosters a sense of peace and security within the family but also models the importance of turning to GOD in times of need. Another example might be a healthcare professional who, while treating patients, silently prays for their healing, invoking the presence of Christ in their work. In this way, the professional integrates their faith into their vocation, becoming a conduit of GOD's healing power.

Balancing spiritual commitments with secular responsibilities is another challenge. The key lies in recognizing that healing is not just about performing miracles but about embodying the love and compassion of Christ in every aspect of life. This can be done by approaching daily tasks with a spirit of service, seeing each interaction as an opportunity to bring healing and wholeness to others.

Practical Spiritual Tools

To help readers embrace their role as healers in the spirit of Jesus, here are some practical spiritual tools:

1. **Intercessory Prayer:**

   - *Instructions:* Set aside time each day to pray specifically for the healing of others. Create a list of people in your life who are in need of physical, emotional, or spiritual healing. As you pray, visualize them being surrounded by GOD's healing light, restored to wholeness.
   - *Application:* Integrate this practice into your daily routine, perhaps during morning or evening prayers. Over time, you will develop a greater awareness of the needs around you and a deeper trust in GOD's healing power.

2. **Laying on of Hands:**

    - *Instructions:* If appropriate, and with the person's consent, place your hands on someone who is in need of healing while praying for them. This practice, rooted in the early Church, symbolizes the transmission of GOD's healing grace through the physical touch.

    - *Application:* Use this practice in personal or communal prayer settings, such as small group meetings or family gatherings. Remember that the power lies not in your hands but in GOD's presence working through you.

3. **Healing Meditation:**

    - *Instructions:* Find a quiet place where you can sit comfortably. Begin by taking deep breaths, inviting the Holy Spirit to fill you with peace. Visualize Jesus standing beside you, His hands extended towards you, radiating healing energy. Allow His presence to touch any areas of your life where you need healing—whether physical, emotional, or spiritual.

    - *Application:* Practice this meditation regularly, especially during times of stress or illness. It can be a powerful way to experience the healing presence of Christ in your own life.

4. **Acts of Compassion:**

    - *Instructions:* Identify simple acts of kindness you can perform in your daily life, such as helping a neighbor, volunteering at a charity, or offering encouragement to someone in need. Each act, no matter how small, is a way of participating in Jesus' healing ministry.

    - *Application:* Make it a habit to perform at least one act of compassion each day. Over time, you will become more attuned to the opportunities for healing that surround you and more responsive to the needs of others.

By integrating these spiritual tools into your daily life, you can actively participate in the healing ministry of Jesus. Whether through prayer, meditation, or simple acts of kindness, you can become a vessel of GOD's healing grace, bringing hope and restoration to those around you.

Exercise: Becoming a Vessel of Healing

Objective: To help you understand and actively participate in the healing ministry of Jesus by applying the concepts and spiritual tools discussed in this chapter to your daily life.

Instructions:

1. **Reflect on Jesus as the Healer:**

    - Spend 10 minutes in silent reflection, focusing on Jesus' role as the healer. Consider the ways He brought healing to those around Him—physically, emotionally, and spiritually.

    - Write down your thoughts in a journal. Reflect on how Jesus' healing ministry speaks to you personally and how you might be called to participate in this ministry.

2. **Identify a Healing Opportunity:**

    - Think of someone in your life who is in need of healing. This could be a friend, family member, or even yourself. Consider whether the need is physical, emotional, or spiritual.

    - Write down this person's name and their specific need. Commit to focusing your efforts on bringing healing to this situation over the next week.

3. **Practice Intercessory Prayer:**

    - Each day, set aside 5-10 minutes to pray specifically for the person you identified. Ask GOD to bring healing and wholeness to their life. Visualize them surrounded by GOD's healing light, restored and at peace.

    - Record your prayer intentions in your journal, noting any insights or feelings that arise during your prayer time.

4. **Offer an Act of Compassion:**

    - Identify a simple act of compassion that you can perform for the person you are praying for. This could be a phone call to check in, a handwritten note of encouragement, or offering practical help with a task.

    - Carry out this act of compassion with the intention of being a vessel of GOD's healing grace. Reflect on how this action impacts your relationship with the person and your own spiritual growth.

5. **Healing Meditation:**

    - At the end of each day, practice a healing meditation. Find a quiet place, sit comfortably, and take deep breaths. Visualize Jesus standing beside you, His hands extended towards you, radiating healing energy.

    - Allow His presence to touch any areas of your life where you need healing. As you meditate, also extend this healing energy to the person you have been praying for.

    - Journal your experiences, noting any changes in your thoughts, feelings, or circumstances over the course of the week.

6. **Evaluate and Reflect:**

    - At the end of the week, review your journal entries. Reflect on the following questions:

        - ✓ How did focusing on Jesus as the healer change your perspective on healing?

        - ✓ What impact did intercessory prayer and acts of compassion have on the person you were praying for? On yourself?

- ✓ How did the healing meditation influence your sense of peace and connection with GOD?
- Write a summary of your reflections, noting any areas where you felt particularly connected to the healing ministry of Jesus.

Outcome: By completing this exercise, you should gain a deeper understanding of how you can participate in the healing ministry of Jesus in your everyday life. The practices of intercessory prayer, acts of compassion, and healing meditation will help you become a more effective vessel of GOD's healing grace, not only for others but also in your own spiritual journey.

NOTES:

Chapter 16: Jesus and Teachings of "A Course in Miracles"

Understanding Jesus Through the Lens of "A Course in Miracles"

"A Course in Miracles" (ACIM) presents a unique perspective on the teachings of Jesus, focusing on the transformative power of love, forgiveness, and the inner journey toward spiritual awakening. This chapter explores how the teachings of ACIM align with and differ from traditional Christian theology, particularly within the Catholic faith, and how these teachings can be integrated into the spiritual lives of modern-day Catholics. By examining key theological concepts and offering practical tools, this chapter aims to help readers deepen their relationship with Jesus and experience the miracles of daily life.

Theological Insights

At the heart of "A Course in Miracles" is the concept of Christ Consciousness, which reflects the divine presence within each person, emphasizing that we are all inherently connected to GOD. ACIM teaches that Jesus is not only the Son of GOD but also a guide who shows us the way back to our true nature, which is love. This idea aligns with the Catholic understanding of Jesus as both fully divine and fully human, a mediator between GOD and humanity who reveals the path to salvation.

In the Gospels, Jesus teaches about the Kingdom of GOD, emphasizing that it is not a physical place but a state of being characterized by love, peace, and unity with GOD. *"The Kingdom of GOD is within you"* (Luke 17:21)[1], Jesus tells us, pointing to an inner reality that ACIM echoes by teaching that salvation comes from recognizing the divine presence within ourselves and others. This perspective encourages Catholics to see beyond the external world and cultivate an inner relationship with GOD, where true peace and healing are found.

The Holy Trinity - Father, Son, and Holy Spirit - is another core concept in both Catholic theology and ACIM. In traditional Catholic doctrine, the Trinity represents the unity of GOD in three distinct persons. ACIM presents a similar idea by emphasizing the interconnectedness of all beings through the shared presence of Christ within us. While ACIM may not explicitly frame this in terms of the Trinity, the underlying message of unity and oneness resonates with the Christian understanding of GOD's nature.

These theological insights challenge Catholics to expand their understanding of Jesus and His teachings, encouraging a more personal and experiential approach to faith. By embracing the concept of Christ Consciousness and recognizing the divine presence within, Catholics can deepen their spiritual practice and experience a closer connection to GOD in their daily lives[2].

Application in Modern Life

Integrating the teachings of "A Course in Miracles" into daily life can provide Catholics with valuable tools for navigating the challenges of modern life. One of the central teachings of ACIM is the power of forgiveness, which is seen as the key to inner peace and spiritual growth. Forgiveness, according to ACIM, is not merely about letting go of grievances but recognizing the inherent innocence in others, which reflects their true nature as children of GOD.

For modern Catholics, this teaching can be transformative. In a world where conflicts and misunderstandings are common, practicing forgiveness as taught by Jesus and emphasized in ACIM can lead to healing and reconciliation in relationships. For example, a person struggling with resentment toward a coworker might apply this teaching by choosing to see the divine presence in the other person, recognizing that their actions stem from fear or misunderstanding rather than malice. This shift in perception can dissolve the barriers of anger and open the way for genuine compassion and understanding.

Balancing spiritual commitments with secular responsibilities is another challenge that many Catholics face. ACIM offers practical guidance by teaching that every situation, no matter how mundane, is an opportunity for spiritual growth. By approaching daily tasks with mindfulness and a spirit of service, Catholics can transform ordinary activities into acts of worship and deepen their connection with GOD.

Consider the example of a parent juggling work, household duties, and caring for children. By applying the principles of ACIM, such as seeing each task as an opportunity to express love and serve others, the parent can infuse their day with a sense of purpose and spiritual significance. This approach not only reduces stress but also fosters a deeper awareness of GOD's presence in everyday life.

Practical Spiritual Tools

To help readers integrate the teachings of Jesus and "A Course in Miracles" into their daily lives, here are some practical spiritual tools:

1. **Forgiveness Practice:**

    - ***Instructions:*** Each day, take a few minutes to reflect on any grievances or judgments you may be holding against others. Ask GOD to help you see the situation through the eyes of Christ, recognizing the inherent innocence and divine nature of the other person. Offer a prayer of forgiveness, releasing the grievance and asking for healing for both yourself and the other person.
    - ***Application:*** Make this practice a daily habit, particularly at the end of the day, to cleanse your mind and heart of any lingering negativity. Over time, you will notice a greater sense of peace and freedom in your relationships.

2. **Mindful Service:**

    - ***Instructions***: Approach your daily tasks, whether at work, home, or in the community, with the intention of serving GOD through serving others. Before starting a task, take a moment to dedicate it to GOD, asking that your actions be guided by love and aligned with His will.
    - ***Application:*** This practice can be applied to any activity, from cooking dinner to attending a meeting. By infusing your actions with a spirit of love and service, you transform ordinary tasks into opportunities for spiritual growth and connection with GOD.

3. **Christ Consciousness Meditation:**

    - ***Instructions:*** Find a quiet place to sit comfortably. Close your eyes and take a few deep breaths, centering yourself in the present moment. Visualize Jesus standing before you, radiating love and light. As you breathe in, imagine that you are absorbing this light into your heart, filling you with Christ's presence. As you breathe out, imagine that this light is extending to others, connecting you with the divine presence in all beings.
    - ***Application:*** Practice this meditation daily, either in the morning to start your day with a sense of

connection or in the evening to reflect on your day with gratitude and love.

4. **Daily Reflection Journal:**

   - ***Instructions:*** At the end of each day, spend a few minutes reflecting on how you applied the teachings of Jesus and ACIM throughout the day. Write down any experiences of forgiveness, moments of mindful service, or insights gained from your meditation practice. Consider how these practices are transforming your life and deepening your relationship with GOD.
   - ***Application:*** Keeping a daily reflection journal helps you stay mindful of your spiritual journey and provides a space to document your growth and challenges. Over time, this practice will enhance your self-awareness and strengthen your commitment to living in alignment with Christ's teachings.

By incorporating these spiritual tools into daily routines, readers can deepen their understanding of Jesus' teachings and the insights offered by "A Course in Miracles." These practices provide a practical framework for experiencing the transformative power of love, forgiveness, and inner peace, leading to a more profound and joyful connection with GOD.

Exercise: Integrating the Teachings of Jesus and "A Course in Miracles" into Daily Life

Objective: To help you internalize and apply the teachings of Jesus as presented in "A Course in Miracles" (ACIM), fostering personal spiritual growth and deeper relationships with others through love, forgiveness, and mindfulness.

Instructions:

1. **Daily Forgiveness Reflection:**
   - ***Duration:*** 10 minutes each day.
   - ***Instructions:*** At the end of each day, reflect on any conflicts, frustrations, or judgments you encountered. Write down these situations in a journal, noting how they made you feel. Then, using the principles from ACIM, consciously choose to forgive those involved, including yourself if necessary. Visualize releasing these negative emotions and replacing them with love and understanding.
   - ***Outcome:*** Over the week, observe how your practice of forgiveness affects your relationships and your inner peace. Journal any changes in your perceptions or emotions.

2. **Mindful Presence in Daily Tasks:**
   - ***Duration:*** Throughout the day.
   - ***Instructions:*** Approach each task, whether mundane or significant, with the awareness that you are serving GOD through your actions. Before beginning any task, pause for a moment to center yourself, set an intention to perform the task with love, and silently dedicate it to GOD.
   - ***Outcome:*** Notice how this mindful approach transforms your attitude toward daily responsibilities.

Reflect on any increase in your sense of purpose or connection to GOD throughout your day.

3. **Christ Consciousness Meditation:**

   - *Duration:* 15 minutes each day.

   - *Instructions:* Find a quiet space and sit comfortably. Close your eyes and focus on your breath. Visualize Jesus standing before you, radiating love and light. As you breathe in, imagine absorbing this light into your heart, and as you breathe out, imagine this light extending from you to others, connecting you with the divine in all beings. Conclude with a prayer asking to carry this consciousness into your daily interactions.

   - *Outcome:* After a week of practicing this meditation, journal any experiences of increased compassion, love, or unity with others. Reflect on how this meditation has influenced your daily life and relationships.

4. **Weekly Reflection and Integration:**

   - *Duration:* 30 minutes at the end of the week.

   - *Instructions:* Review your journal entries from the week. Reflect on the overall impact of the forgiveness practice, mindful presence, and Christ Consciousness meditation on your life. Consider how these practices have helped you integrate the teachings of Jesus and ACIM into your daily routine. Identify any areas where you struggled and plan how to address these challenges in the coming week.

   - *Outcome:* Write a summary of your week's experiences, noting any spiritual growth, changes in perception, or improvements in your relationships. Use this reflection to refine your practices for the next week, setting specific goals for further integration.

Outcome: By completing this exercise, you will gain practical experience in applying the teachings of Jesus and "A Course in Miracles" to your daily life. The practices of forgiveness, mindfulness, and meditation will help you cultivate a deeper relationship with GOD, enhance your inner peace, and improve your interactions with others. This exercise aims to make these spiritual teachings a living reality in your everyday experiences.

NOTES:

Chapter 17: The Holy Trinity – GOD, Jesus, and The Holy Spirit

Exploring the Mystery and Unity of The Holy Trinity

The Holy Trinity is a foundational doctrine in Christianity, representing the complex and beautiful unity of GOD as Father, Son, and Holy Spirit. This chapter delves into the theological depth of The Trinity, offering insights into how this central belief can enrich the spiritual lives of modern-day Catholics. By understanding The Trinity, Catholics can deepen their relationship with GOD, find guidance in their daily lives, and grow in their spiritual journey.

Theological Insights

The doctrine of The Holy Trinity teaches that there is one GOD in three persons: GOD the Father, GOD the Son (Jesus Christ), and GOD the Holy Spirit. These three persons are distinct yet co-equal, co-eternal, and consubstantial, meaning they share the same divine essence. This concept, though mysterious, reveals the richness of GOD's nature and His relationship with humanity.

GOD the Father is the Creator, the source of all life and the foundation of all that exists. He is often seen as the loving and omnipotent guide who governs the universe with wisdom and care. The Father's role within The Trinity underscores the idea of a personal GOD who desires a relationship with His creation.

Jesus Christ, the Son, is the embodiment of GOD's love and salvation. Fully divine and fully human, Jesus bridges the gap between GOD and humanity. His incarnation, death, and resurrection are central to Christian faith, offering a path to redemption and eternal life. Jesus' role as the Son within The Trinity emphasizes His unique position as both GOD and the Savior of the world. In John 10:30[1], Jesus states, *"I and the Father are one,"* highlighting His unity with the Father .

The Holy Spirit is the active presence of GOD in the world today. The Spirit is often associated with guidance, inspiration, and the sanctification of believers. Through The Holy Spirit, Christians are empowered to live out their faith, grow in holiness, and participate in the life of the Church. In John 14:26[2], Jesus describes The Holy Spirit as the Advocate who will teach and remind the disciples of all that He has said.

The Trinity is not just a theological concept but a model for understanding relationships - both within the GOD-head and in our own lives. The Father, Son, and Holy Spirit are distinct yet united, each playing a unique role while sharing a common purpose. This unity in diversity serves as a profound example for human relationships, where differences can coexist in harmony.

For modern-day Catholics, The Trinity is a source of comfort, guidance, and inspiration. It reminds us that GOD is both transcendent and immanent - He is beyond us, yet intimately involved in our lives. Understanding The Trinity helps Catholics connect more deeply with each person of the GOD-head, fostering a more robust and personal faith.

Application in Modern Life

The mystery of The Trinity, while profound, offers practical insights that can be applied to everyday life. Understanding the relational nature of The Trinity can help Catholics navigate the complexities of modern relationships, whether in families, workplaces, or communities.

One common challenge for Catholics today is balancing spiritual commitments with secular responsibilities. The doctrine of The Trinity can guide this balance by reminding believers that GOD is present in all aspects of life, not just in explicitly religious activities. The Father's role as Creator emphasizes the sacredness of all creation, suggesting that work, family, and social responsibilities are not separate from our spiritual lives but integral to them.

Consider the example of a working professional who struggles to find time for prayer amidst a busy schedule. By viewing work as a participation in GOD's creative activity, this individual can transform their daily tasks into acts of worship. Offering each task to GOD in prayer and seeking the guidance of The Holy Spirit in decision-making, allows for a harmonious integration of faith and work.

Another example is in relationships. The unity and mutual love within The Trinity provide a model for human relationships. In a marriage, for instance, the love and cooperation between the Father, Son, and Holy Spirit can inspire couples to strive for unity and mutual respect, even amidst differences. When conflicts arise, spouses can look to The Trinity as a model for resolving disagreements with love and understanding, seeking to reflect the unity that exists within GOD Himself.

Practical Spiritual Tools

To help readers deepen their understanding and experience of The Trinity, here are some practical spiritual tools:

1. **Trinitarian Prayer:**

    - ***Instructions:*** Begin your day by invoking The Holy Trinity. Start with a prayer to GOD the Father, thanking Him for the gift of life. Continue with a prayer to Jesus, asking for guidance and strength throughout the day. Conclude with a prayer to the Holy Spirit, seeking inspiration and the grace to live according to GOD's will.
    - ***Application:*** This practice can be incorporated into your morning routine. By consciously engaging with each person of The Trinity, you will cultivate a deeper sense of GOD's presence throughout the day.

2. **Lectio Divina with a Trinitarian Focus:**

    - ***Instructions:*** Choose a passage of scripture that highlights the role of the Father, Son, or Holy Spirit.

Read the passage slowly, allowing the words to resonate in your heart. Reflect on how The Trinity is present in the passage and what GOD is saying to you through it.
- **Application:** Use this practice weekly, focusing on different aspects of The Trinity. Over time, you will develop a more nuanced understanding of how The Trinity operates in scripture and in your life.

3. **Trinitarian Meditation:**

    - **Instructions:** Find a quiet place to sit comfortably. Close your eyes and take deep breaths, focusing on the presence of GOD within and around you. Begin by meditating on GOD the Father as the source of all life, then on Jesus as your Savior and guide, and finally on The Holy Spirit as the source of inspiration and strength. Allow yourself to experience the unity and love of The Trinity within your own being.
    - **Application:** Practice this meditation regularly, especially during moments of stress or decision-making. It can help you feel grounded in the love and unity of The Trinity, providing clarity and peace.

4. **Family or Community Prayer to The Trinity:**

    - **Instructions:** Gather with your family or a small group and pray together to The Holy Trinity. Each person can take turns addressing the Father, Son, and Holy Spirit in their prayers, expressing gratitude, asking for guidance, and seeking blessings for the community.

- **Application:** This practice can be integrated into family prayer time or small group meetings. It helps build a sense of communal unity, mirroring the unity of The Trinity, and fosters spiritual growth in a shared context.

By incorporating these spiritual tools into daily routines, readers can deepen their relationship with The Holy Trinity and experience its transformative power in their lives. The Trinity, while a profound mystery, is also a source of endless inspiration and guidance for living a fulfilling, meaningful, and joyous life.

Exercise: Living in the Presence of The Holy Trinity

Objective: To deepen your understanding and experience of The Holy Trinity by integrating the concepts discussed in this chapter into your daily life. This exercise aims to help you cultivate a more personal and practical relationship with GOD as Father, Son, and Holy Spirit.

Instructions:

1. **Morning Invocation of The Trinity:**
   - **Duration:** 5 minutes each morning.
   - **Instructions:** Start each day by invoking The Holy Trinity. Begin with a prayer to GOD the Father, thanking Him for the gift of life and asking for His guidance throughout the day. Next, pray to Jesus,

the Son, asking for His presence to help you live according to His teachings. Conclude with a prayer to The Holy Spirit, asking for inspiration and strength to face the day's challenges.

- **Outcome**: This daily practice will help you begin each day with a conscious awareness of The Trinity's presence in your life, fostering a sense of spiritual guidance and purpose.

2. **Trinitarian Reflection Journal:**
   - **Duration:** 10 minutes each evening.
   - **Instructions:** At the end of each day, reflect on how you experienced the presence of The Trinity in your daily activities. Write down specific moments where you felt guided by the Father, supported by Jesus, or inspired by The Holy Spirit. Reflect on how these experiences impacted your decisions, interactions, and overall sense of peace.
   - **Outcome:** Keeping a journal will help you track your spiritual growth and deepen your awareness of The Trinity's active role in your life.

3. **Weekly Trinitarian Meditation:**
   - **Duration:** 20 minutes once a week.
   - **Instructions:** Find a quiet place to meditate on The Holy Trinity. Begin by focusing on GOD the Father,

contemplating His role as Creator and Provider. Move on to meditate on Jesus, the Son, considering His sacrifice and teachings. Finally, focus on The Holy Spirit, reflecting on how the Spirit guides, inspires, and empowers you. Allow yourself to feel the unity and love of The Trinity within you.

- *Outcome:* This meditation practice will help you develop a deeper connection with each person of The Trinity, enhancing your overall spiritual life.

4. **Trinity-Inspired Acts of Service:**
   - *Duration:* Ongoing throughout the week.
   - *Instructions:* Identify one act of service you can perform in each role of The Trinity: as a provider (Father), as a servant-leader (Son), and as an inspirer (Holy Spirit). For example, you might offer support to someone in need (Father), volunteer your time to help others (Son), or share words of encouragement or wisdom (Holy Spirit).
   - *Outcome:* By aligning your actions with the roles of The Trinity, you will actively live out your faith in a way that reflects the love, service, and inspiration of GOD in the world.

5. **Group or Family Trinitarian Prayer:**

    - *Duration:* 15 minutes once a week.

    - *Instructions:* Gather with your family or a small group to pray together to The Holy Trinity. Each person can take turns offering prayers to the Father, Son, and Holy Spirit, focusing on gratitude, guidance, and blessings. Encourage each member to share how they've experienced The Trinity during the week.

    - *Outcome:* This communal prayer practice will strengthen the spiritual bonds within your family or group, fostering a shared understanding and appreciation of The Trinity's presence in your lives.

Outcome: By completing this exercise, you will gain a deeper understanding of The Holy Trinity and its relevance to your daily life. The practices of daily invocation, reflection, meditation, service, and communal prayer will help you cultivate a more intimate and practical relationship with GOD as Father, Son, and Holy Spirit. This exercise is designed to make the mystery of The Trinity a living reality in your spiritual journey, enriching your faith and guiding your actions.

NOTES:

Chapter 18: The Core Beliefs of Catholicism

Understanding the Pillars of Catholic Faith

The core beliefs of Catholicism form the foundation upon which the entire faith is built. These beliefs, deeply rooted in scripture and tradition, guide the lives of Catholics, shaping their understanding of GOD, the Church, and their role in the world. This chapter explores the fundamental doctrines of the Catholic Church, providing theological insights, practical applications, and spiritual tools to help modern Catholics live out their faith with purpose and conviction.

Theological Insights

At the heart of Catholicism is the belief in The Holy Trinity - one GOD in three persons: Father, Son, and Holy Spirit. This doctrine is central to understanding the nature of GOD as both a unity and a community of love. The Father is the Creator, the source of all life; the Son, Jesus Christ, is the Redeemer, who through His life, death, and resurrection, reconciled humanity with GOD; The Holy Spirit is the Sanctifier, who empowers and guides the faithful in their spiritual journey. The mystery of The Trinity is profound, yet it offers a model for understanding the relationships within the Church and within families, emphasizing unity in diversity.

Another core belief is the Incarnation, the doctrine that GOD became man in the person of Jesus Christ. This belief underscores the dignity of human nature and the closeness of GOD to His creation. Jesus, fully divine and fully human, lived among us, taught us, suffered, died, and rose again for our salvation. This mystery of the Incarnation reveals GOD's immense love for humanity and His desire to be in relationship with us. As John 1:14 states, *"And the Word became flesh and dwelt among us, full of grace and truth.*[1]*"*

Catholics also hold a deep reverence for the sacraments, which are outward signs of inward grace, instituted by Christ to give life to the Church.

The Seven Sacraments:

1. Baptism

2. Confirmation

3. Eucharist

4. Penance

5. Anointing of the Sick

6. Holy Orders
(Ordains Bishops, Priests, and Deacons,
giving them the power and grace to perform their duties.)

7. Matrimony

Are central to the spiritual life of Catholics. Each sacrament serves as a conduit of GOD's grace, nurturing the believer's faith and relationship with GOD. The Eucharist, in particular, is the "source and summit of the Christian life," as it embodies the real presence of Christ and commemorates His sacrifice on the cross[2].

The Catholic belief in the communion of saints emphasizes the spiritual solidarity among all believers, both living and deceased. This belief encourages Catholics to seek the intercession of saints, who are seen as exemplars of faith and close companions in the spiritual journey. The communion of saints reflects the Church's understanding of community, where the faithful support each other through prayer and example, transcending the boundaries of time and space.

The teachings on Christ Consciousness, while not traditionally expressed in Catholic terminology, can be understood as the call for every Catholic to embody the love, wisdom, and presence of Christ in their daily lives. This concept resonates with the Catholic belief in the universal call to holiness, where every believer is called to imitate Christ and participate in His mission to bring GOD's love to the world.

Application in Modern Life

Integrating these core beliefs into daily life is essential for modern Catholics seeking to live out their faith authentically. However, this can be challenging in a world that often prioritizes material success and individualism over spiritual growth and community.

One of the main challenges for Catholics today is balancing their spiritual commitments with the demands of work, family, and social life. Understanding that GOD is present in every aspect of life, not just in religious activities, can help Catholics navigate this balance. For instance, by recognizing work as a participation in GOD's creative action, Catholics can approach their jobs with a sense of purpose and dedication, offering their efforts as a form of worship.

Consider the example of a Catholic professional who struggles to maintain a consistent prayer life due to a busy schedule. By integrating short, intentional prayers throughout the day - such as a morning offering, a prayer before meals, and a brief reflection at the end of the day - this person can maintain a connection with GOD amidst their daily responsibilities. This practice not only sustains their spiritual life but also infuses their work with a sense of divine presence.

Another area where Catholics can apply their faith is in their relationships. The belief in The Holy Trinity and the communion of saints highlights the importance of community and mutual support. In practical terms, this means that Catholics are called to foster relationships based on love, respect, and service. Whether in marriage, friendship, or community life, Catholics can draw inspiration from The Trinity's model of unity and the saints' example of selfless love.

For instance, a married couple might reflect on the Trinitarian nature of their relationship, recognizing that their love for each other is a reflection of GOD's love. By regularly praying together, participating in the sacraments, and supporting each other's spiritual growth, they can strengthen their marriage and draw closer to GOD.

Practical Spiritual Tools

To help readers integrate these core beliefs into their daily lives, here are some practical spiritual tools:

1. **Daily Prayer Routine:**

    - ***Instructions:*** Establish a daily prayer routine that includes morning prayers, grace before meals, and an evening reflection. Incorporate the core beliefs into your prayers, such as thanking GOD the Father for creation, asking Jesus for guidance in your actions, and seeking the Holy Spirit's inspiration.

    - ***Application:*** This routine helps maintain a connection with GOD throughout the day and reinforces the central beliefs of your faith.

2. **Sacramental Preparation and Participation:**

    - ***Instructions:*** Regularly participate in the sacraments, especially the Eucharist and Reconciliation. Before receiving the sacraments, spend time in prayer and reflection, focusing on their significance and the grace they impart.

- ***Application:*** Frequent participation in the sacraments strengthens your relationship with GOD and nourishes your spiritual life.

3. **Community Involvement:**

    - ***Instructions:*** Engage with your local parish community through volunteering, attending Mass regularly, and participating in parish activities. Build relationships with fellow Catholics, drawing inspiration from the communion of saints.

    - ***Application:*** Active involvement in your parish fosters a sense of belonging and provides opportunities to live out your faith in community.

4. **Scripture Reflection:**

    - ***Instructions:*** Set aside time each week to read and reflect on scripture, particularly passages that highlight the core beliefs of the Catholic faith. Use the Lectio Divina method to meditate on the Word of GOD and discern its relevance to your life.

    - ***Application:*** Regular scripture reflection deepens your understanding of GOD's word and strengthens your faith.

By incorporating these spiritual tools into daily routines, readers can live out the core beliefs of Catholicism in a meaningful and practical way. These practices provide a foundation for spiritual growth, helping Catholics navigate the complexities of modern life while staying rooted in their faith.

Exercise: Living Out the Core Beliefs of Catholicism

Objective: To help you internalize and apply the fundamental beliefs of Catholicism in your daily life, fostering a deeper understanding of your faith and its practical implications.

Instructions:

1. **Daily Reflection on The Trinity:**
   - *Duration:* 5-10 minutes each morning.
   - *Instructions:* Begin each day by reflecting on the Holy Trinity. Start with a prayer to GOD the Father, thanking Him for creation and His constant guidance. Then, pray to Jesus Christ, asking for His presence and example to guide your actions. Finally, invoke The Holy Spirit, seeking inspiration and strength for the day ahead.
   - *Outcome:* This practice will help you cultivate an awareness of The Trinity's presence in your life and set a spiritual tone for your day.

2. **Sacrament Preparation and Participation:**

    - *Duration:* Weekly participation.

    - *Instructions:* Choose one sacrament, such as the Eucharist or Reconciliation, to focus on for the week. Prepare by spending time in prayer and reflection on the significance of the sacrament and what it means to receive GOD's grace through it. Participate in the sacrament with intentionality, fully engaging in the experience.

    - *Outcome:* By preparing for and actively participating in the sacraments, you will deepen your understanding of their importance and feel more connected to your faith.

3. **Weekly Scripture Reflection:**

    - *Duration:* 20 minutes once a week.

    - *Instructions:* Select a scripture passage that relates to one of the core beliefs discussed in this chapter, such as the Incarnation or the communion of saints. Read the passage slowly, meditate on its meaning, and reflect on how it applies to your life. Consider using the Lectio Divina method to guide your reflection.

- **Outcome:** Regular scripture reflection will help you internalize the core beliefs and see their relevance in your daily life.

4. **Community Service Inspired by the Eucharist:**
   - **Duration:** 1-2 hours each month.
   - **Instructions:** Reflect on the Eucharist as the "source and summit of Christian life" and consider how you can extend this understanding into acts of service. Choose a service activity, such as volunteering at a food bank, visiting the sick, or helping at a parish event, as a way to live out the Eucharistic call to serve others.
   - **Outcome:** Engaging in community service will help you put your faith into action and experience the joy of serving others as Christ did.

5. **Relationship Reflection and Improvement:**
   - **Duration:** 15 minutes once a week.
   - **Instructions:** Reflect on your relationships, considering how the core beliefs of Catholicism, such as the Trinity and the universal call to holiness, can improve how you interact with others. Identify one relationship where you can apply these beliefs more fully, such as through increased patience, forgiveness, or support. Take practical steps to

enhance that relationship during the week.

- ***Outcome:*** This exercise will help you bring your faith into your relationships, fostering stronger, more loving connections with others.

Outcome: By completing this exercise, you will gain a deeper understanding of the core beliefs of Catholicism and how they can be lived out in practical ways. The daily reflection, sacramental participation, scripture study, community service, and relationship improvement practices will help you integrate your faith into all aspects of your life, leading to spiritual growth and a more meaningful connection with GOD and others.

Chapter 19: Understanding The Sacraments

Exploring the Significance of the Seven Sacraments in the Catholic Faith

The Sacraments are central to Catholic life, serving as visible signs of GOD's invisible grace. They are profound encounters with the divine, designed to strengthen the believer's relationship with GOD and the Church. In this chapter, we will explore the significance of The Seven Sacraments, with a special focus on the Eucharist and Reconciliation. By understanding these sacred rites, modern Catholics can deepen their spiritual lives and integrate The Sacraments more fully into their daily practices.

Theological Insights

The Sacraments are deeply rooted in the theological concepts of the Incarnation and The Holy Trinity. Through the Incarnation, GOD became man in the person of Jesus Christ, fully embracing human nature while remaining fully divine. This mystery of faith is foundational to understanding The Sacraments, as it highlights GOD's desire to be intimately present in the lives of His people. The Sacraments are tangible expressions of this divine presence, where GOD's grace is conferred through physical signs and actions.

The Holy Trinity - Father, Son, and Holy Spirit - is also integral to The Sacraments. Each Sacrament is an encounter with the Trinity: The Father, who bestows His grace; The Son, who instituted The Sacraments and is present in them; and The Holy Spirit, who empowers and sanctifies the faithful through these sacred rites. For example, in the sacrament of Baptism, The Holy Spirit descends upon the believer, making them a new creation in Christ and a member of The Body of Christ, The Church.

The Eucharist, often referred to as the "source and summit of the Christian life," is the central sacrament in Catholic worship. In The Eucharist, Catholics believe that the bread and wine become The Body and Blood of Christ, a doctrine known as **Transubstantiation**. This mystery is supported by Jesus' words at the Last Supper: *"This is my body, which is given for you. Do this in remembrance of me"* (Luke 22:19)[1]. The Eucharist is not merely a symbol but a real presence of Christ, offering believers spiritual nourishment and a profound union with GOD.

Reconciliation, also known as Confession, is another vital Sacrament that emphasizes GOD's mercy and forgiveness. Through this Sacrament, Catholics confess their sins to a priest, who, acting in the person of Christ, offers **absolution** and **reconciles** the penitent with GOD and the Church. This Sacrament reflects the ongoing need for conversion and renewal in the Christian life. As Jesus said, *"If you forgive the* *sins of any, they are forgiven them; if you retain the sins of any, they are retained"* (John 20:23)[2].

These Sacraments, along with the others - Baptism, Confirmation, Anointing of the Sick, Holy Orders, and Matrimony - form a cohesive framework for spiritual growth and communal life in the Church. They are not isolated rituals but interconnected experiences that guide Catholics through every stage of life, from birth to death, and beyond.

Application in Modern Life

Understanding The Sacraments is one thing; integrating them into daily life is another. For many modern Catholics, the challenge lies in balancing the spiritual richness of The Sacraments with the demands of a busy, secular world. However, The Sacraments are not meant to be confined to church services; they are intended to permeate every aspect of a believer's life, providing strength, guidance, and grace for daily living.

The Eucharist, for example, can be more than just a Sunday obligation. By consciously reflecting on the Eucharist throughout the week, Catholics can carry the presence of Christ with them into their work, relationships, and personal struggles. One practical way to do this is by making a habit of Eucharistic adoration, spending time in prayer before the Blessed Sacrament, either in a church or a designated chapel. This practice helps to keep the reality of Christ's presence at the forefront of one's life, fostering a deeper spiritual connection that influences daily decisions and actions.

Reconciliation, too, can be more than an occasional practice. Regular confession, such as monthly or even bi-weekly, allows Catholics to continually assess their spiritual health and seek GOD's grace for ongoing conversion. This Sacrament is particularly helpful in dealing with persistent sins or struggles, offering a fresh start and renewed commitment to living according to GOD's will.

Consider the example of a Catholic business leader who faces ethical challenges in their work environment. By regularly participating in the Sacraments, particularly the Eucharist and Reconciliation, this individual can draw on the grace received to make decisions that reflect their faith. The Eucharist strengthens their resolve to act with integrity, while Reconciliation provides the humility and accountability needed to correct mistakes and seek GOD's guidance.

Another example could be a young couple preparing for marriage. By understanding the Sacrament of Matrimony not just as a one-time event but as a lifelong commitment, they can approach their relationship with a deeper sense of purpose. Regular participation in the Eucharist helps them to center their marriage on Christ, while Reconciliation allows them to address conflicts and challenges with a spirit of forgiveness and renewal.

Practical Spiritual Tools

To help readers deepen their understanding and experience of the sacraments, here are some practical spiritual tools:

1. **Daily Sacramental Reflection:**

   - *Instructions:* Spend a few minutes each day reflecting on the significance of The Sacraments in your life. Choose one Sacrament to focus on each week. For example, meditate on the Eucharist by reading scripture passages related to the Last Supper or by praying the Anima Christi prayer after receiving Communion.

   - *Application:* This practice will help you stay connected to the grace of The Sacraments and integrate their meaning into your daily life.

2. **Frequent Eucharistic Adoration:**

   - *Instructions:* Set aside time each week for Eucharistic adoration. If possible, visit a church or chapel where the Blessed Sacrament is exposed. Spend this time in silent prayer, focusing on the presence of Christ in the Eucharist and offering your daily concerns to Him.

   - *Application:* Regular adoration deepens your relationship with Christ and helps you carry the peace of the Eucharist into your daily life.

3. **Regular Examination of Conscience:**

    - ***Instructions:*** Develop a habit of examining your conscience at the end of each day. Reflect on your actions, thoughts, and words, considering where you have lived according to GOD's will and where you have fallen short. Use this reflection to prepare for regular confession.
    - ***Application:*** Regular examination of conscience fosters spiritual growth and prepares you to receive The Sacrament of Reconciliation with a contrite heart.

4. **Sacramental Journaling:**

    - ***Instructions:*** Keep a journal dedicated to your experiences with the sacraments. After participating in a Sacrament, such as the Eucharist or Reconciliation, write down your thoughts, feelings, and any spiritual insights you gained. Review your entries regularly to track your spiritual growth.
    - ***Application:*** Journaling helps you internalize the grace received through The Sacraments and encourages ongoing reflection and spiritual development.

By incorporating these spiritual tools into your daily routine, you can deepen your experience of The Sacraments and allow their grace to transform your life. The Sacraments are not just rituals but living encounters with GOD, designed to nourish your soul and guide you on the path to holiness.

Exercise: Deepening Your Experience of The Sacraments

Objective: To help you understand and more fully integrate The Sacraments into your daily life, fostering a deeper connection with GOD and a richer spiritual life.

Instructions:

1. **Eucharistic Reflection:**
   - *Duration:* 10 minutes after each Mass.
   - *Instructions:* After receiving The Eucharist at Mass, spend 10 minutes in silent reflection. Focus on the presence of Christ within you. Contemplate how The Eucharist nourishes your soul and how you can carry Christ's presence into your daily life. Write down any insights or resolutions in a journal dedicated to your spiritual journey.
   - *Outcome:* This practice will deepen your appreciation of The Eucharist and help you to live out its significance in your daily actions and decisions.

2. **Regular Confession and Examination of Conscience:**
   - ***Duration:*** 15 minutes weekly, with Confession monthly.

   - ***Instructions:*** Each week, set aside time to examine your conscience, reflecting on your actions, thoughts, and words. Consider how you have lived according to GOD's will and where you have fallen short. Prepare to receive the sacrament of Reconciliation by acknowledging your sins and seeking GOD's forgiveness. Aim to go to Confession at least once a month.

   - ***Outcome:*** Regular participation in Reconciliation will help you maintain spiritual clarity, grow in holiness, and experience the healing grace of GOD's forgiveness.

3. **Sacramental Integration into Daily Life:**
   - ***Duration:*** Ongoing throughout the week.
   - ***Instructions:*** Identify one Sacrament each week to focus on and find ways to integrate its significance into your daily life. For example, after receiving The Eucharist, practice acts of charity and kindness, reflecting Christ's presence in you. If you focus on Matrimony, dedicate time to strengthening your relationship with your spouse through shared prayer

or acts of love.

- **Outcome:** By consciously integrating The Sacraments into your daily activities, you will foster a continuous awareness of GOD's grace and presence in your life.

4. **Community Service Inspired by The Sacraments:**
   - **Duration:** 1-2 hours monthly.
   - **Instructions:** Choose a community service activity that reflects The Sacramental life of the Church. For example, volunteer at a food bank as a way of living out the Eucharistic call to feed the hungry or visit the sick and elderly as an extension of the Anointing of the Sick. Offer your service in the spirit of the sacraments, seeking to bring GOD's love to others.
   - **Outcome:** This exercise will help you live out The Sacraments in practical ways, deepening your commitment to serving others as Christ did.

5. **Sacramental Meditation:**
   - **Duration:** 15 minutes weekly.
   - **Instructions:** Spend time in meditation, focusing on a particular Sacrament. For example, meditate on the meaning of Baptism and your identity as a child

of GOD, or reflect on the Eucharist and how Christ nourishes your soul. Use this time to connect with GOD and allow The Sacrament to transform your heart and mind.

- ***Outcome:*** Regular Sacramental meditation will help you internalize the spiritual realities of the sacraments, leading to a more profound and personal relationship with GOD.

Outcome: By engaging in this exercise, you will deepen your understanding of The Sacraments and experience their transformative power in your life. The practices of reflection, confession, daily integration, community service, and meditation will help you live out The Sacraments more fully, fostering spiritual growth and a closer relationship with GOD. This exercise is designed to make The Sacraments a living and active part of your faith journey.

Chapter 20: The Nicene Creed – The Profession of Faith

Understanding and Living the Nicene Creed

The Nicene Creed is one of the most important and enduring statements of Christian faith, recited by Catholics around the world during Mass. It encapsulates the core beliefs of Christianity, affirming the doctrines of The Holy Trinity, the nature of Jesus Christ, The Church, and the promise of eternal life. This chapter explores the theological significance of the Nicene Creed, its relevance to modern-day Catholics, and how it can be integrated into daily life as a guide for living out one's faith.

Theological Insights

The Nicene Creed, formulated at the First Council of Nicaea in 325 AD and later expanded at the Council of Constantinople in 381 AD, serves as a definitive statement of Christian orthodoxy. It was developed to address and refute heresies, particularly Arianism, which denied the full divinity of Jesus Christ. The Creed begins with a profound declaration of belief in one GOD, the Father Almighty, the Creator of heaven and earth, affirming the monotheistic foundation of Christianity[2].

The Creed then professes faith in Jesus Christ, the only Son of GOD, "begotten, not made, consubstantial with The Father." This statement is crucial because it affirms the full divinity of

Jesus, acknowledging that He is of the same essence as the Father, not a created being. This is supported by scripture, such as John 1:1-3[1], which states, *"In the beginning was the Word, and the Word was with GOD, and the Word was GOD. He was in the beginning with GOD; all things were made through Him, and without Him was not anything made that was made."* The Creed also highlights the Incarnation, stating that Jesus "came down from heaven" and "became man" for the salvation of humanity, which is the central mystery of the Christian faith.

The Holy Spirit, the "Lord, the giver of life," is also affirmed in the Creed as proceeding from the Father and the Son, emphasizing the unity and co-equality of The Holy Trinity. The Spirit's role in inspiring the prophets and sustaining the Church is acknowledged, underscoring the ongoing presence of GOD in the world today.

The Creed concludes with a profession of faith in "one, holy, catholic, and apostolic Church," the communion of saints, the forgiveness of sins, the resurrection of the dead, and life everlasting. These statements affirm the communal and eschatological aspects of the faith, reminding believers of their connection to the broader Church and their ultimate destiny in GOD's eternal kingdom.

For modern-day Catholics, The Nicene Creed serves as both a summary of core beliefs and a declaration of identity. It is not merely a historical document but a living expression of faith that continues to shape and guide the Church's teaching and practice. Understanding the theological depth of The Creed can help Catholics engage more fully with their faith, grounding them in the truths that have been handed down through the centuries.

Application in Modern Life

Reciting The Nicene Creed during Mass is a communal act of faith, but its significance extends far beyond the liturgy. For modern Catholics, The Creed can serve as a spiritual anchor, providing clarity and direction in a complex and often confusing world. By regularly reflecting on The Creed, believers can strengthen their understanding of the faith and apply its truths to their daily lives.

One of the challenges many Catholics face is maintaining a balance between spiritual commitments and the demands of everyday life. The Creed offers a framework for prioritizing these commitments by reminding believers of the fundamental truths that should guide their decisions and actions. For example, the affirmation of GOD as The Creator can inspire a sense of stewardship and responsibility toward the environment and the world around us. Similarly, belief in the Incarnation can encourage Catholics to recognize the dignity and worth of every person, leading to more compassionate and just relationships.

Consider the example of a Catholic business owner who strives to live out their faith in a competitive and often cutthroat industry. By grounding their decisions in the principles of The Creed - such as the inherent dignity of all people, the call to honesty and integrity, and the belief in a just and merciful GOD -

they can navigate ethical dilemmas with confidence and clarity. The Creed provides a moral compass, guiding them to act in ways that reflect their faith, even in difficult circumstances.

Another example could be a young parent teaching their children about the faith. By explaining The Creed in simple terms and relating its teachings to everyday experiences, the parent can help their children develop a strong and enduring foundation of faith. For instance, discussing the belief in one GOD can lead to conversations about gratitude for creation and the importance of prayer, while the doctrine of The Holy Spirit can be linked to recognizing GOD's presence and guidance in daily life.

Practical Spiritual Tools

To help readers integrate The Nicene Creed into their daily lives, here are some practical spiritual tools:

1. **Daily Reflection on the Creed:**

    - ***Instructions***: Set aside time each day to reflect on a specific line or section of The Nicene Creed. Consider what it means for your life and how you can live out that belief in your daily actions. For example, when reflecting on *"I believe in one GOD, the Father Almighty,"* consider how you can trust in GOD's providence and express gratitude for His creation.

- **Application:** This practice will help deepen your understanding of The Creed and reinforce its truths in your everyday life.

2. **Creed-Based Prayer:**

    - **Instructions:** Use The Nicene Creed as the basis for your daily prayers. Start by reciting The Creed, then expand on each section with personal prayers. For example, after professing belief in Jesus Christ, you might thank Him for His sacrifice and ask for the grace to follow His example.

    - **Application:** Incorporating The Creed into your prayer life will help you internalize its teachings and strengthen your spiritual connection to GOD.

3. **Teaching the Creed:**

    - **Instructions:** If you have children or teach catechism, use The Nicene Creed as a teaching tool. Break it down into simple concepts and relate it to the children's experiences. For example, explain the concept of The Trinity by comparing it to a family unit, where each person is distinct but part of the same family.

    - **Application:** Teaching The Creed helps solidify your own understanding while passing on the faith to the next generation.

4. **Creed-Inspired Actions:**

    - ***Instructions:*** Choose one line from The Creed each week and focus on living it out through specific actions. For example, if focusing on "the resurrection of the dead and the life of the world to come," consider how you can live with hope and encourage others who are struggling.

    - ***Application:*** This exercise helps translate The Creed's theological concepts into practical, everyday actions that reflect your faith.

By incorporating these spiritual tools into your daily routine, you can make the Nicene Creed a living part of your faith journey. The Creed is not just a statement of beliefs but a guide for how to live out those beliefs in a meaningful and impactful way.

Exercise: Living the Nicene Creed

Objective: To help you deepen your understanding of The Nicene Creed and integrate its teachings into your daily life, fostering a more profound connection with your faith and its core beliefs.

Instructions:

1. **Daily Creed Reflection:**
    - ***Duration:*** 5-10 minutes each morning.

- *Instructions:* Begin each day by reciting The Nicene Creed slowly and thoughtfully. Choose one line or section to focus on for the day. Reflect on its meaning and how it applies to your life. For example, if you focus on *"I believe in one GOD, the Father Almighty, Creator of heaven and earth,"* consider how you can express gratitude for GOD's creation or trust in His providence.

- *Outcome:* This daily reflection will help you internalize The Creed's teachings and start each day grounded in your faith.

2. **Weekly Application of a Creed Concept:**

    - *Duration:* Ongoing throughout the week.

    - *Instructions:* Each week, choose a specific line or concept from The Creed to apply in your daily life. For instance, if you focus on *"the resurrection of the dead and the life of the world to come,"* think about how you can live with hope and inspire hope in others. Actively seek opportunities to embody this belief in your actions, whether through words of encouragement, acts of kindness, or personal reflection on eternal life.

    - *Outcome:* By applying The Creed's teachings in practical ways, you'll begin to see how these core beliefs influence and enrich your everyday decisions and interactions.

3. **Creed Journaling:**
    - ***Duration:*** 15 minutes once a week.
    - ***Instructions:*** Set aside time each week to journal about your reflections on The Nicene Creed. Write about how the specific line or concept you focused on influenced your thoughts, actions, and experiences. Consider how this understanding has deepened your faith or challenged you to grow spiritually.
    - ***Outcome:*** Regular journaling will help you track your spiritual growth and provide insights into how The Creed is shaping your faith journey.

4. **Creed Discussion Group:**
    - ***Duration:*** 1 hour monthly.
    - ***Instructions:*** Organize or join a small discussion group to explore The Nicene Creed with others. Each member can share their reflections on different sections of The Creed and how they are applying it in their lives. Discuss challenges, insights, and ways to support one another in living out The Creed's teachings.

- ***Outcome:*** Engaging in group discussions will deepen your understanding of The Creed and provide communal support for integrating its teachings into your life.

5. **Creed-Based Prayer Practice:**
   - ***Duration:*** 10 minutes before bedtime.
   - ***Instructions:*** Incorporate The Nicene Creed into your nightly prayer routine. After reciting The Creed, offer prayers of thanksgiving, repentance, and petition based on its teachings. For example, after professing belief in *"one holy, catholic, and apostolic Church,"* pray for the unity of the Church and for guidance in contributing to its mission.
   - ***Outcome:*** This prayer practice will reinforce The Creed's teachings and help you end each day with a reaffirmation of your faith.

Outcome: By completing this exercise, you will gain a deeper understanding of The Nicene Creed and its relevance to your daily life. The practices of reflection, application, journaling, group discussion, and prayer will help you live out The Creed's teachings in a tangible and meaningful way, strengthening your connection to the core beliefs of your faith and fostering continuous spiritual growth.

NOTES:

Chapter 21: Core Prayers of Catholic Devotional Practice

Theme: Deepening Faith Through Core Catholic Prayers

Prayer is the lifeblood of the Catholic spiritual life, providing a direct line of communication with GOD. The core prayers of Catholic devotional practice are not just words to be recited; they are profound expressions of faith, hope, and love that connect believers with the divine. This chapter explores the theological significance of these prayers, their relevance to modern-day Catholics, and how they can be integrated into daily life to foster a deeper relationship with GOD.

Theological Insights

The core prayers of Catholicism, such as the Our Father, Hail Mary, and the Glory Be, are rich in theological meaning. They encapsulate the key beliefs of the faith, drawing the believer into a deeper understanding of GOD and His relationship with humanity.

The Our Father, also known as **The Lord's Prayer**, is the prayer Jesus taught His disciples (Matthew 6:9-13)[1]. It is a perfect summary of the Gospel, expressing the believer's trust in GOD as Father, acknowledging His holiness, and aligning oneself with His will. The prayer's petition for daily bread is both a request for physical sustenance and a spiritual plea for The Eucharist, the "Bread of Life" (John 6:35)[2]. The Our Father also emphasizes the importance of forgiveness, a central tenet of Christian life, as we ask GOD to forgive our trespasses as we forgive those who trespass against us.

The Hail Mary is a prayer of devotion to the Blessed Virgin Mary, rooted in scripture (Luke 1:28, 42)[3]. It begins with the angel Gabriel's greeting to Mary, *"Hail, full of grace, the Lord is with you,"* and Elizabeth's exclamation, *"Blessed are you among women, and blessed is the fruit of your womb"* (Luke 1:28, 42). The Hail Mary is both a prayer of praise and a request for Mary's intercession, recognizing her unique role in salvation history as the Mother of GOD. This prayer reflects the Catholic belief in the communion of saints, wherein Mary, as the most exalted of the saints, is a powerful advocate for the faithful.

The Glory Be is a doxology, a short hymn of praise to The Holy Trinity. It honors GOD as Father, Son, and Holy Spirit, acknowledging the eternal nature of The Trinity: "As it was in the beginning, is now, and ever shall be, world without end." This prayer underscores the centrality of the Trinity in Catholic faith, reminding believers of GOD's unchanging presence throughout time and their place within His divine plan.

These prayers, deeply rooted in scripture and tradition, serve as foundational elements of Catholic devotional life. They connect believers with the core tenets of the faith, guiding them in their spiritual journey and helping them to live out their beliefs in practical ways.

Application in Modern Life

In the fast-paced world of today, maintaining a consistent prayer life can be challenging. However, these core prayers offer Catholics a way to stay connected to their faith, no matter how busy life becomes. By incorporating these prayers into daily routines, Catholics can create a rhythm of prayer that anchors them in GOD's presence.

One common challenge is finding time for prayer amidst work, family, and social obligations. The Our Father, Hail Mary, and Glory Be are concise yet profound prayers that can be easily integrated into daily life. For example, a Catholic professional might start their day by reciting The Our Father during their morning commute, asking for GOD's guidance and protection throughout the day. Similarly, parents can teach their children to pray The Hail Mary before bed, fostering a habit of prayer that will grow with them.

Another challenge is staying focused during prayer, especially in a world full of distractions. The repetition of these core prayers can help quiet the mind and center the heart on GOD. For instance, praying The Rosary, which involves repeating the Hail Mary while meditating on the mysteries of Christ's life, can be a powerful way to deepen one's prayer life. The Rosary combines vocal prayer with meditation, allowing the believer to enter into a contemplative state where they can encounter GOD more intimately.

Consider the example of a Catholic nurse who, amidst the stress and demands of their job, uses the Glory Be as a short prayer of praise and thanksgiving throughout the day. Whether after a successful procedure or a moment of peace in a hectic shift, this prayer becomes a way to acknowledge GOD's presence and give glory to Him in the midst of daily responsibilities.

Practical Spiritual Tools

To help readers integrate these core prayers into their daily lives, here are some practical spiritual tools:

1. **Daily Prayer Routine:**

    - ***Instructions:*** Establish a daily prayer routine that includes The Our Father, Hail Mary, and Glory Be. Begin the day with the Our Father, asking for GOD's guidance and strength. Incorporate The Hail Mary at midday, seeking Mary's intercession for any challenges you face. End the day with The Glory Be, offering thanks and praise to GOD for His blessings.

    - ***Application:*** This routine will help you stay connected to GOD throughout the day and deepen your relationship with Him.

2. **Praying the Rosary:**

    - ***Instructions:*** Set aside time each day or week to pray the Rosary. Begin with The Sign of the Cross, then proceed with the Apostles' Creed, The Our Father, three Hail Mary's, and The Glory Be. Continue through the decades, meditating on the mysteries of Christ's life as you pray.

    - ***Application:*** Praying The Rosary regularly fosters a deeper connection with Christ and His Mother, and helps you develop a habit of meditation and contemplation.

3. **Prayer Breaks:**

    - ***Instructions:*** Throughout your day, take short breaks to recite one of the core prayers. Whether at work, at home, or on the go, these moments of prayer can help you refocus and re-center on GOD. For example, before a meeting, recite The Our Father to seek GOD's guidance, or say the Hail Mary before making a difficult decision.

    - ***Application:*** These prayer breaks serve as reminders of GOD's constant presence and provide spiritual support in daily tasks.

4. **Family Prayer Time:**

    - ***Instructions:*** Incorporate the core prayers into your family's daily routine. Pray The Our Father together in the morning, The Hail Mary in the evening, and The Glory Be at the end of the day. Encourage family members to share their intentions before each prayer, fostering a sense of unity and mutual support.

    - ***Application:*** Family prayer time strengthens the bonds between family members and creates a spiritual foundation that can be passed on to future generations.

By incorporating these spiritual tools into your daily routine, you can make the core prayers of Catholic devotional practice a living part of your faith journey. These prayers are not just words to be recited; they are powerful expressions of faith that connect you with GOD, The Church, and the broader Catholic tradition.

Exercise: Integrating Core Catholic Prayers into Daily Life

Objective: To help you deepen your understanding and experience of the core Catholic prayers by incorporating them into your daily routine, enhancing your spiritual life, and strengthening your connection with GOD.

Instructions:

1. **Morning Prayer Routine:**
   - *Duration:* 10 minutes each morning.
   - *Instructions:* Begin each day by setting aside 10 minutes for prayer. Start with The Our Father, followed by The Hail Mary, and conclude with The Glory Be. As you pray, focus on the meaning of each word, offering your day to GOD and asking for His guidance, protection, and blessings.
   - *Outcome:* This routine will help you start your day with a clear spiritual focus, aligning your intentions with GOD's will.

2. **Midday Prayer Pause:**
   - *Duration:* 5 minutes during lunch or a break.
   - *Instructions:* During your lunch break or a moment of rest, take 5 minutes to recite one of the core prayers. Reflect on the challenges and blessings of the morning and ask for GOD's continued presence and Mary's intercession in the rest of your day.

- **Outcome:** This practice will help you stay spiritually centered and mindful of GOD's presence throughout the day.

3. **Evening Prayer Reflection:**
   - **Duration:** 10 minutes before bed.
   - **Instructions:** End your day by reflecting on how GOD was present in your life. Recite The Our Father, Hail Mary, and Glory Be, giving thanks for the day's blessings and seeking forgiveness for any shortcomings. Offer any worries or concerns to GOD, entrusting them to His care.
   - **Outcome:** This evening reflection will bring closure to your day, fostering a sense of peace and spiritual renewal before sleep.

4. **Weekly Rosary Meditation:**
   - **Duration:** 20-30 minutes once a week.
   - **Instructions:** Choose a quiet time each week to pray the Rosary. Begin with The Apostles' Creed, followed by The Our Father, three Hail Mary's, and The Glory Be. As you proceed through The Decades, meditate on The Mysteries of Christ's life, asking for the grace to live out these mysteries in your own life.
   - **Outcome:** Regular Rosary meditation will deepen your connection with Christ and Mary, helping you to

reflect on The Mysteries of the faith and apply them to your daily experiences.

5. **Family Prayer Time:**

    - **Duration:** 15 minutes daily.

    - **Instructions:** Gather with your family each evening for prayer. Recite The Our Father, Hail Mary, and Glory Be together, encouraging each family member to share their intentions. This time can also include a brief discussion of a particular prayer or its meaning, helping to reinforce its significance.

    - **Outcome:** Family prayer time will strengthen the spiritual bonds within your family, creating a shared practice of faith that supports each member's spiritual growth.

Outcome: By completing this exercise, you will not only enhance your understanding of the core Catholic prayers but also integrate them into your daily life in a meaningful way. The practices of morning, midday, and evening prayers, along with weekly Rosary meditation and family prayer time, will help you maintain a constant awareness of GOD's presence, deepen your relationship with Him, and foster spiritual growth in both personal and communal contexts.

NOTES:

Chapter 22: The Liturgical Calendar

Understanding the Rhythms of the Liturgical Year

The Liturgical Calendar is more than just a schedule of church services; it is a spiritual journey that guides Catholics through the life of Christ, the mysteries of the faith, and the communion of saints. By observing the liturgical seasons, feasts, and saints' days, Catholics are invited to enter more deeply into the mysteries of the faith, align their lives with the rhythms of the Church, and grow in holiness. This chapter explores the theological significance of the Liturgical Calendar, its relevance to modern-day Catholics, and how it can be integrated into daily life to foster continuous spiritual growth.

Theological Insights

The Liturgical Calendar is designed to lead the faithful through the key events in the life of Jesus Christ, the foundational mysteries of the Christian faith, and the celebration of The Saints who have lived out these mysteries. The calendar is divided into seasons: **Advent, Christmas, Ordinary Time, Lent, the Sacred Paschal Triduum,** and **Easter**. Each season has its own theological focus, guiding the believer through a cycle of preparation, celebration, and reflection.

Advent is the season of preparation for the coming of Christ. It is a time of anticipation and hope, as Catholics reflect on the first coming of Jesus in Bethlehem and look forward to His second coming in glory. The Advent Wreath, with its four candles, symbolizes the light of Christ gradually overcoming the darkness, a theme echoed in John 1:5, *"The light shines in the darkness, and the darkness has not overcome it"*[1].

Christmas celebrates the Incarnation, the mystery of GOD becoming man in the person of Jesus Christ. This season is marked by joy and thanksgiving for the gift of the Savior, who is *"Emmanuel," meaning "GOD with us"* (Matthew 1:23)[2]. The Christmas season extends to The Feast of the Baptism of the Lord, reminding Catholics of their own Baptism and call to follow Christ.

Ordinary Time is not a time of lesser importance but a period of growth and maturation in the Christian life. It focuses on the teachings and miracles of Jesus, encouraging believers to apply His lessons in their daily lives. This season represents the "ordinary" aspects of the Christian journey - living out faith in everyday circumstances.

Lent is a season of Penance, Reflection, and Renewal, leading up to the Passion, Death, and Resurrection of Jesus Christ. Catholics are called to enter into the mystery of Christ's suffering, embracing practices of Prayer, Fasting, and Almsgiving. Lent is a time of spiritual purification, preparing the heart to receive the fullness of Easter joy.

The **Sacred Paschal Triduum** - Holy Thursday, Good Friday, and Holy Saturday - is the climax of the Liturgical Year. These three days commemorate The Last Supper, The Passion and

Death of Jesus, and His rest in the tomb. The Triduum is a time of intense reflection on the mystery of Redemption, culminating in the Easter Vigil, where The Resurrection of Christ is celebrated with great joy.

Easter is the season of resurrection, celebrating the victory of Christ over sin and death. It is a time of rejoicing and renewal, as Catholics are reminded of the new life they have received in Christ. The Easter season lasts for 50 days, ending with Pentecost, the feast of The Holy Spirit's descent upon The Apostles and the birth of the Church.

Throughout the Liturgical Year, the Church also celebrates **Feasts** and **Saints' Days**. These special days honor The Saints - men and women who have lived exemplary lives of holiness - and key events in The Life of Christ and The Blessed Virgin Mary. Celebrating these days helps Catholics to remember The Communion of Saints, the ongoing presence of GOD in history, and the call to holiness in their own lives.

For modern-day Catholics, The Liturgical Calendar offers a way to structure their spiritual lives around the mysteries of the faith, aligning their personal rhythms with The Church's seasons of preparation, celebration, and reflection.

Application in Modern Life

Integrating the Liturgical Calendar into daily life can be a powerful way for Catholics to maintain a deep and vibrant faith. However, in a world filled with distractions and competing demands, this can be challenging. The Liturgical Calendar provides a framework that helps Catholics stay grounded in their faith, offering regular opportunities to renew their commitment to GOD and grow in holiness.

One practical way to integrate The Liturgical Calendar into daily life is by observing the major liturgical seasons. For example, during Advent, families can light an Advent Wreath each evening, pray together, and reflect on the readings of the day. This practice helps to create a sense of anticipation and prepares the heart to welcome Christ at Christmas.

During Lent, Catholics might choose to participate in traditional practices such as fasting on Fridays, attending Stations of the Cross, or setting aside time each day for Prayer and Reflection. These practices help to cultivate a spirit of penance and renewal, aligning the believer with the suffering and sacrifice of Christ.

In the Easter Season, Catholics are encouraged to live with a spirit of joy and thanksgiving, reflecting on the resurrection and its implications for their lives. This might involve attending daily Mass, participating in Easter Devotions, or finding ways to share the joy of the resurrection with others through acts of kindness and service.

Feasts and Saints' Days offer additional opportunities for spiritual growth. For example, on the feast of a favorite saint, a Catholic might read about the saint's life, pray a special prayer, or engage in an activity that honors the saint's example. These celebrations help to keep the memory of the saints alive and inspire believers to follow their example of holiness.

Practical Spiritual Tools

To help readers integrate the Liturgical Calendar into their daily lives, here are some practical spiritual tools:

1. **Liturgical Calendar Planning:**

    - ***Instructions:*** At the beginning of each liturgical season, take time to plan how you will observe it. Identify key practices, prayers, and devotions that align with the season's themes. For example, plan to attend extra Masses during Advent or set aside time for daily Lenten reflections.

    - ***Application:*** This planning helps you stay intentional about living according to the Liturgical Calendar, ensuring that your spiritual life remains focused and vibrant.

2. **Seasonal Prayer and Reflection:**

    - ***Instructions:*** Choose a specific Prayer or Scripture passage to focus on for each Liturgical Season. For example, during Lent, you might reflect daily on The Passion narratives in The Gospels. During Easter, you might focus on the resurrection accounts and The Acts of the Apostles.

- **Application:** This practice deepens your connection with the themes of each season, helping you to grow spiritually in a structured and meaningful way.

3. **Observance of Feasts and Saints' Days:**

    - **Instructions:** Make a habit of observing the major Feasts and Saints' days throughout the year. This could include attending Mass, reading about the life of a Saint, or Praying a Novena leading up to a particular feast day.

    - **Application:** Regularly observing these days keeps you connected to the broader Catholic tradition and inspires you to live out your faith more fully.

4. **Family Liturgical Practices:**

    - **Instructions:** Involve your family in celebrating The Liturgical Calendar. Create family traditions around key seasons, such as making an Advent Wreath, celebrating a special meal on feast days, or praying the Rosary together during the month of May, dedicated to Mary.

    - **Application:** These practices help to build a strong spiritual foundation for your family, ensuring that The Faith is passed on to the next generation.

By incorporating these spiritual tools into your daily routine, you can make The Liturgical Calendar a living part of your faith journey. The calendar is not just a series of dates and observances; it is a spiritual map that guides you through the mysteries of the faith, helping you to grow closer to GOD and live out your Catholic identity more fully.

Exercise: Living the Liturgical Calendar

Objective: To help you understand and integrate The Liturgical Calendar into your daily life, fostering a deeper connection with the rhythms of the Church and growing in your faith throughout the year.

Instructions:

1. **Seasonal Planning and Reflection:**
   - ***Duration:*** 30 minutes at the start of each liturgical season.

   - ***Instructions:*** At the beginning of each liturgical season (Advent, Christmas, Lent, Easter, and Ordinary Time), set aside 30 minutes to plan how you will observe the season. Reflect on the themes of the season and decide on specific spiritual practices, such as attending daily Mass, adding extra prayer time, or engaging in acts of charity. Write down your plan and commit to following it throughout the season.

- **Outcome:** This planning will help you stay intentional about your spiritual growth, ensuring that each season of The Liturgical Calendar becomes an opportunity for deeper reflection and commitment.

2. **Daily Prayer and Scripture Reading:**
   - **Duration:** 10-15 minutes daily.
   - **Instructions:** Each day, set aside 10-15 minutes to pray and read the scripture passages related to the current liturgical season. Use a Catholic Daily Missal or an online resource to find the appropriate readings. Reflect on how the themes of the season apply to your life and ask GOD to help you live out these themes in your daily actions.
   - **Outcome:** Regular engagement with the daily readings and prayers will deepen your understanding of The Liturgical Calendar and strengthen your connection to the Church's teachings.

3. **Observance of Feast Days and Saints' Days:**
   - **Duration:** 15 minutes on selected feast days.
   - **Instructions:** Choose a few key feast days or saints' days to observe more closely during each season. On these days, read about the significance of the feast or the life of the saint, pray a special

prayer, and consider attending Mass if possible. Reflect on how the example of the saint or the significance of the feast can inspire you in your own faith journey.

- **Outcome:** Observing Feast days and Saints' Days will keep you connected to the wider Church and inspire you to emulate the holiness of the Saints in your own life.

4. **Family and Community Involvement:**
   - **Duration:** 1 hour weekly.

   - **Instructions:** Involve your family or community in observing The Liturgical Calendar. Plan a weekly family or community activity that reflects the current season, such as creating an Advent Wreath, organizing a Lenten service project, or celebrating a feast day with a special meal. Use these activities as opportunities to discuss the significance of the season and how it applies to your lives.

   - **Outcome:** Engaging your family or community in The Liturgical Calendar will strengthen your collective faith, create lasting spiritual traditions, and ensure that the teachings of The Church are passed on to future generations.

5. **Liturgical Season Review:**

    - ***Duration:*** 30 minutes at the end of each season.

    - ***Instructions:*** At the end of each liturgical season, take 30 minutes to review how you observed the season. Reflect on what practices were most meaningful, what challenges you faced, and how the season helped you grow in your faith. Write down your reflections and consider how you can carry forward the lessons learned into the next season.

    - ***Outcome:*** Regular review and reflection will help you to continually grow in your understanding of The Liturgical Calendar, making each season a stepping stone in your spiritual journey.

Outcome: By completing this exercise, you will gain a deeper understanding of The Liturgical Calendar and learn how to integrate its rhythms into your daily life. The practices of seasonal planning, daily prayer, observance of feast days, family involvement, and regular review will help you live out the teachings of The Church more fully, fostering continuous spiritual growth and a closer relationship with GOD.

Chapter 23: What Does it Mean to Be Catholic?

Embracing the Catholic Identity in Modern Life

Being Catholic is more than adhering to a set of beliefs; it is a way of life that permeates every aspect of a person's existence. This chapter explores what it means to live as a Catholic today, examining the theological foundations of the faith and offering practical guidance on how to integrate Catholic principles into daily life. By understanding the essence of Catholic identity, modern believers can navigate the complexities of contemporary life with faith, integrity, and purpose.

Theological Insights

At the heart of Catholic identity is the belief in the Holy Trinity - one GOD in three persons: Father, Son, and Holy Spirit. This mystery is central to the Catholic faith, reflecting the nature of GOD as a community of love. The doctrine of the Trinity teaches that GOD is relational, and this relational nature is reflected in the Church, which is seen as the Body of Christ on earth. As St. Paul writes, *"Now you are the body of Christ, and individually members of it"* (1 Corinthians 12:27)[1]. This concept underscores the communal aspect of Catholic life, where individual believers are interconnected and called to live in communion with one another.

Another foundational belief is the Incarnation - the mystery of GOD becoming human in the person of Jesus Christ. This doctrine highlights the dignity of human life and the closeness of GOD to humanity. As the Catechism of the Catholic Church states, *"The Word became flesh to make us partakers of the divine nature"* (CCC 460)[2]. The Incarnation is not just a historical event; it has ongoing implications for how Catholics view themselves and the world. It affirms that GOD is intimately involved in the human experience, and that every aspect of life - work, relationships, suffering, joy - can be a means of encountering GOD.

The Sacramental nature of Catholicism is another key aspect of what it means to be Catholic. The Church teaches that The Sacraments are *"efficacious signs of grace, instituted by Christ and entrusted to the Church, by which divine life is dispensed to us"* (CCC 1131) . Through The Sacraments, especially The Eucharist, Catholics experience the real presence of Christ and are nourished by His grace. The Eucharist, in particular, is the *"source and summit of the Christian life,"* uniting believers with Christ and with one another in a profound way (CCC 1324) .

For modern Catholics, these theological insights are not abstract concepts but living truths that shape their identity and guide their actions. Understanding the nature of GOD, the significance of The Incarnation, and the power of The Sacraments provides a foundation for living out the Catholic faith in a meaningful and authentic way.

Application in Modern Life

Living as a Catholic in today's world presents unique challenges. The demands of work, family, and society often pull believers in different directions, making it difficult to maintain a consistent spiritual life. However, integrating Catholic principles into daily routines can help Catholics navigate these challenges with grace and purpose.

One of the key challenges modern Catholics face is balancing spiritual commitments with secular responsibilities. The fast pace of life can make it easy to neglect prayer, Mass attendance, and other spiritual practices. However, by prioritizing these practices, Catholics can ensure that their faith remains at the center of their lives. For example, setting aside time each morning for Prayer or Scripture reading can provide spiritual nourishment and set a positive tone for the day.

Consider the example of a busy professional who struggles to find time for spiritual practices. By integrating short prayers throughout the day - such as saying a Hail Mary during a commute or offering a quick prayer before a meeting - this individual can maintain a connection with GOD even in the midst of a hectic schedule. Additionally, attending daily Mass or making a weekly visit to a church for Eucharistic adoration can offer moments of peace and spiritual renewal.

Another challenge is living out Catholic values in a secular world. Issues such as social justice, ethical decision-making, and family life can be difficult to navigate, especially when they conflict with societal norms. However, by grounding their actions in Catholic teachings, believers can approach these issues with clarity and conviction. For instance, a Catholic business owner might choose to implement fair labor practices and environmentally sustainable policies, even if it means sacrificing some profit. By doing so, they live out the Church's teachings on the dignity of work and care for creation.

Relationships are another area where Catholic principles can be integrated. The Church teaches that love and respect should guide all human interactions, reflecting the love of Christ for His Church. In practical terms, this means prioritizing family time, practicing forgiveness, and offering support to those in need. A Catholic parent might make it a point to pray with their children before bed, discuss the importance of kindness and honesty, and volunteer as a family to serve the community.

Practical Spiritual Tools

To help readers deepen their Catholic identity and integrate it into their daily lives, here are some practical spiritual tools:

1. **Daily Prayer and Reflection:**

    - ***Instructions:*** Set aside 10-15 minutes each morning or evening for prayer and reflection. Begin with a simple prayer, such as The Our Father or Hail Mary, and follow with a short reading from the Gospels. Reflect on how the passage applies to your life and ask GOD for the grace to live out the day with faith and integrity.

- **Application:** This practice will help you stay grounded in your faith and provide spiritual strength for the challenges of daily life.

2. **Sacramental Participation:**

   - **Instructions:** Make a commitment to regularly participate in the Sacraments, especially The Eucharist and Reconciliation. Attend Mass at least weekly and consider going to Confession monthly. Before receiving the Sacraments, spend time in prayer and examination of conscience, preparing your heart to receive GOD's grace.

   - **Application:** Regular participation in the Sacraments will deepen your relationship with Christ and nourish your spiritual life.

3. **Service and Social Justice:**

   - **Instructions:** Identify an area of need in your community and commit to serving in some capacity, whether through volunteering, donating, or advocating for justice. Reflect on Catholic social teachings, such as the dignity of the human person and the preferential option for the poor and seek to apply these principles in your service.

- **Application:** Engaging in service and social justice will help you live out your faith in concrete ways, making a positive impact on others and the world.

4. **Faith in the Workplace:**

    - **Instructions:** Integrate your faith into your work by setting ethical standards that reflect Catholic teachings. Practice honesty, integrity, and fairness in all your dealings, and seek to create a work environment that respects the dignity of every person.
    - **Application:** Bringing your faith into the workplace will help you maintain consistency between your beliefs and actions, making your work an extension of your spiritual life.

By incorporating these spiritual tools into your daily routine, you can live out your Catholic identity more fully. Being Catholic is not just about attending Mass or following rules; it is about embracing a way of life that reflects the love, truth, and grace of GOD in every aspect of your existence. Through prayer, Sacraments, service, and ethical living, you can deepen your relationship with GOD and make a meaningful impact on the world around you.

Exercise: Living Out Your Catholic Identity

Objective: To help you understand and fully embrace your Catholic identity by integrating core Catholic principles into your daily life, thereby deepening your faith and making a positive impact on those around you.

Instructions:

1. **Daily Reflection on Catholic Identity:**
   - ***Duration:*** 10 minutes each morning or evening.
   - ***Instructions:*** Begin or end each day with a brief reflection on what it means to be Catholic. Choose a specific aspect of Catholic teaching or a virtue (such as love, humility, or service) to focus on. Reflect on how you can embody this teaching or virtue in your daily activities, relationships, and decisions. Write down one practical way you will live out this aspect of your Catholic identity during the day.
   - ***Outcome:*** This daily reflection will help you to consciously integrate Catholic values into your life, reinforcing your faith and guiding your actions.

2. **Weekly Sacrament Focus:**
   - ***Duration:*** 15-30 minutes each week.
   - ***Instructions:*** Choose one Sacrament to focus on each week. Spend time in prayer and study to deepen your understanding of the Sacrament's significance. If possible, participate in the Sacrament during the week (e.g., attend Mass for the Eucharist, go to

Confession). Reflect on how the grace of this Sacrament can transform your life and relationships.

- **Outcome:** This weekly focus will help you experience the Sacraments more deeply and integrate their grace into your everyday life.

3. **Service and Outreach Activity:**

   - **Duration:** 1-2 hours monthly.

   - **Instructions:** Identify a need in your community and commit to a monthly service or outreach activity that addresses this need. Whether it's volunteering at a food bank, visiting the elderly, or participating in a parish ministry, approach this service with the intention of living out the Church's teachings on social justice and the dignity of the human person.

   - **Outcome:** Regular service will help you put your faith into action, allowing you to live out your Catholic identity by serving others and contributing to the common good.

4. **Catholic Values in the Workplace:**

   - **Duration:** Ongoing throughout the workweek.

   - **Instructions:** Reflect on how you can bring Catholic values into your work environment. This might involve setting ethical standards, fostering a spirit of collaboration and respect, or addressing issues of justice and fairness. Choose one specific action each week that reflects your Catholic values, such as speaking out against unethical practices, offering support to a colleague, or promoting sustainability.

- **Outcome:** By integrating your faith into your work, you will create a consistent and authentic Catholic identity that influences all areas of your life, including your professional environment.

5. **Family Faith Practice:**

- **Duration:** 1 hour weekly.

- **Instructions:** Involve your family in living out your Catholic identity. Set aside one hour each week for a family faith activity, such as praying The Rosary together, reading a passage from The Bible, or discussing a Catholic teaching or Saint. Use this time to strengthen the spiritual foundation of your family and to ensure that Catholic values are being passed on to the next generation.

- **Outcome:** This practice will reinforce your family's Catholic identity, creating a strong, faith-filled home environment that supports each member's spiritual growth.

Outcome: By completing this exercise, you will gain a deeper understanding of what it means to be Catholic and how to live out your faith in practical, everyday ways. The practices of daily reflection, Sacramental focus, service, workplace integration, and family faith activities will help you fully embrace your Catholic identity, leading to a more meaningful and impactful spiritual life.

Chapter 24: Learning, Reading, and Contemplating Sacred Texts

Engaging with Sacred Texts to Deepen Faith and Spiritual Growth

Sacred texts, particularly The Holy Bible, are central to the life of every Catholic. They serve as the primary source of divine revelation and a guide for living a life aligned with GOD's will. This chapter explores the importance of learning, reading, and contemplating these sacred texts, providing theological insights, practical applications, and spiritual tools for integrating Scripture into daily life. By engaging deeply with sacred texts, modern Catholics can strengthen their faith, gain wisdom, and foster a closer relationship with GOD.

Theological Insights

At the heart of Catholic belief is the understanding that The Bible is the inspired Word of GOD, written by human authors under the guidance of The Holy Spirit. As the Catechism of the Catholic Church states, *"GOD is the author of Sacred Scripture because He inspired its human authors; He acts in them and by means of them"* (CCC 105)[1]. This dual authorship - divine and human - means that while The Bible reflects the historical and cultural contexts of its writers, it also conveys eternal truths that are relevant to every generation.

The Bible is composed of the Old and New Testaments, each with its distinct role in salvation history. The Old Testament recounts GOD's covenant with His people, preparing the way for the coming of Jesus Christ. The New Testament reveals the fulfillment of that covenant through the life, death, and resurrection of Jesus, and the establishment of the Church. As St. Augustine famously said, *"The New Testament lies hidden in the Old, and the Old Testament is unveiled in the New"*[2].

A key theological concept related to the reading of sacred texts is the nature of Jesus Christ as the Word of GOD made flesh. In the prologue of John's Gospel, we read, *"In the beginning was the Word, and the Word was with GOD, and the Word was GOD"* (John 1:1)[3]. This identification of Jesus with the divine Word emphasizes that to know Christ is to know The Scriptures, and to read the Scriptures is to encounter Christ. This concept is central to the Catholic approach to Scripture, which is not just an intellectual exercise but a spiritual encounter with the living GOD.

The Holy Trinity - Father, Son, and Holy Spirit - also plays a vital role in understanding the sacred texts. The Father reveals His will through the Word, The Son embodies that Word, and The Holy Spirit illuminates the minds and hearts of believers to understand and apply it. This Trinitarian approach ensures that reading The Bible is a dynamic and transformative experience, drawing believers into a deeper relationship with the Triune GOD.

For modern Catholics, these theological insights are crucial for approaching The Bible with the reverence and expectation that it deserves. Understanding the Bible as the living Word of GOD, inspired by The Holy Spirit and centered on Christ, frames it as a guide not only for religious practice but for all aspects of life.

Application in Modern Life

In today's fast-paced world, finding time to engage meaningfully with sacred texts can be challenging. However, integrating Scripture into daily life is essential for maintaining a vibrant faith and navigating the complexities of modern living. The Bible offers wisdom, comfort, and guidance that are applicable to every situation, but accessing these treasures requires intentional effort.

One common challenge is balancing the demands of work, family, and social responsibilities with the need for spiritual nourishment. Many Catholics find it difficult to carve out time for regular Bible reading or reflection. Yet, by viewing Scripture as a source of strength and direction, it becomes easier to prioritize this practice. For instance, setting aside time each morning or evening for Scripture reading can provide a spiritual anchor that steadies you throughout the day.

Consider the example of a working parent who struggles to find quiet moments for personal prayer and reflection. By integrating short Scripture passages into their daily routine - such as reading a Psalm with morning coffee or reflecting on a Gospel passage before bed - this individual can stay connected to

GOD's Word amid the busyness of life. Over time, these small but consistent practices can lead to deeper spiritual growth and a more centered life.

Another challenge is understanding and interpreting The Bible in a way that is relevant to modern life. Many Catholics feel intimidated by The Bible's complexity or uncertain about how to apply ancient texts to contemporary issues. However, The Church provides numerous resources to help believers navigate these challenges, including study guides, commentaries, and the insights of Church Fathers and theologians. Engaging with these resources can enhance your understanding of Scripture and enable you to apply its teachings to your personal and professional life.

For example, a young adult facing ethical dilemmas at work might turn to the Beatitudes in the Gospel of Matthew (Matthew 5:3-12) for guidance on living with integrity and compassion. By reflecting on these teachings and seeking The Holy Spirit's guidance, they can make decisions that align with their faith and demonstrate Christian values in the workplace.

Practical Spiritual Tools

To help readers deepen their engagement with sacred texts, here are some practical spiritual tools:

1. **Daily Scripture Reading:**

- **Instructions:** Set aside 10-15 minutes each day to read a passage from the Bible. Start with the Gospels, Psalms, or the letters of St. Paul. Reflect on the passage's meaning and how it applies to your life. Consider keeping a journal to record your thoughts and any insights you gain during your reading.

- **Application:** Regular Scripture reading will help you grow in your knowledge of the Bible and deepen your relationship with GOD.

2. **Lectio Divina:**

    - **Instructions:** Practice Lectio Divina, a traditional method of prayerful Scripture reading. Begin by reading a short passage slowly (Lectio), meditate on its meaning (Meditatio), pray about how GOD is speaking to you through the text (Oratio), and then rest in GOD's presence (Contemplatio). This practice can be done individually or in a group.

    - **Application:** Lectio Divina helps you engage deeply with Scripture, allowing GOD's Word to penetrate your heart and transform your life.

3. **Scripture Study Group:**

    - **Instructions:** Join or start a Scripture study group in your parish or community. Meet regularly to read and discuss passages from The Bible, using study guides or Church documents to deepen your understanding. Encourage group members to share how they apply Scripture in their daily lives.

- **Application:** Participating in a Scripture study group provides fellowship and support, helping you to grow in your understanding of The Bible and its relevance to modern life.

4. **Incorporating Scripture into Daily Routines:**

- **Instructions:** Find ways to incorporate Scripture into your daily routines. This could include listening to audio recordings of The Bible during your commute, placing Scripture verses around your home, or reciting a favorite verse during moments of stress or decision-making.

- **Application:** Integrating Scripture into daily life ensures that GOD's Word remains at the forefront of your mind and heart, guiding your thoughts and actions.

By adopting these spiritual tools, you can deepen your engagement with sacred texts and allow them to shape your life in meaningful ways. The Bible is not just a book to be read but a living Word to be encountered, offering wisdom, guidance, and strength for every situation. Through regular reading, prayerful contemplation, and community study, you can grow in your faith and draw closer to GOD.

Exercise: Engaging with Sacred Texts for Spiritual Growth

Objective: To deepen your understanding and application of sacred texts by establishing regular reading, contemplation, and discussion practices that integrate Scripture into your daily life.

Instructions:

1. **Daily Scripture Reading and Reflection:**
    - *Duration:* 15 minutes daily.
    - *Instructions:* Choose a specific time each day, such as morning or evening, to read a passage from The Bible. Start with the Gospels or Psalms if you are new to regular Scripture reading. After reading, spend a few minutes reflecting on the passage. Ask yourself how it applies to your current life situation and what GOD might be saying to you through this Scripture.
    - *Outcome:* This daily practice will help you develop a consistent habit of engaging with sacred texts, making Scripture a regular part of your spiritual nourishment.

2. **Lectio Divina Practice:**
    - *Duration:* 30 minutes weekly.
    - *Instructions:* Set aside time once a week to practice Lectio Divina. Begin by selecting a short Scripture passage. Follow the four steps:

- ✓ ***Lectio (Read):*** Slowly read the passage, paying attention to any words or phrases that stand out.

- ✓ ***Meditatio (Meditate):*** Reflect on the meaning of the passage and how it speaks to your life.

- ✓ ***Oratio (Pray):*** Respond to GOD in prayer, sharing your thoughts, feelings, and desires inspired by the passage.

- ✓ ***Contemplatio (Contemplate):*** Rest in GOD's presence, allowing the passage to sink deeply into your heart.

- **Outcome:** This contemplative practice will deepen your understanding of Scripture and enhance your personal relationship with GOD.

3. **Scripture Study Group Participation:**

    - **Duration:** 1 hour weekly.

    - **Instructions:** Join or form a Scripture study group within your parish or community. Commit to meeting weekly to read and discuss specific books or passages from The Bible. Use study guides or Church-approved commentaries to aid in understanding the historical and theological context of the Scriptures. Encourage each member to share personal insights and applications.

- **Outcome:** Group study will provide a supportive environment for learning, foster a deeper understanding of Scripture, and help you apply biblical teachings to your daily life.

4. **Scripture Integration in Daily Routines:**
    - **Duration:** Ongoing throughout the day.
    - **Instructions:** Incorporate Scripture into your daily routines by placing Bible verses in strategic locations around your home or workplace (e.g., on your desk, mirror, or refrigerator). Choose verses that resonate with your current spiritual journey or challenges you face. Recite these verses during moments of stress, decision-making, or reflection.
    - **Outcome:** This practice will keep GOD's Word at the forefront of your mind throughout the day, helping you make decisions and respond to situations in a way that aligns with your faith.

5. **Scripture Journaling:**
    - **Duration:** 15 minutes weekly.
    - **Instructions:** At the end of each week, spend time journaling about your experiences with Scripture. Write about what passages stood out to you, how

they impacted your thoughts or actions, and any insights you gained. Reflect on how you can continue to apply these teachings in the coming week.

- ***Outcome:*** Journaling will help you process and internalize what you've learned from Scripture, reinforcing its lessons and tracking your spiritual growth over time.

Outcome: By completing this exercise, you will not only deepen your understanding of sacred texts but also integrate their teachings into your everyday life. The practices of daily reading, contemplative prayer, group study, Scripture integration, and journaling will help you engage with The Bible in a meaningful way, fostering continuous spiritual growth and a stronger relationship with GOD.

Chapter 25: Going to Mass

Embracing the Sacredness of The Eucharist and the Mass

The Mass is the cornerstone of Catholic worship, a profound encounter with Jesus Christ through The Eucharist and communal prayer. This chapter delves into the theological significance of the Mass, its relevance to modern Catholics, and practical ways to integrate its sacredness into daily life. By understanding and fully participating in the Mass, Catholics can deepen their relationship with GOD and strengthen their spiritual lives.

Theological Insights

At the heart of the Catholic faith is the belief in the Real Presence of Jesus Christ in the Eucharist. This belief is rooted in Jesus' words at the Last Supper: *"This is my body, which is given for you. Do this in remembrance of me"* (Luke 22:19)[1]. The Catholic Church teaches that during the consecration at Mass, the bread and wine are transformed into the Body and Blood of Christ - a doctrine known as *transubstantiation*. This mystery of faith is a central tenet of Catholicism, emphasizing that The Eucharist is not merely symbolic but a true and substantial presence of Christ.

The Mass is also a re-presentation of the one sacrifice of Christ on Calvary. As the Catechism of the Catholic Church explains, *"The sacrifice of Christ and the sacrifice of The Eucharist are one single sacrifice: 'The victim is one and the same: the same now offers through the ministry of priests, who then offered himself on the cross; only the manner of offering is different'"* (CCC 1367)[2]. This understanding underscores the profound connection between The Eucharist and the salvific work of Christ, making the Mass the source and summit of Christian life.

The communal nature of the Mass is another essential aspect of its theological significance. The Mass is not just a private devotion but a public act of worship that unites the faithful with one another and with the entire Church, both in Heaven and on earth. As St. Paul writes, *"Because there is one bread, we who are many are one body, for we all partake of the one bread"* (1 Corinthians 10:17)[3]. This unity reflects the communal nature of the Church, which is the Body of Christ, and highlights the importance of participating in the Mass as a member of the Church community.

For modern Catholics, understanding these theological concepts is crucial for appreciating the significance of the Mass. The Eucharist is not just a ritual but an encounter with the living Christ, a participation in His sacrifice, and a communal celebration of faith.

Application in Modern Life

In today's fast-paced world, finding time to attend Mass regularly can be challenging. Work schedules, family commitments, and social activities often compete for our attention, making it difficult to prioritize Mass. However, attending Mass is essential for spiritual nourishment and maintaining a strong connection with GOD.

One of the common challenges faced by modern Catholics is maintaining a sense of reverence and focus during Mass. The distractions of daily life can make it difficult to fully engage in the liturgy. However, by approaching the Mass with a prepared and prayerful heart, Catholics can enter more deeply into the sacred mysteries being celebrated. Arriving a few minutes early to pray and reflect on the readings can help set the tone for a more meaningful participation in the Mass.

Consider the example of a busy professional who struggles to find time for Mass during the week. By intentionally setting aside time on Sundays—and perhaps even one weekday - this individual can make Mass a non-negotiable part of their routine. This commitment not only honors GOD but also provides a regular opportunity to receive the grace and strength needed to navigate the demands of modern life.

Another challenge is balancing the spiritual richness of the Mass with the responsibilities and distractions of daily life. After leaving Mass, it's easy to slip back into the busyness of the week and forget the spiritual nourishment received. To counteract this, Catholics can adopt practices that extend the experience of the Mass into their everyday lives. For example, reflecting on the homily or readings throughout the week, or making a habit of visiting a church for silent prayer, can help keep the grace of the Mass alive.

Real-life examples of integrating the Mass into daily life can be inspiring. Take, for instance, a young mother who, despite her hectic schedule, prioritizes attending Mass with her children. She uses the time before Mass to teach her children about the significance of The Eucharist and the importance of participating in the liturgy. This not only strengthens her own faith but also instills a sense of reverence and love for the Mass in her children.

Practical Spiritual Tools

To help readers deepen their understanding and participation in the Mass, here are some practical spiritual tools:

1. **Pre-Mass Preparation:**

   - ***Instructions:*** Spend 10-15 minutes before Mass in quiet prayer and reflection. Read The Scripture passages for the day and meditate on their meaning. Ask The Holy Spirit to help you fully engage in the liturgy and to open your heart to the grace of The Eucharist.
   - ***Application:*** This preparation will help you enter The Mass with a prayerful and attentive heart, enhancing your participation and deepening your experience of The Eucharist.

2. **Post-Mass Reflection:**

   - *Instructions:* After Mass, take a few moments to reflect on the experience. Consider the homily, the prayers, and the Eucharist. Ask yourself how the grace received at Mass can guide your actions and decisions in the coming week. Keep a journal to record your reflections and any insights gained.

   - *Application:* Regular post-Mass reflection helps to internalize the spiritual nourishment received and encourages ongoing growth in faith.

3. **Daily Connection with the Eucharist:**

   - *Instructions:* If attending daily Mass is not possible, find ways to connect with The Eucharist during the week. This could include visiting a church for Eucharistic adoration, spending time in silent prayer, or reading and reflecting on the daily Mass readings at home.

   - *Application:* These practices will help you maintain a strong connection with The Eucharist and the grace it provides, even outside of Sunday Mass.

4. **Community Involvement:**

   - *Instructions:* Engage more deeply with your parish community by participating in ministries or volunteer opportunities. Serving as a lector, Eucharistic Minister, or in other parish roles can enhance your experience of the Mass and strengthen your sense of belonging to the Church.

- *Application:* Active involvement in the parish community fosters a deeper connection with The Church and enhances your participation in the Mass as a communal celebration of faith.

By incorporating these spiritual tools into your routine, you can make the Mass a central part of your spiritual life. The Eucharist is a profound gift, offering an encounter with Christ, a participation in His sacrifice, and a source of grace for everyday living. Through regular attendance, prayerful preparation, and ongoing reflection, you can deepen your relationship with GOD and grow in holiness.

Exercise: Deepening Your Participation in the Mass

Objective: To enhance your understanding and experience of the Mass by integrating its spiritual significance into your daily life, thereby deepening your relationship with GOD and the Church community.

Instructions:

1. **Pre-Mass Spiritual Preparation:**
    - *Duration:* 15 minutes before Mass.
    - *Instructions:* Arrive at church at least 15 minutes early. Spend this time in quiet prayer, asking GOD to

prepare your heart for the Mass. Read the scripture readings for the day and reflect on how they might apply to your life. Consider any intentions you want to bring to The Eucharist. Conclude your preparation with a prayer asking the Holy Spirit to help you fully engage in the liturgy.

- **Outcome:** This preparation will help you enter the Mass with a focused and prayerful mindset, enhancing your participation and receptivity to GOD's grace.

2. **Active Participation During Mass:**
   - **Duration:** Throughout the Mass.
   - **Instructions:** During The Mass, consciously engage with each part of the liturgy. Listen attentively to the readings and homily, participate fully in the prayers and responses, and approach The Eucharist with reverence and gratitude. Pay attention to the words and actions of the Mass, allowing them to deepen your connection with Christ and the Church.
   - **Outcome:** Active participation will transform your experience of the Mass from a routine obligation to a profound encounter with GOD, enriching your spiritual life.

3. **Post-Mass Reflection:**

    - *Duration:* 10-15 minutes after Mass.

    - *Instructions:* After the Mass, spend a few moments in quiet reflection. Consider what stood out to you during The Liturgy - whether it was a particular reading, the homily, or the experience of receiving The Eucharist. Reflect on how The Mass has touched your heart and what GOD might be calling you to do in response. Write down your thoughts in a journal.

    - *Outcome:* Regular post-Mass reflection will help you internalize the spiritual nourishment received and encourage continuous growth in your faith.

4. **Midweek Eucharistic Connection:**

    - *Duration:* 10 minutes, midweek.

    - *Instructions:* If attending daily Mass is not possible, set aside time during the week to reconnect with the Eucharist. Visit a church for Eucharistic adoration, spend time in silent prayer at home, or read and reflect on the upcoming Sunday's readings. Consider how the grace of The Eucharist can continue to guide your thoughts, words, and actions throughout the week.

- *Outcome:* This practice will keep The Mass alive in your heart throughout the week, helping you to draw strength from The Eucharist even outside of Sunday Mass.

5. **Community Engagement:**
    - *Duration:* 1 hour monthly.
    - *Instructions:* Commit to engaging more deeply with your parish community. This could involve volunteering for a ministry, joining a prayer group, or participating in a parish event. Consider how you can contribute to the communal life of the Church and how your participation in the Mass can extend to service within the parish.
    - *Outcome:* Community engagement will strengthen your connection to The Church, enhance your sense of belonging, and provide opportunities to live out the grace of the Mass in tangible ways.

Outcome: By completing this exercise, you will deepen your understanding and experience of the Mass, transforming it from a weekly obligation into a central, life-giving part of your spiritual journey. The practices of pre-Mass preparation, active participation, post-Mass reflection, midweek connection, and community engagement will help you fully integrate The Mass into your daily life, fostering continuous spiritual growth and a closer relationship with GOD and The Church.

Chapter 26: Volunteering at Church

Embracing Service as a Path to Spiritual Growth and Community Building

Volunteering at church is more than just a way to give back; it is a powerful expression of faith and a vital component of spiritual growth. This chapter explores the theological foundations of service in the Church, the importance of volunteering in fostering a strong Catholic community, and practical ways to integrate this service into your daily life. By actively participating in church ministries, modern Catholics can deepen their relationship with GOD, strengthen their parish communities, and live out their faith in tangible ways.

Theological Insights

At the heart of Christian service is the example set by Jesus Christ, who came *"not to be served, but to serve, and to give his life as a ransom for many"* (Matthew 20:28)[1]. This profound act of self-giving is the model for all Christian service. In the Catholic tradition, service is not merely a good deed but a participation in the mission of Christ. It is an expression of the Christ Consciousness - understanding that Christ's love and compassion should flow through us into the world, touching the lives of others.

The nature of The Holy Trinity also provides a framework for understanding the communal aspect of service. The Trinity - Father, Son, and Holy Spirit - exists in a perfect relationship of love and mutual giving. This divine relationship is the model for the Church, which is called to be a community of love and service. St. Paul writes, *"Now you are the body of Christ and individually members of it"* (1 Corinthians 12:27)[2], emphasizing that each member of The Church has a unique role to play in building up The Body of Christ. Volunteering at church is a way to fulfill this role, contributing to the life and mission of the Church.

The Eucharist, the source and summit of Christian life, also has profound implications for service. When Catholics receive The Body and Blood of Christ, they are united more closely to Him and to one another. This unity compels them to act in love and service, carrying the grace of the Eucharist into the world. As the Catechism of the Catholic Church states, *"The Eucharist commits us to the poor"* (CCC 1397)[3]. This means that participating in the Eucharist should naturally lead to acts of charity and service, as Catholics are called to embody Christ's love in their interactions with others.

In a modern context, these theological insights remind Catholics that volunteering at church is not just an optional activity but a vital expression of their faith. It is a way to live out the teachings of Christ, contribute to the life of the Church, and grow in holiness.

Application in Modern Life

Balancing the demands of modern life with the call to volunteer at church can be challenging. Work, family responsibilities, and social commitments often leave little time for additional activities. However, integrating service into your life can bring significant spiritual benefits and a deeper sense of purpose.

One common challenge is finding the time to volunteer amidst a busy schedule. It's important to remember that volunteering does not always require a large time commitment. Even small acts of service, such as helping with a church event or assisting in a ministry for an hour a week, can make a significant impact. The key is to find opportunities that align with your interests and talents, making service a natural and fulfilling part of your life.

Consider the example of a young professional who feels overwhelmed by work and social obligations but wants to contribute to their parish. By volunteering as a lector or usher, they can participate in the liturgy without a significant time commitment. This involvement not only deepens their connection to the Mass but also strengthens their sense of belonging in the parish community.

Another challenge is maintaining a balance between spiritual commitments and other responsibilities. Volunteering at church should enhance your spiritual life, not detract from it. It's important to approach service with the right mindset - seeing it as a way to grow closer to GOD and contribute to the community, rather than just another task on a to-do list. Setting aside regular time for prayer and reflection can help you stay grounded and ensure that your service is spiritually enriching.

Real-life examples can illustrate how integrating church volunteering into daily life can be transformative. Take, for instance, a retired couple who decide to dedicate part of their time to coordinating the parish food pantry. Their service not only provides vital assistance to those in need but also deepens their own faith and strengthens their relationship with each other. Through their commitment, they experience the joy of giving and the fulfillment of living out their Catholic values.

Practical Spiritual Tools

To help readers integrate volunteering at church into their spiritual lives, here are some practical spiritual tools:

1. **Discernment of Talents and Interests:**

    - ***Instructions:*** Spend time in prayer and reflection to discern how your talents and interests can best serve your parish community. Consider the needs of your parish and how you can contribute meaningfully. You might start by making a list of your skills and interests, then look for volunteer opportunities that match them.

    - ***Application:*** By aligning your talents with parish needs, you will find volunteering more fulfilling and impactful.

2. **Scheduled Volunteer Time:**

    - ***Instructions:*** Just as you schedule time for work, family, and leisure, schedule regular time for volunteering. Whether it's an hour a week or a few hours a month, put it on your calendar and treat it as a commitment. Communicate with your family or employer to ensure that this time is respected.

    - ***Application:*** Consistent volunteer time ensures that you remain engaged and that your service becomes a regular part of your life.

3. **Spiritual Reflection on Service:**

    - ***Instructions:*** After each volunteering experience, take a few minutes to reflect on how it impacted you spiritually. Ask yourself how your service brought you closer to GOD, what challenges you faced, and what joys you experienced. Consider keeping a journal to record these reflections and track your spiritual growth over time.
    - ***Application:*** Regular reflection helps you stay spiritually connected to your service and ensures that it remains a meaningful part of your faith journey.

4. **Incorporating Family and Community:**

    - ***Instructions:*** If possible, involve your family or friends in your volunteer activities. Serving together can strengthen your relationships and create a shared sense of purpose. Whether it's volunteering at a parish event, participating in a ministry, or organizing a community service project, find ways to make volunteering a group effort.

- ***Application:*** Family and community involvement in service can enhance your experience, making it a source of joy and a powerful witness of faith.

By incorporating these spiritual tools into your life, you can make volunteering at church a vital and fulfilling part of your spiritual journey. Service is not just about giving your time; it's about growing closer to GOD, building up The Body of Christ, and living out the teachings of Jesus in your everyday life. Through regular, prayerful, and joyful service, you can deepen your faith, strengthen your parish community, and experience the transformative power of Christian love.

Exercise: Integrating Service into Your Spiritual Life

Objective: To help you understand the spiritual significance of volunteering at church and to integrate service into your daily life as a means of growing in faith and building community.

Instructions:

1. **Identify Your Talents and Interests:**
    - ***Duration:*** 30 minutes.

- ***Instructions***: Begin by reflecting on your talents, skills, and interests. Make a list of the things you enjoy doing and areas where you excel. Then, consider how these can be used in service to your parish community. Look for volunteer opportunities that align with your list, whether it's teaching, organizing events, participating in liturgical roles, or helping with charitable activities.
- ***Outcome:*** This exercise will help you identify the best ways to serve, ensuring that your volunteering is both meaningful and fulfilling.

2. **Commit to a Volunteering Schedule:**
   - ***Duration:*** Ongoing.
   - ***Instructions:*** Once you've identified a suitable volunteer opportunity, commit to a regular schedule. Whether it's weekly, bi-weekly, or monthly, block out specific times on your calendar dedicated to your chosen volunteer activity. Treat this time with the same importance as work or family commitments. If possible, communicate your schedule to your family or employer to ensure support and understanding.
   - ***Outcome:*** A regular volunteering schedule will help you integrate service into your life consistently, making it a natural part of your routine.

3. **Prayerful Preparation and Reflection:**

    - ***Duration:*** 10 minutes before and after each volunteer activity.

    - ***Instructions:*** Before you begin your volunteer work, spend a few minutes in prayer, asking GOD to guide your efforts and to work through you to benefit others. After you've completed your service, take a few minutes to reflect on the experience. Ask yourself what you learned, how you felt, and how the experience brought you closer to GOD. Consider keeping a journal to record your reflections.

    - ***Outcome:*** Prayerful preparation and reflection will help you stay spiritually connected to your service, ensuring that it contributes to your personal growth and relationship with GOD.

4. **Involve Others in Your Service:**

    - ***Duration:*** Ongoing.

    - ***Instructions:*** Encourage family members, friends, or fellow parishioners to join you in your volunteer activities. This could involve inviting them to help with a specific event, participate in a ministry, or start a new service project together. Discuss how serving together can strengthen your relationships and provide mutual spiritual support.

- **Outcome:** Involving others in your service fosters community and helps build stronger bonds within your parish, creating a shared sense of purpose and mission.

5. **Service Impact Reflection:**
   - **Duration:** 30 minutes monthly.
   - **Instructions:** At the end of each month, take time to reflect on the impact of your volunteer work. Consider how your service has benefited others, how it has affected your own spiritual life, and what new insights or experiences you've gained. Use this time to evaluate whether you want to continue in your current role or explore new volunteer opportunities.
   - **Outcome:** Regular reflection on the impact of your service will help you stay motivated, recognize the value of your contributions, and ensure that your volunteering remains a meaningful part of your spiritual journey.

Outcome: By completing this exercise, you will not only deepen your understanding of the spiritual significance of volunteering at church but also effectively integrate service into your life. Through identifying your talents, committing to a regular schedule, prayerful reflection, involving others, and evaluating the impact of your service, you will grow in faith, strengthen your parish community, and experience the joy of living out your Catholic values in practical ways.

NOTES:

Chapter 27: Fellowship with Others – Locally, Nationally, Worldwide

Embracing Christian Fellowship Across All Levels

The theme of this chapter is the significance of Christian fellowship and how it extends beyond the local parish to include national and global communities. Fellowship is not just a social activity; it is a vital expression of our unity in Christ and an essential part of living out our faith. By engaging in fellowship at various levels, Catholics can grow in their spiritual lives, support one another, and contribute to the broader mission of the Church.

Theological Insights

The concept of fellowship is deeply rooted in Christian theology, particularly in the understanding of the Church as the Body of Christ. St. Paul writes, *"For just as the body is one and has many members, and all the members of the body, though many, are one body, so it is with Christ"* (1 Corinthians 12:12)[1]. This passage highlights the interconnectedness of all believers, who are united in Christ regardless of geographical or cultural differences. The Holy Trinity itself is a model of perfect communion and fellowship - Father, Son, and Holy Spirit exist in a relationship of love and mutual self-giving. This divine relationship serves as a blueprint for Christian fellowship, where believers are called to live in unity and love with one another.

Jesus emphasized the importance of fellowship in His teachings, particularly in the Great Commandment: *"You shall love your neighbor as yourself"* (Matthew 22:39)[2]. This commandment calls Christians to form relationships based on love, respect, and mutual care. Fellowship, therefore, is not just about social interaction but about living out the love of Christ in community with others. It is through fellowship that the Church becomes a living expression of GOD's love in the world.

In the modern context, the concept of fellowship has expanded beyond the confines of the local parish to include national and global connections. The Catholic Church is a universal community, and Catholics are called to engage with and support their brothers and sisters around the world. This global fellowship is a powerful witness to the unity of The Church and the universality of its mission.

Application in Modern Life

In today's world, where individualism and isolation are prevalent, fostering meaningful fellowship can be challenging. However, by prioritizing relationships and community, Catholics can overcome these challenges and experience the fullness of life in Christ.

One of the common challenges faced by modern Catholics is finding time for fellowship amid busy schedules. Balancing work, family, and social commitments can make it difficult to engage in community activities. However, integrating fellowship into daily life is essential for spiritual growth and well-being. Practical steps include participating in parish events, joining a small group or prayer group, and volunteering for community service projects. These activities not only provide opportunities for fellowship but also allow Catholics to live out their faith in concrete ways.

Consider the example of a young professional who, despite a demanding job, makes time to attend a weekly Bible study group. This commitment provides a space for spiritual growth, mutual support, and deepening relationships with others who share the same faith. The benefits of this fellowship extend beyond the weekly meetings, as the relationships formed in the group become a source of encouragement and strength in daily life.

Fellowship also plays a crucial role in addressing the challenges of modern life, such as loneliness, stress, and the pressures of secular society. Engaging in fellowship provides a sense of belonging and community, which is vital for mental and emotional health. Moreover, it offers a support system that helps individuals navigate the difficulties of life with the help of others who share their values and beliefs.

On a national and global level, fellowship takes on a broader dimension. Catholics are called to be aware of and engage with the needs and concerns of the Church around the world. This can be achieved through participation in national Church events, supporting missionary activities, and engaging with global

Catholic organizations. By doing so, Catholics contribute to the universal mission of the Church and demonstrate the unity of the Body of Christ.

Practical Spiritual Tools

To help readers integrate fellowship into their spiritual lives, here are some practical spiritual tools:

1. **Join a Parish Group:**

    - ***Instructions:*** Identify a group within your parish that aligns with your interests or needs, such as a Bible study, prayer group, or service ministry. Commit to attending regularly and actively participating in group activities. This involvement will provide a sense of community and accountability in your spiritual journey.

    - ***Outcome:*** Regular participation in a parish group fosters deep connections with others and strengthens your sense of belonging within the Church.

2. **Volunteer for Community Service:**

    - ***Instructions:*** Look for opportunities to volunteer in your parish or local community. This could involve helping with a food pantry, visiting the elderly, or participating in a parish outreach program. Volunteering allows you to live out your faith in service to others and to form meaningful relationships with those you serve alongside.

- **Outcome:** Volunteering enhances your connection to the broader community and provides tangible ways to express your faith through action.

3. **Engage in Global Catholic Fellowship:**

   - **Instructions:** Stay informed about global issues affecting The Church and consider how you can contribute. This could involve supporting a Catholic missionary organization, participating in a global prayer initiative, or connecting with Catholics in other parts of the world through online communities or social media.

   - **Outcome:** Engaging in global fellowship broadens your perspective and helps you understand and participate in the universal mission of the Church.

4. **Host a Fellowship Event:**

   - **Instructions:** Organize a small gathering for fellow parishioners, friends, or family to share a meal, pray together, or discuss a spiritual topic. This event could be as simple as a potluck dinner or a more structured prayer meeting. The goal is to create an environment where relationships can deepen, and faith can be shared.

- ***Outcome:*** Hosting fellowship events strengthens community bonds and encourages open, faith-filled conversations in a relaxed setting.

5. **Practice Intentional Prayer for Others:**

    - ***Instructions:*** Make a habit of praying regularly for the members of your parish, national Church, and the global Catholic community. You can keep a prayer journal to record your intentions and the needs of those around you. This practice helps you stay connected to others through prayer and fosters a sense of spiritual solidarity.

    - ***Outcome:*** Intentional prayer for others deepens your empathy and connection to the wider Church community, reinforcing the bonds of fellowship.

By incorporating these spiritual tools into your daily routine, you can make fellowship a central part of your spiritual life. Whether locally, nationally, or globally, fellowship is essential for living out the Christian faith. It is through fellowship that Catholics grow in their relationship with GOD, support one another, and contribute to the mission of the Church. By actively engaging in fellowship, you participate in the life of the Church and experience the richness of Christian community.

Exercise: Building and Strengthening Fellowship

Objective: To help readers actively engage in and strengthen their fellowship with others at the local, national, and global levels, fostering deeper connections and a stronger sense of community within the Church.

Instructions:

1. **Local Fellowship Commitment:**
   - ***Duration:*** Weekly for 1 month.
   - ***Instructions:*** Commit to participating in a local parish group or activity each week for one month. This could include attending a Bible study, joining a prayer group, or volunteering at a parish event. After each session, reflect on your experience by asking yourself:
     - ✓ What did I learn from this fellowship experience?
     - ✓ How did it help me grow in my faith?
     - ✓ How can I continue to contribute to this community?
   - ***Outcome:*** By the end of the month, you should feel more connected to your parish community and have a deeper understanding of the importance of local fellowship in your spiritual life.

2. **National Fellowship Engagement:**
   - ***Duration:*** Once per month.
   - ***Instructions:*** Identify a national Catholic event, conference, or initiative that aligns with your interests.

Participate either in person or virtually. This could be a national retreat, a conference on Catholic social teaching, or a virtual prayer event. After participating, journal about the following:

- ✓ How did this experience broaden my understanding of the Church's mission?
- ✓ What new connections or insights did I gain?
- ✓ How can I apply what I learned to my local community or personal spiritual journey?

- **Outcome:** Engaging with national-level events will help you see your role in the broader Church community and inspire new ways to contribute to the Church's mission.

3. **Global Fellowship Awareness and Action:**
   - **Duration:** 1 hour per week for 1 month.
   - **Instructions:** Choose a global Catholic initiative or organization to support, such as a missionary project, humanitarian aid program, or global prayer network. Spend at least one hour per week learning about the initiative, praying for those involved, and considering ways to support it (e.g., through donations, advocacy, or spreading awareness). Reflect on your experience by considering:
     - ✓ How does this global initiative align with the Church's mission and my personal faith journey?

- ✓ What impact can I have, even from afar, on the global Church community?
- ✓ How can I share this initiative with others in my local parish or community?
- **Outcome**: This exercise will deepen your awareness of the global Church, foster a sense of solidarity with Catholics worldwide, and encourage you to take concrete actions in support of global fellowship.

4. **Host a Fellowship Gathering:**
   - **Duration:** 2-3 hours, one-time event.
   - **Instructions:** Organize and host a fellowship gathering with members of your parish or local Catholic community. The gathering could be a simple meal, a discussion on a spiritual topic, or a prayer session. Encourage attendees to share their experiences of faith and fellowship. After the event, reflect on:
     - ✓ What was the most meaningful part of the gathering for me and for others?
     - ✓ How did this event help build or strengthen relationships within my community?
     - ✓ What can I do to continue fostering fellowship in my parish?
   - **Outcome:** Hosting a fellowship gathering will help you take an active role in building community, deepening relationships, and encouraging others to engage in fellowship.

5. **Intentional Prayer for Fellowship:**
    - ***Duration:*** Daily for 2 weeks.
    - ***Instructions:*** Dedicate a portion of your daily prayer time specifically to praying for the strengthening of fellowship in your parish, the national Church, and the global Catholic community. Include specific intentions for people or groups you've encountered through your fellowship activities. Reflect on:
        - ✓ How has intentional prayer for fellowship impacted my sense of connection to the Church?
        - ✓ What insights or inspirations have arisen during this prayer time?
        - ✓ How can I continue to support and build fellowship through prayer?
    - ***Outcome:*** Consistent, intentional prayer will help you cultivate a deeper spiritual connection with the broader Church and inspire you to take further steps in building and nurturing fellowship.

Outcome: By engaging in this exercise, you will develop a stronger sense of community at the local, national, and global levels. You will gain practical experience in building and nurturing fellowship, understand the broader implications of Christian community, and integrate these experiences into your spiritual life. This exercise will not only deepen your own faith but also contribute to the growth and unity of the Church as a whole.

Chapter 28: Service to Others – Elderly, Single Parents, Children, etc.

Living Out Faith Through Acts of Service

The theme of this chapter is the call to service as a fundamental expression of Christian love and discipleship. Service to others - especially the elderly, single parents, children, and other vulnerable groups—is a concrete way to live out the teachings of Jesus Christ and to embody the love of GOD in our daily lives. This chapter explores the theological foundations of service, offers practical guidance for integrating service into modern life, and provides spiritual tools to help readers deepen their commitment to serving others.

Theological Insights

Service to others is deeply rooted in Christian theology, particularly in the teachings and example of Jesus Christ. In the Gospels, Jesus consistently demonstrates a life of service, teaching His disciples that *"the Son of Man came not to be served but to serve, and to give his life as a ransom for many"* (Mark 10:45)[1]. This statement encapsulates the essence of Christian service: selfless love and sacrifice for the good of others. The nature of Jesus as both fully human and fully divine is central to this understanding, as He embodies the perfect model of service, showing us that to serve others is to serve GOD.

The concept of Christ Consciousness, which emphasizes the awareness of the divine presence within all beings, further underscores the importance of service. When we serve others, especially those in need, we are acknowledging and honoring the presence of Christ within them. This aligns with Jesus' teaching in Matthew 25:40[2], where He says, *"Truly I tell you, whatever you did for one of the least of these brothers and sisters of mine, you did for me."* This passage highlights that service to others is not just a moral duty but a spiritual act that connects us directly to Christ.

The Holy Trinity also provides a theological framework for understanding service. The relationship between the Father, Son, and Holy Spirit is one of perfect love and mutual self-giving. As Christians, we are called to mirror this divine relationship by living in loving service to others. This means recognizing the inherent dignity of every person, created in the image of GOD (Imago Dei), and responding to their needs with compassion and generosity.

In contemporary Catholic teaching, the importance of service is further emphasized through the Church's social doctrine, which calls for a preferential option for the poor and vulnerable. This principle teaches that in our service, we should prioritize those who are most in need, such as the elderly, single parents, and children. By doing so, we fulfill the Gospel call to love our neighbor and to work for justice and peace in our communities.

Application in Modern Life

In today's fast-paced and often self-centered world, integrating service to others into our daily lives can be challenging. However, by viewing service as an integral part of our spiritual journey, we can find ways to balance our responsibilities while making meaningful contributions to the lives of others.

One of the key challenges modern Catholics face is finding the time and energy to serve others while managing personal and professional commitments. To overcome this, it's important to recognize that service doesn't always require large time commitments or dramatic gestures. Small, consistent acts of kindness - such as visiting an elderly neighbor, offering support to a single parent, or volunteering at a local youth group - can have a profound impact. The key is to start with what you can do and to build a habit of service into your daily routine.

Consider the example of a busy professional who volunteers at a local senior center on weekends. While their workweek is demanding, they find fulfillment in spending a few hours each week engaging with the elderly, offering companionship, and assisting with activities. This service not only benefits the seniors but also enriches the volunteer's spiritual life, providing a sense of purpose and connection to the broader community.

For those with families, involving children in acts of service can be a powerful way to teach the values of compassion and empathy. Simple activities like making cards for residents of a nursing home, preparing meals for a family in need, or participating in a community cleanup can be meaningful experiences that instill the importance of service in young hearts.

Balancing service with personal and professional responsibilities requires intentionality and planning. It's helpful to set aside specific times for service activities and to treat them as important commitments. Additionally, integrating service into your existing routines - such as bringing your children along when visiting the elderly or combining social activities with charitable causes - can make it easier to maintain a consistent practice of service.

Practical Spiritual Tools

To help readers integrate service into their spiritual lives, here are some practical spiritual tools:

1. **Daily Prayer for Service Opportunities:**
   - ***Instructions***: Begin each day with a short prayer asking GOD to open your heart to opportunities for service. Ask for the grace to recognize the needs of those around you and the courage to respond generously. This prayer can be as simple as, "Lord,

help me to see and serve You in others today."

- **Outcome:** Regular prayer for service opportunities helps attune your heart to the needs of others and fosters a spirit of readiness to serve.

2. **Service Reflection Journal:**

    - **Instructions:** Keep a journal where you reflect on your service experiences. After each act of service, take a few minutes to write about what you did, how it impacted those you served, and how it affected your own spiritual growth. Consider what GOD might be teaching you through these experiences.

    - **Outcome:** A service reflection journal helps you stay mindful of the spiritual significance of your actions and encourages ongoing personal and spiritual development.

3. **Family Service Projects:**

    - **Instructions:** Choose a service project that your entire family can participate in, such as organizing a food drive, visiting a nursing home, or helping a single parent with childcare. Make it a regular activity, whether monthly or quarterly, and use the experience as an opportunity to discuss the importance of serving others.

- **Outcome:** Family service projects strengthen family bonds while teaching children the values of compassion, generosity, and community involvement.

4. **Service Prayer Chain:**

    - **Instructions:** Start a prayer chain within your parish or community focused on service. Each person in the chain commits to praying for the service activities of others, asking GOD to bless their efforts and bring forth good fruit. Participants can share prayer requests related to their service work and offer support to one another.

    - **Outcome:** A service prayer chain creates a supportive community of prayer that reinforces the spiritual foundation of service and fosters a sense of shared mission.

5. **Service Sabbatical:**

    - **Instructions:** If possible, take a short sabbatical from your regular routine to dedicate time to service. This could be a few days or a week spent volunteering at a shelter, participating in a mission trip, or supporting a community project. Use this time to immerse yourself in service and deepen your relationship with GOD through acts of love.

- ***Outcome:*** A service sabbatical offers a focused opportunity to grow spiritually through intensive service, providing fresh insights and inspiration for ongoing service activities.

By incorporating these spiritual tools into your life, you can make service a central part of your spiritual journey. Service to others is not just a charitable act; it is a profound expression of your faith and a way to live out the teachings of Christ in your daily life. Through consistent, prayerful service, you can deepen your relationship with GOD, build stronger communities, and make a lasting impact on the lives of those around you.

Exercise: Integrating Service into Daily Life

Objective: To help readers actively engage in service to others, particularly the elderly, single parents, and children, by integrating acts of service into their daily lives and fostering a habit of selfless giving.

Instructions:

1. **Identify Local Needs:**
    - ***Duration:*** 30 minutes.
    - ***Instructions****:* Spend some time researching the needs within your local community. Identify specific groups or individuals who might benefit from your service, such as elderly neighbors, single parents who need support, or local children's programs. Make a list

of these opportunities and choose one or two that resonate with you.

- *Outcome:* By identifying local needs, you become more aware of the opportunities for service in your immediate environment, making it easier to take the first steps toward helping others.

2. **Create a Service Plan:**

   - *Duration:* 1 hour.

   - *Instructions:* Based on the needs you identified, create a simple service plan. This plan should include:

     ✓ Specific actions you will take (e.g., visiting an elderly person weekly, offering babysitting for a single parent, or volunteering at a children's shelter).
     ✓ The frequency and duration of your service.
     ✓ Any resources or support you might need.

   - *Outcome:* A clear service plan helps you commit to regular acts of service, ensuring that your intentions translate into consistent, meaningful actions.

3. **Set Up a Service Journal:**

   - *Duration:* Ongoing.

   - *Instructions:* Start a journal dedicated to your service activities. After each act of service, take 5-10 minutes to reflect on the experience. Write about what you did, how the person or group responded, and how it impacted you spiritually. Include any insights or lessons you learned.

- **Outcome:** Keeping a service journal will help you track your progress, reflect on the spiritual significance of your actions, and identify areas for growth and improvement.

4. **Involve Others in Your Service:**
   - **Duration:** Ongoing.
   - **Instructions:** Invite friends, family members, or parishioners to join you in your service activities. This could involve organizing a group visit to a nursing home, coordinating a meal train for a single parent, or starting a volunteer group at your parish. Share your service plan and encourage others to create their own.
   - **Outcome:** Involving others in your service work fosters a sense of community and amplifies the impact of your efforts, making it a collective expression of faith and love.

5. **Monthly Reflection and Adjustment:**
   - **Duration:** 1 hour, once a month.
   - **Instructions:** At the end of each month, set aside time to review your service journal and reflect on your experiences. Consider the following questions:

- ✓ How has my service impacted those I've helped?
- ✓ How has serving others affected my spiritual life and relationship with GOD?
- ✓ Are there any changes or adjustments I need to make to my service plan?
- ✓ What new opportunities for service can I explore?

- *Outcome:* Regular reflection allows you to evaluate the effectiveness of your service, make necessary adjustments, and remain committed to growing in your role as a servant of Christ.

Outcome: By completing this exercise, you will develop a habit of serving others that is both consistent and impactful. You will gain a deeper understanding of the needs in your community, learn how to balance service with other responsibilities, and experience the spiritual growth that comes from living out the Gospel through acts of love and compassion. This exercise will not only benefit those you serve but also enrich your own spiritual journey as you grow closer to GOD through service.

Chapter 29: Church Ministries – Prayer Ministry, Sick Ministry, Youth Ministry, Food Pantry, etc.

The Vital Role of Church Ministries in Living Out the Gospel

The theme of this chapter is the essential role that church ministries play in the life of the Catholic community. These ministries - such as prayer ministry, sick ministry, youth ministry, and food pantries - are vital expressions of the Church's mission to serve others, foster spiritual growth, and build a strong, supportive community. This chapter explores the theological foundations of these ministries, their relevance to modern-day Catholics, and practical ways to get involved and deepen one's faith through service.

Theological Insights

Church ministries are rooted in the mission of Jesus Christ, who came to serve and not to be served (Mark 10:45)[1]. This mission is carried forward by the Church, which is called to be the hands and feet of Christ in the world. The ministries of the Church are diverse but share a common purpose: to bring the love, healing, and presence of Christ to those in need.

The concept of Christ Consciousness, which emphasizes the awareness of Christ's presence within us and others, is central to understanding the importance of church ministries. When we engage in ministry, we are not only serving others but also recognizing and honoring the presence of Christ in those we serve. This is particularly evident in ministries that care for the sick, feed the hungry, and guide the young, as Jesus taught, *"Truly, I say to you, as you did it to one of the least of these my brothers, you did it to me"* (Matthew 25:40)[2].

The Holy Trinity also offers a model for ministry. The relationship between the Father, Son, and Holy Spirit is one of perfect unity, love, and mutual self-giving. Church ministries reflect this divine relationship by fostering communities of care and service where individuals work together for the common good. Each ministry is an expression of the Church's commitment to live out the Gospel and to manifest the love of GOD in concrete ways.

For modern-day Catholics, participation in church ministries is a way to live out their baptismal call to be active members of the Body of Christ. The Catechism of the Catholic Church teaches that every Christian is called to be a *"living stone"* in the building up of the Church (CCC 1267)[3]. Ministries provide a practical way to respond to this call by contributing to the life and mission of the Church in tangible, meaningful ways.

Application in Modern Life

In today's world, where individualism and secularism often overshadow communal and spiritual values, church ministries provide a countercultural witness to the power of community and service. However, many Catholics struggle with balancing their involvement in church ministries with the demands of modern life. Work, family responsibilities, and social commitments can make it challenging to find time for ministry.

One way to overcome these challenges is to integrate ministry into everyday life. Rather than viewing ministry as an additional burden, it can be seen as an opportunity to live out one's faith in practical, life-giving ways. For example, prayer ministry can be incorporated into daily routines through regular prayer times, offering intercessory prayers for others, and participating in prayer groups. Similarly, those involved in the sick ministry can make visiting the sick a regular part of their schedule, seeing it as a form of Christian service that also nourishes their own spiritual life.

Youth ministry is another vital area where Catholics can make a significant impact. By mentoring young people, leading youth groups, or simply being present in their lives, adults can help guide the next generation in their faith journey. This ministry is particularly important in a time when young people face numerous challenges and are often searching for meaning and purpose.

Food pantries and similar ministries provide essential support to those in need and offer Catholics a concrete way to live out the Gospel call to feed the hungry. Volunteering at a food pantry, organizing food drives, or simply donating regularly are practical ways to contribute. These acts of service not only meet physical needs but also demonstrate the love and care of the Church for the most vulnerable.

Balancing these commitments with personal and professional responsibilities requires intentionality and discernment. It's important to choose ministries that align with one's gifts, interests, and availability, ensuring that the service is sustainable and fulfilling. It's also essential to maintain a healthy balance between ministry work and other aspects of life, avoiding burnout by setting realistic expectations and taking time for personal prayer and reflection.

Practical Spiritual Tools

To help readers integrate ministry into their spiritual lives, here are some practical spiritual tools:

1. **Ministry Discernment Prayer:**

    - *Instructions:* Spend time in prayer asking GOD to guide you in choosing a ministry that aligns with your gifts and passions. Reflect on the needs of your community and where you feel called to serve. Consider using the Ignatian practice of discernment, which involves prayerfully weighing the options and seeking inner peace about the decision.

    - *Outcome:* Discernment prayer helps you make thoughtful, Spirit-led decisions about where and how to serve in the Church.

2. **Weekly Ministry Reflection:**

    - *Instructions:* Set aside time each week to reflect on your ministry work. Write about your experiences, the people you served, and how the work has impacted your faith. Consider any challenges you faced and how you can address them moving forward. Use this time to reconnect with the spiritual purpose behind your service.

    - *Outcome:* Regular reflection helps you stay grounded in the spiritual significance of your ministry and fosters ongoing growth and commitment.

- **Ministry Accountability Partner:**

    - *Instructions:* Find a fellow parishioner or friend who is also involved in ministry and agree to support each other in your service work. Check in regularly to share experiences, offer encouragement, and pray for each other. This partnership can provide motivation and help you stay committed to your ministry work.

    - *Outcome:* Having an accountability partner strengthens your resolve to serve and provides a source of mutual support and encouragement.

3. **Incorporate Ministry into Family Life:**

    - *Instructions:* If possible, involve your family in your ministry work. This could include volunteering together at a food pantry, praying as a family for the sick, or participating in youth ministry activities. Involving family members not only lightens the load but also teaches them the value of service and builds a shared sense of purpose.

- *Outcome:* Integrating ministry into family life enriches your family's faith journey and strengthens your collective commitment to serving others.

4. **Annual Ministry Retreat:**

- *Instructions:* Consider attending or organizing an annual retreat focused on your ministry area. This retreat could include time for prayer, reflection, and learning about new ways to serve. Use the retreat to recharge spiritually and to gain new insights and inspiration for your ministry work.

- *Outcome:* A retreat provides a dedicated time for spiritual renewal, helping you to return to your ministry work with fresh energy and a renewed sense of purpose.

By engaging in these spiritual practices, you can make church ministry a central part of your spiritual life. Whether you are involved in prayer ministry, sick ministry, youth ministry, or a food pantry, your service is a powerful way to live out the Gospel and to contribute to the life of the Church. Through ministry, you not only serve others but also grow closer to GOD, deepen your faith, and become a vital part of the Church's mission to bring Christ's love to the world.

Exercise: Engaging in Church Ministry

Objective: To help readers actively participate in church ministries by identifying their unique gifts, choosing a ministry that aligns with their strengths, and committing to regular involvement. This exercise is designed to deepen their understanding of ministry work and its impact on both the individual and the community.

Instructions:

1. **Identify Your Gifts and Interests:**
   - *Duration:* 30 minutes.
   - *Instructions:* Reflect on your personal strengths, skills, and interests. Consider how these could be used in service to your parish and the broader Church community. Make a list of your top three gifts (e.g., teaching, compassion, organization) and think about which ministries might benefit from these abilities.
   - *Outcome:* By identifying your gifts, you'll be better equipped to choose a ministry where you can serve effectively and joyfully.

2. **Research Available Ministries:**
   - *Duration:* 1 hour.
   - *Instructions:* Contact your parish office or visit the parish website to learn about the different ministries

available, such as prayer ministry, sick ministry, youth ministry, or food pantry. Take note of the ministries that align with your gifts and interests. If possible, speak with ministry leaders to gain a better understanding of what is involved.

- *Outcome:* Gaining a clear understanding of the available ministries will help you make an informed decision about where to serve.

3. **Commit to a Ministry:**
   - *Duration:* 1 month (initial commitment).
   - *Instructions:* Choose one ministry to commit to for at least one month. During this time, attend meetings, participate in activities, and get to know other ministry members. Keep a journal to reflect on your experiences, noting any challenges, rewards, and spiritual growth.
   - *Outcome:* A month-long commitment allows you to immerse yourself in the ministry, helping you to determine if it's the right fit for your gifts and interests.

4. **Reflect and Evaluate:**
   - *Duration:* 30 minutes.
   - *Instructions:* At the end of the month, review your journal entries and reflect on your ministry experience. Consider the following questions:

- ✓ How did this ministry align with my gifts and interests?
- ✓ What impact did my involvement have on others and on my own spiritual life?
- ✓ Should I continue with this ministry, or explore other options?
- **Outcome:** Reflection helps you assess the effectiveness and fulfillment of your ministry work, guiding you in your decision to continue or explore new opportunities.

5. **Deepen Your Involvement:**
   - **Duration:** Ongoing.
   - **Instructions:** If you decide to continue with the chosen ministry, look for ways to deepen your involvement. This could include taking on a leadership role, inviting others to join, or starting a new initiative within the ministry. Set specific goals for your involvement, such as increasing your time commitment or expanding the reach of the ministry.
   - **Outcome:** Deepening your involvement in ministry work enhances your contribution to the community and fosters further spiritual growth.

6. **Share Your Experience:**
   - **Duration:** 1 hour.
   - **Instructions:** Prepare a short presentation or written testimony about your ministry experience and share it

with your parish community. This could be done during a ministry meeting, parish event, or through the parish newsletter. Focus on how the ministry has impacted your life and the lives of others and encourage others to get involved.

- *Outcome:* Sharing your experience can inspire others to join in ministry work, building a stronger, more active church community.

Outcome: By completing this exercise, you will not only deepen your understanding of church ministries but also actively contribute to the life of your parish. This experience will help you grow spiritually, connect with others in meaningful ways, and fulfill your call to serve as part of The Body of Christ. Through regular reflection and evaluation, you'll ensure that your ministry work remains fulfilling and impactful, both for yourself and for those you serve.

Chapter 30: Catholic Classes, Workshops, and Seminars

Empowering Faith through Education and Formation

The theme of this chapter revolves around the importance of continuous learning and spiritual formation within the Catholic faith. Catholic classes, workshops, and seminars serve as vital avenues for deepening one's understanding of theology, spirituality, and the practical aspects of living a Catholic life. These educational opportunities empower believers to integrate their faith into every aspect of their lives, helping them to navigate the challenges of modern-day living with a Christ-centered approach. This chapter explores the theological basis for lifelong learning, offers practical insights into the modern techniques used in faith-based education, and provides tools to help Catholics engage more fully with their faith through structured learning experiences.

Theological Insights

The Catholic tradition has always placed a strong emphasis on the importance of education in the faith. The Great Commission, as recorded in Matthew 28:19-20, commands the disciples to *"go and make disciples of all nations, baptizing them in the name of the Father and of the Son and of the Holy Spirit, and teaching them to obey everything I have commanded you."* This directive underscores the importance of teaching and learning within the Christian life, making education a fundamental aspect of discipleship.

The Holy Trinity - Father, Son, and Holy Spirit - serves as a model for all educational endeavors within the Church. The Father, as the source of all wisdom, The Son as the Word made flesh and ultimate teacher, and The Holy Spirit as the guide and inspirer of truth, together emphasize the divine foundation of all true knowledge. In the Catholic context, this means that education is not merely about acquiring knowledge but about entering into a deeper relationship with GOD and understanding His will for our lives.

The concept of Christ Consciousness further illuminates the purpose of Catholic education. Christ Consciousness refers to the awareness of the divine presence within and around us, guiding our actions and thoughts. Through Catholic classes, workshops, and seminars, believers are invited to cultivate this awareness, allowing the teachings of Christ to permeate their lives more fully. By engaging in these learning opportunities, Catholics can better understand their faith and how it applies to contemporary issues, helping them to live out their vocation with greater clarity and purpose[2].

Modern-day techniques in educational settings, such as interactive workshops, online seminars, and experiential learning, are being increasingly utilized within the Church to enhance the effectiveness of faith formation. These methods align with the Church's mission to reach people where they are and to make the teachings of Christ accessible and relevant in a rapidly changing world.

Application in Modern Life

For modern Catholics, finding time for spiritual education amidst the demands of daily life can be challenging. However, integrating faith-based learning into one's routine is essential for personal growth and for living out the Catholic faith authentically. Catholic classes, workshops, and seminars provide structured opportunities for this growth, offering spaces where individuals can explore their faith more deeply and connect with others on the same journey.

One of the key challenges for many Catholics today is balancing their spiritual commitments with the responsibilities of work, family, and social life. Catholic education can serve as a tool for achieving this balance, offering practical insights and strategies for integrating faith into everyday activities. For example, a workshop on time management from a Catholic perspective might include discussions on prioritizing prayer, balancing work and rest, and serving others in one's daily routine.

Online classes and webinars have become particularly valuable in this regard, offering flexibility for those with busy schedules. These digital formats allow Catholics to engage with their faith at their own pace, accessing resources and learning opportunities from the comfort of their homes. For instance, a working parent might enroll in an online course on Catholic parenting, learning how to instill faith values in their children while managing the challenges of modern family life.

Experiential learning is another modern technique that has proven effective in Catholic education. Retreats, pilgrimage experiences, and hands-on service projects offer participants the chance to live out their faith in concrete ways, fostering a deeper connection to the teachings of Christ. These experiences not only enhance understanding but also encourage participants to apply what they have learned in their personal and professional lives.

A real-life example of this integration can be seen in the story of a young professional who attended a Catholic leadership workshop. Through this experience, she learned how to incorporate her faith into her work environment, leading with integrity, compassion, and a sense of purpose rooted in the Gospel. This transformation not only impacted her career but also deepened her relationship with GOD, as she began to see her work as a vocation rather than just a job.

Practical Spiritual Tools

To help readers engage more fully with Catholic classes, workshops, and seminars, here are some practical spiritual tools:

1. **Spiritual Learning Plan:**

    - *Instructions:* Create a personal spiritual learning plan that outlines your goals for faith education over the next year. Include specific topics you wish to explore, such as theology, scripture, or Catholic social teaching, and identify classes, workshops, or seminars that align with these interests. Schedule time each week for study and reflection.

    - *Outcome:* A spiritual learning plan helps you stay focused on your educational goals and ensures that you are continually growing in your faith.

2. **Interactive Faith Journaling:**

    - *Instructions:* During your participation in a class, workshop, or seminar, keep a journal where you record key insights, questions, and reflections. After each session, spend time in prayer, asking GOD to help you apply what you have learned to your daily life. Revisit your journal regularly to track your growth and identify areas for further exploration.

    - *Outcome:* Faith journaling deepens your engagement with the material and helps you integrate new knowledge into your spiritual practice.

3. **Group Study and Discussion:**

    - ***Instructions:*** Form or join a study group with fellow parishioners who are also interested in deepening their faith through Catholic education. Meet regularly to discuss what you have learned, share insights, and support each other in applying these lessons to your lives. Consider rotating leadership roles to encourage active participation from all members.

    - ***Outcome:*** Group study fosters community, accountability, and deeper understanding through shared learning experiences.

4. **Digital Faith Retreat:**

    - ***Instructions:*** If in-person retreats are not feasible, create a personal digital retreat using online resources. Choose a topic, such as deepening prayer life or understanding the sacraments, and set aside a weekend for focused study and reflection. Include time for prayer, meditation, and journaling to fully immerse yourself in the experience.

    - ***Outcome:*** A digital retreat allows for intensive spiritual growth and reflection, even within the constraints of a busy schedule.

5. **Service-Based Learning:**

    - ***Instructions:*** Combine education with action by participating in a service project related to what you are learning. For example, if you are studying Catholic social teaching, volunteer at a local charity or food pantry. Reflect on how your service connects to the teachings of Christ and enhances your understanding of the material.

    - ***Outcome:*** Service-based learning helps bridge the gap between knowledge and action, reinforcing the practical implications of your faith.

By engaging in these tools and techniques, you can make Catholic education a dynamic and transformative part of your spiritual life. Whether through classes, workshops, or seminars, these learning opportunities offer invaluable resources for deepening your faith, enhancing your understanding of Catholic teachings, and living out the Gospel in everyday life.

Exercise: Designing Your Personal Catholic Learning Pathway

Objective: To help readers create a personalized and actionable learning plan that integrates Catholic classes, workshops, and seminars into their spiritual journey, enhancing their understanding and application of the faith in daily life.

Instructions:

1. **Assess Your Current Knowledge:**
   - *Duration:* 20 minutes.
   - *Instructions:* Reflect on your current understanding of Catholic teachings and practices. Identify areas where you feel confident and areas where you would like to deepen your knowledge. Write down at least three topics or aspects of the faith that you wish to explore further (e.g., understanding the sacraments, deepening your prayer life, learning about Catholic social teaching).
   - *Outcome:* This assessment will help you focus on specific areas for growth and set clear learning goals.

2. **Research Available Resources:**
   - *Duration:* 1 hour.
   - *Instructions:* Look into available Catholic classes, workshops, seminars, and online courses that align with the topics you identified. Use parish bulletins, diocesan websites, and Catholic educational

platforms to find opportunities. Make a list of at least three options for each topic, including details such as dates, locations, formats (online or in-person), and costs.

- **Outcome:** Researching available resources will give you a broad view of the educational opportunities available to you and allow you to select the best fit for your needs.

3. **Create Your Learning Schedule:**
   - **Duration:** 30 minutes.
   - **Instructions:** Based on your research, create a learning schedule that outlines when and how you will participate in the selected classes, workshops, or seminars. Be realistic about your time commitments and consider integrating these activities into your weekly routine. For example, you might decide to attend a workshop on the sacraments once a month or to complete an online course on prayer over the next six weeks.
   - **Outcome:** A clear and organized schedule will help you stay committed to your learning goals and ensure that you make consistent progress.

4. **Participate and Engage Fully:**
   - *Duration:* Ongoing.
   - *Instructions:* As you attend the selected classes, workshops, or seminars, actively participate by taking notes, asking questions, and engaging in discussions. Apply what you learn in your daily life, whether through prayer, reflection, or action. Consider keeping a journal to document your experiences and insights.
   - *Outcome:* Active participation will deepen your understanding and help you integrate new knowledge into your spiritual practice.

5. **Reflect and Adjust:**
   - *Duration:* 30 minutes, monthly.
   - *Instructions:* At the end of each month, review your progress. Reflect on what you've learned, how it has impacted your faith, and whether you are meeting your learning goals. If necessary, adjust your schedule or explore new topics that have emerged from your learning experience. Continue this reflection process throughout your learning journey.
   - *Outcome:* Regular reflection ensures that your learning remains relevant and impactful, allowing you to continually grow in your faith.

6. **Share Your Journey:**
    - ***Duration:*** 1 hour.
    - ***Instructions:*** Consider sharing your learning journey with others in your parish or faith community. This could be done through a short presentation, a discussion group, or a written testimony in the parish bulletin. Focus on how the educational experiences have enriched your faith and how they can benefit others.
    - ***Outcome:*** Sharing your journey reinforces your learning and encourages others to engage in their own faith education, fostering a community of lifelong learners.

Outcome: By completing this exercise, you will create a personalized Catholic learning pathway that helps you deepen your faith and apply it more effectively in your daily life. Through thoughtful planning, active participation, and regular reflection, you will grow in your understanding of Catholic teachings and become more engaged in living out your faith. This exercise also encourages you to share your journey with others, contributing to the spiritual growth of your community.

NOTES:

Chapter 31: Catholic Spiritual Direction and Mentoring

Guiding Souls on the Path to Holiness

The theme of this chapter centers on the importance of spiritual direction and mentoring within the Catholic tradition. These practices are essential tools for deepening one's relationship with GOD and navigating the complexities of the spiritual life. In a world filled with distractions and challenges, spiritual direction and mentoring provide Catholics with the guidance needed to grow in holiness and live out their faith more fully. This chapter explores the theological foundations of spiritual direction, discusses its relevance to modern-day Catholics, and offers practical tools for integrating these practices into everyday life.

Theological Insights

Spiritual direction is deeply rooted in the Catholic tradition, drawing from the Church's understanding of the human person as a spiritual being created in the image of GOD (Genesis 1:27)[1]. The purpose of spiritual direction is to help individuals discern GOD's will in their lives, grow in virtue, and deepen their relationship with Christ. The role of a spiritual director is akin to that of a shepherd, guiding the soul through the various stages of spiritual growth.

The Holy Trinity - Father, Son, and Holy Spirit - serves as the ultimate model for all spiritual relationships. In the context of spiritual direction, The Holy Spirit plays a particularly significant role. As Jesus promised, The Holy Spirit is the "Counselor" and "Spirit of truth" who leads believers into all truth (John 16:13)[2]. The Spiritual Director, guided by The Holy Spirit, helps the "Directee" to recognize the movements of grace in their life and to respond to them with greater fidelity.

Christ Consciousness, the awareness of Christ's presence within and around us, is also central to the practice of spiritual direction. This concept emphasizes that spiritual growth is not merely about acquiring knowledge but about deepening one's experiential awareness of GOD's presence. Through spiritual direction, Catholics are encouraged to cultivate this awareness, allowing Christ to shape their thoughts, actions, and desires.

Mentoring, while similar to spiritual direction, often focuses on practical guidance in living out the faith. Catholic mentoring relationships, whether formal or informal, are characterized by a shared commitment to grow in holiness. Mentors provide wisdom, support, and encouragement, helping mentees to integrate their faith into all aspects of their lives. The relationship between St. Paul and Timothy, as described in the New Testament, serves as a biblical example of mentoring (2 Timothy 2:2)[3]. Paul's guidance and instruction to Timothy highlight the importance of passing on the faith through personal relationships.

In modern contexts, spiritual direction and mentoring have adapted to meet the needs of Catholics in various life circumstances. Techniques such as regular one-on-one meetings, online spiritual direction sessions, and group mentoring are now commonly used to accommodate busy schedules and diverse lifestyles. These methods ensure that spiritual guidance remains accessible and relevant in today's fast-paced world.

Application in Modern Life

In the hustle and bustle of modern life, many Catholics struggle to find the time and space for spiritual growth. Spiritual direction and mentoring offer structured opportunities to prioritize one's relationship with GOD amidst the demands of daily life. These practices provide a framework for making decisions, overcoming spiritual obstacles, and maintaining a balanced life centered on Christ.

One of the primary challenges faced by modern Catholics is the tension between spiritual commitments and secular responsibilities. Spiritual direction can help individuals navigate this tension by providing clarity and focus. For example, a young professional might seek spiritual direction to discern how to live out their faith in the workplace, balancing ambition with humility and service. Through regular meetings with a spiritual director, this individual can develop a plan for integrating prayer, sacramental life, and Christian virtues into their professional life.

Mentoring, on the other hand, is particularly valuable for those in transitional phases of life, such as young adults entering the workforce, newly married couples, or parents raising children in the faith. A mentor can offer practical advice and share personal experiences, helping the mentee to apply Catholic teachings in real-life situations. For instance, a newly married couple might seek guidance from a mentor couple on how to build a strong, faith-centered marriage. Through regular conversations and shared activities, the mentor couple can provide insights on communication, prayer, and family life, helping the younger couple to navigate the joys and challenges of marriage.

Online spiritual direction and mentoring have become increasingly popular, especially in the wake of the COVID-19 pandemic. These digital platforms allow for greater flexibility, enabling Catholics to receive guidance from experienced spiritual directors and mentors regardless of geographical location. Online sessions can include video calls, email exchanges, and the use of spiritual exercises tailored to the directee's or mentee's needs. This accessibility ensures that more Catholics can benefit from these practices, even with the constraints of a busy lifestyle.

Practical Spiritual Tools

To help readers incorporate spiritual direction and mentoring into their spiritual lives, here are some practical spiritual tools:

1. **Daily Examen:**
    - ***Instructions***: Incorporate the Ignatian practice of the Examen into your daily routine. At the end of each day, take 10-15 minutes to review your day in the

presence of GOD. Reflect on moments of grace and challenges and ask for the Holy Spirit's guidance in recognizing GOD's presence in your life. Share these reflections with your spiritual director or mentor during your next meeting.

- **Outcome:** The Daily Examen helps you cultivate awareness of GOD's presence and provides a foundation for deeper conversations in spiritual direction or mentoring.

2. **Spiritual Journal:**

    - **Instructions:** Keep a journal dedicated to your spiritual direction or mentoring journey. After each session, write down key insights, spiritual movements, and action steps. Use this journal to track your spiritual growth over time and to identify recurring themes or challenges. Review your journal regularly to prepare for upcoming sessions.

    - **Outcome:** A spiritual journal deepens your self-awareness and enhances the effectiveness of spiritual direction or mentoring by providing a record of your journey.

3. **Regular Check-ins:**

    - **Instructions:** Schedule regular check-ins with your spiritual director or mentor, whether in person or online. These sessions should be frequent enough to maintain momentum but flexible enough to accommodate your schedule. During check-ins, discuss your progress, challenges, and any new questions or insights that have arisen since your last meeting.

- **Outcome:** Regular check-ins ensure continuity in your spiritual growth and provide ongoing support and accountability.

4. **Prayerful Decision-Making:**

- **Instructions:** When faced with important decisions, use a prayerful decision-making process guided by your spiritual director or mentor. Begin by praying for wisdom and clarity. Discuss your options with your director or mentor, considering how each choice aligns with your spiritual goals and values. Make a decision in a spirit of trust and surrender to GOD's will.

- **Outcome:** Prayerful decision-making helps you align your choices with GOD's will and strengthens your reliance on divine guidance.

5. **Mentorship Reflection Guide:**

- **Instructions:** If you are in a mentoring relationship, create a reflection guide for your mentee that includes questions and exercises to help them integrate their faith into specific areas of their life. For example, if mentoring a young adult, include questions about balancing faith and work, or if mentoring a new parent, focus on raising children in the faith. Review their responses during your sessions.

- *Outcome:* A mentorship reflection guide provides structure to the mentoring relationship and helps the mentee apply Catholic teachings in practical ways.

By engaging in these spiritual practices, you can make spiritual direction and mentoring central to your faith journey. Whether you are seeking guidance through formal spiritual direction or informal mentoring, these practices offer invaluable support for growing closer to GOD, discerning His will, and living out your Catholic faith with greater intentionality and purpose.

Exercise: Developing a Personalized Spiritual Growth Plan

Objective: To help readers create a personalized and actionable spiritual growth plan that incorporates the guidance of spiritual direction or mentoring. This exercise will empower readers to deepen their relationship with GOD, align their daily lives with their faith, and achieve specific spiritual goals.

Instructions:

1. **Reflect on Your Current Spiritual State:**
   - *Duration:* 20 minutes.
   - *Instructions:* Begin by reflecting on your current spiritual life. Consider your prayer habits, your

relationship with GOD, your engagement with the sacraments, and your areas of spiritual struggle. Write down your reflections, focusing on where you feel strong in your faith and where you need growth.

- **Outcome:** This reflection will give you a clear understanding of your current spiritual state, providing a foundation for setting future goals.

2. **Set Specific Spiritual Goals:**
   - **Duration:** 30 minutes.
   - **Instructions:** Based on your reflection, identify three to five specific spiritual goals you want to achieve over the next six months. These could include improving your prayer life, attending Mass more regularly, overcoming a particular sin, or deepening your understanding of a specific aspect of the faith. Write these goals down, making sure they are clear, measurable, and realistic.
   - **Outcome:** Setting specific goals will help you focus your spiritual growth efforts and measure your progress.

3. **Identify Spiritual Practices to Support Your Goals:**
   - **Duration:** 30 minutes.
   - **Instructions:** For each of your spiritual goals, identify at least one spiritual practice that will help you

achieve it. For example, if your goal is to deepen your prayer life, you might commit to daily meditation, attending Adoration weekly, or using the Examen. If your goal is to grow in understanding of the faith, you might enroll in a Catholic class or read a specific spiritual book.

- *Outcome:* Identifying specific practices ensures that you have actionable steps to take toward achieving your spiritual goals.

4. **Schedule Regular Spiritual Direction or Mentoring Sessions:**
   - *Duration:* 10 minutes.
   - *Instructions:* If you haven't already, find a spiritual director or mentor who can guide you in your spiritual journey. Schedule regular sessions (e.g., bi-weekly or monthly) to discuss your progress, challenges, and insights. Use these sessions to receive feedback, adjust your goals as needed, and stay accountable.
   - *Outcome:* Regular spiritual direction or mentoring sessions provide ongoing support, guidance, and accountability, helping you stay on track with your spiritual growth plan.

5. **Incorporate Daily and Weekly Check-Ins:**
   - *Duration:* 10 minutes daily, 20 minutes weekly.

- **Instructions:** At the end of each day, take 10 minutes to review your day in light of your spiritual goals. Reflect on what went well and where you need improvement. At the end of each week, spend 20 minutes reviewing your progress toward your goals, adjusting your spiritual practices if necessary, and preparing for your next spiritual direction or mentoring session.

- **Outcome:** Daily and weekly check-ins help you stay mindful of your spiritual growth and ensure continuous progress.

6. **Engage in a Monthly Retreat Day:**

    - **Duration:** 1 day per month.

    - **Instructions:** Set aside one day each month for a personal retreat focused on your spiritual growth plan. Use this time for extended prayer, reflection, spiritual reading, and reviewing your progress. Consider incorporating activities such as silence, nature walks, or journaling to deepen your retreat experience.

    - **Outcome:** A monthly retreat day provides a dedicated time for spiritual renewal, allowing you to refocus and reenergize your efforts toward your spiritual goals.

7. **Evaluate and Adjust Your Plan:**

    - **Duration:** 30 minutes every three months.

- ***Instructions:*** Every three months, take time to evaluate your overall progress. Reflect on what goals you have achieved, what challenges you faced, and what areas still need attention. Based on your evaluation, adjust your spiritual practices, goals, or even your approach to spiritual direction or mentoring as necessary.

- ***Outcome:*** Regular evaluation ensures that your spiritual growth plan remains relevant and effective, allowing you to adapt to new challenges and opportunities for growth.

Outcome: By completing this exercise, you will create a comprehensive and personalized spiritual growth plan that integrates spiritual direction or mentoring. This plan will help you achieve specific spiritual goals, deepen your relationship with GOD, and live out your Catholic faith with greater intentionality. The structure provided by regular check-ins, retreats, and evaluations will ensure continuous progress and sustained spiritual growth.

NOTES:

Chapter 32: Catholic Church Elders

Honoring the Wisdom and Guidance of Church Elders

The central theme of this chapter is the vital role that elders play within The Catholic Church, both as bearers of tradition and as spiritual guides for the younger generations. Catholic elders, through their lived experiences, deep faith, and accumulated wisdom, serve as invaluable resources for the community. This chapter explores the theological foundations of respecting and learning from elders, offers practical advice on engaging with elders in meaningful ways, and provides tools to help integrate the wisdom of elders into daily spiritual life.

Theological Insights

In Catholic tradition, the role of elders is deeply rooted in Scripture and the teachings of the Church. The Bible frequently emphasizes the importance of honoring and learning from those who have walked the path of faith before us. In the Old Testament, Proverbs 16:31[1] states, *"Gray hair is a crown of glory; it is gained in a righteous life,"* highlighting the respect that is due to those who have lived a life of virtue. In the New Testament, St. Paul advises Timothy, a young leader in the Church, to respect and value the elders in the community (1 Timothy 5:1-2)[2], recognizing their role as pillars of wisdom and faith.

The concept of The Holy Trinity - Father, Son, and Holy Spirit - provides a model for understanding the relationship between generations in The Church. Just as The Trinity reflects a perfect communion of love and mutual respect among distinct persons, so too should the Church embody a communion between its members, where the wisdom of the elders is cherished and integrated into the life of the community. This Trinitarian model encourages us to see our elders as reflections of GOD's enduring faithfulness and as instruments through which The Holy Spirit continues to guide The Church.

Christ Consciousness, the awareness of Christ's presence within and around us, also informs our approach to elders. By recognizing Christ in every person, especially those who have faithfully served The Church for many years, we honor their dignity and the unique contributions they bring to the body of Christ. Elders are often seen as the living embodiment of Christ's teachings, having applied His words to their lives over decades of faithfulness[3].

In modern contexts, working with elders involves not only respecting their wisdom but also actively engaging them in the life of the Church. This includes incorporating modern techniques such as intergenerational programs, digital literacy initiatives for elders, and creating opportunities for elders to mentor younger members of the Church. These approaches ensure that the wisdom of elders is passed on and that they continue to feel valued and included in the Church's mission.

Application in Modern Life

In today's fast-paced society, where the elderly are often marginalized or overlooked, The Church has a crucial role to play in ensuring that elders are honored and that their contributions are recognized. Integrating the wisdom of elders into the fabric of daily life requires intentionality and creativity.

One of the challenges faced by modern Catholics is maintaining a connection with older generations, especially in an era where families may be geographically dispersed. The Church can serve as a bridge, fostering relationships between young and old through parish programs and community events. For instance, organizing intergenerational prayer groups or Bible study sessions can create opportunities for young people to learn from the experiences and insights of elders. These interactions not only enrich the spiritual lives of the younger participants but also provide elders with a sense of purpose and belonging.

Digital technology also offers new avenues for engaging with elders. Many Catholic parishes are now offering digital literacy workshops to help older members navigate technology, allowing them to participate more fully in the Church's online activities, such as virtual Masses, prayer meetings, and faith formation programs. This inclusion ensures that elders remain connected to their faith community, even when physical attendance may be challenging due to health or mobility issues.

A real-life example of successfully integrating elders into the life of the Church can be seen in a parish that started a mentorship program pairing elders with young adults preparing for Confirmation. The elders shared their personal faith journeys, offered guidance on living a Catholic life, and provided a living witness to the enduring power of faith. The young adults, in turn, gained a deeper appreciation for the richness of the Catholic tradition and the importance of lifelong discipleship. This program not only strengthened the faith of the participants but also built strong intergenerational bonds within the parish community.

Practical Spiritual Tools

To help readers incorporate the wisdom and guidance of Catholic elders into their spiritual lives, here are some practical spiritual tools:

1. **Elder Wisdom Circles:**

    - ***Instructions***: Organize or join an "Elder Wisdom Circle" in your parish, where elders share their life stories, faith experiences, and insights on living out Catholic teachings. These circles can meet monthly and focus on different themes, such as prayer, sacramental life, or social justice. Younger members should actively listen and engage in discussions, asking questions and reflecting on how they can apply the wisdom shared.

- ***Outcome***: Elder Wisdom Circles foster a deep respect for the experience of elders and help younger members integrate this wisdom into their own spiritual practices.

2. **Intergenerational Prayer Partnerships:**

    - ***Instructions:*** Pair up with an elder in your parish as a prayer partner. Commit to praying for each other's intentions regularly and meet at least once a month to pray together, either in person or virtually. Use these meetings as an opportunity to discuss how GOD is working in your lives and to share spiritual insights.

    - ***Outcome:*** Prayer partnerships strengthen the bonds between generations and encourage mutual spiritual growth and support.

3. **Spiritual Journaling with Elders:**

    - ***Instructions:*** If you have a close relationship with an elder, invite them to participate in a joint spiritual journaling project. Each week, choose a scripture passage or Catholic teaching to reflect on. Both you and the elder write down your thoughts, prayers, and reflections, and then share them with each other. Discuss how the passage relates to your lives and what insights you've gained from each other's experiences.

- **Outcome:** Joint spiritual journaling deepens the spiritual connection between generations and allows for the exchange of perspectives and wisdom.

4. **Mentorship Programs:**

    - **Instructions:** Encourage your parish to establish a mentorship program where elders mentor younger Catholics in various aspects of faith and life. Mentors can offer advice on career choices, marriage and family life, or navigating moral dilemmas from a Catholic perspective. Regular check-ins between mentors and mentees ensure ongoing guidance and support.

    - **Outcome:** Mentorship programs help integrate the life experience of elders into the formation of younger Catholics, promoting a holistic approach to faith and life.

5. **Digital Inclusion Initiatives:**

    - **Instructions:** Volunteer to help teach elders in your parish how to use digital tools to stay connected with the Church. Offer workshops on using video conferencing for virtual Mass, accessing online faith resources, or participating in social media groups. Ensure that elders feel confident and empowered to use these tools.

- **Outcome:** Digital inclusion initiatives ensure that elders remain active participants in the Church community, fostering a sense of belonging and continuity of faith.

By implementing these spiritual tools, readers can ensure that the wisdom of Catholic elders continues to play a vital role in the Church and in their personal spiritual journeys. Engaging with elders not only enriches our faith but also builds a stronger, more connected Church community that honors the contributions of every generation.

Exercise: Engaging with Elders for Spiritual Growth
Objective: To help readers actively engage with elders in their community to deepen their spiritual understanding and strengthen intergenerational relationships within the Church. This exercise will foster respect for the wisdom of elders and encourage practical application of their insights into daily life.

Instructions:

1. **Identify an Elder to Connect With:**
    - *Duration:* 15 minutes.
    - *Instructions:* Think of an elder in your parish or community whom you admire or who has been a source of inspiration to you. This could be a grandparent, a long-time parishioner, or someone who has shown great faith throughout their life. Reach out to this person and express your interest in learning from their experiences and wisdom.

- *Outcome:* Identifying and connecting with an elder establishes the foundation for a meaningful and spiritually enriching relationship.

2. **Schedule Regular Meetings:**
   - *Duration:* 10 minutes (to schedule), ongoing meetings.
   - *Instructions:* Set up a schedule for regular meetings with the elder you've connected with. These could be weekly or bi-weekly, depending on your availability and theirs. Meetings can be in person, over the phone, or via video call if necessary. During these meetings, ask the elder to share stories from their life, particularly how their faith has guided them through various challenges.
   - *Outcome:* Regular meetings ensure consistent engagement and allow for a deeper understanding of the elder's spiritual journey.

3. **Create an Elder Wisdom Journal:**
   - *Duration:* 10 minutes per meeting.
   - *Instructions:* After each meeting, take time to write down the key insights, stories, and advice that the elder shared with you. Reflect on how these lessons apply to your own life. Include any questions that

arise from these conversations and bring them up in future meetings.

- **Outcome:** An Elder Wisdom Journal helps you capture the insights gained and provides a resource for ongoing reflection and application in your spiritual life.

4. **Participate in a Shared Spiritual Activity:**
   - **Duration:** 1 hour.
   - **Instructions:** Plan a shared spiritual activity with the elder, such as attending Mass together, participating in Adoration, praying the Rosary, or engaging in a community service project. Use this time to discuss your experiences and how they relate to your faith journeys.
   - **Outcome:** Shared spiritual activities deepen your connection with the elder and provide practical ways to live out the wisdom you've gained.

5. **Host an Elder Wisdom Circle:**
   - **Duration:** 2 hours.
   - **Instructions:** Organize a small group gathering with a few elders from your parish and other interested participants. Create a space where elders can share their faith stories and offer advice to the younger members. Facilitate a discussion that encourages

questions and reflections on how these stories can be applied to everyday life.

- *Outcome:* An Elder Wisdom Circle fosters community, encourages intergenerational dialogue, and provides a platform for elders to share their valuable experiences with a broader audience.

6. **Reflect and Implement Lessons Learned:**
   - *Duration:* 30 minutes.
   - *Instructions:* At the end of each month, review your Elder Wisdom Journal and reflect on the lessons you've learned. Identify specific ways you can implement these lessons in your daily life, whether through changes in your prayer habits, how you approach challenges, or how you interact with others. Write down your action plan and set goals for the coming month.
   - *Outcome:* Regular reflection and implementation of lessons learned ensure that the wisdom gained from elders has a lasting impact on your spiritual growth and daily life.

Outcome: By completing this exercise, you will build a meaningful relationship with a Catholic elder, gain valuable spiritual insights, and find practical ways to incorporate their wisdom into your life. This exercise not only enriches your faith but also strengthens the bonds within your parish community, ensuring that the wisdom of elders continues to guide and inspire future generations.

NOTES:

Chapter 33: Catholicism and The Future

The Church as a Beacon of Hope and Transformation in the Modern World

The theme of this chapter revolves around the potential for The Catholic Church to reclaim its role as a powerful force for good in the world, shaping the future through faith, service, and innovation. As society evolves, The Church must adapt while remaining rooted in the eternal truths of the Gospel. By embracing both tradition and positive change, Catholicism can once again become a leading voice in addressing global challenges, fostering unity, and inspiring moral and spiritual renewal.

Theological Insights

At the heart of Catholicism is the belief in the enduring presence of Jesus Christ in the world, through The Holy Spirit and the Church. The doctrine of **The Holy Trinity** - Father, Son, and Holy Spirit - emphasizes GOD's unchanging nature and His active involvement in creation. This theological foundation assures us that GOD's love and guidance are constants, even in times of uncertainty and change.

The concept of Christ Consciousness, which is the awareness of Christ's presence within us, invites Catholics to view the future with hope and purpose. Christ's teachings, centered on love, compassion, and justice, provide a blueprint for addressing the complex issues of our time, from social inequality to environmental stewardship. By cultivating Christ Consciousness, Catholics can discern GOD's will in their lives and contribute to building a more just and loving world.

The Church's teachings on The Holy Trinity also highlight the importance of community and relationships. Just as The Father, Son, and Holy Spirit exist in a perfect communion of love, the Church is called to foster unity among its members and extend that unity to the broader world. This Trinitarian model encourages Catholics to work together to address the challenges facing humanity, drawing on the strengths and gifts of each person.

Looking to the future, The Church has the potential to play a transformative role by staying true to its theological roots while embracing new ways to engage with the world. This includes harnessing technology to spread the Gospel, fostering dialogue between different faiths and cultures, and advocating for justice and peace on a global scale. As Pope Francis has often emphasized, the Church must be a *"field hospital"* that goes out to meet people where they are, offering healing, hope, and guidance[1].

Application in Modern Life

For The Church to remain relevant and impactful, Catholics must integrate their faith into every aspect of their lives, from personal relationships to professional endeavors. This means finding ways to live out the teachings of Jesus in the modern world, where secular pressures and distractions often pull individuals away from their spiritual commitments.

One of the key challenges for modern Catholics is balancing their spiritual lives with the demands of work, family, and society. This requires a conscious effort to prioritize faith and make time for prayer, worship, and service. By doing so, Catholics can stay grounded in their beliefs and draw strength from their relationship with GOD, even in the midst of a busy and sometimes chaotic world.

Real-life examples abound of individuals and communities successfully integrating their faith into daily life. For instance, Catholic professionals who incorporate ethical principles into their business practices not only succeed in their careers but also witness to The Gospel in the marketplace. Families who make prayer and participation in the sacraments a central part of their lives often find that their relationships are strengthened and their sense of purpose is deepened. Parish communities that engage in social justice initiatives, such as feeding the hungry or advocating for the marginalized, embody the Church's mission to be the hands and feet of Christ in the world.

Looking to the future, The Church can continue to be a positive influence by promoting the spiritual formation of its members, encouraging them to live out their faith in all areas of life. This includes providing resources and opportunities for spiritual growth, such as retreats, small faith groups, and online platforms for prayer and study. By supporting Catholics in their spiritual journey, the Church can empower them to be agents of change in their families, workplaces, and communities.

Practical Spiritual Tools

To help Catholics prepare for the future and contribute to the Church's mission, here are some practical spiritual tools:

1. **Daily Prayer Routine:**

    - ***Instructions**:* Develop a daily prayer routine that includes time for personal reflection, scripture reading, and intercession. Set aside specific times each day for prayer, such as in the morning and evening. Use this time to seek GOD's guidance, offer thanks, and pray for the needs of others.

    - ***Outcome:*** A consistent prayer routine will help you stay connected to GOD and grounded in your faith, enabling you to face the challenges of daily life with peace and confidence.

2. **Engage in Community Service:**

    - ***Instructions:*** Commit to a regular service activity in your parish or community, such as volunteering at a food pantry, participating in a pro-life march, or helping with parish events. Use these opportunities to live out The Gospel's call to love and serve others.

- **Outcome:** Community service not only benefits those in need but also strengthens your faith and deepens your connection to the Church.

3. **Practice Digital Evangelization:**

    - **Instructions:** Use social media and other digital platforms to share your faith and the teachings of The Church. This could include posting inspirational quotes, sharing reflections on the Sunday readings, or engaging in respectful dialogue on religious topics.

    - **Outcome:** Digital evangelization allows you to reach a broader audience and contribute to The Church's mission of spreading the Gospel in the modern world.

4. **Participate in Faith Formation:**

    - **Instructions:** Take advantage of opportunities for ongoing faith formation, such as attending a Catholic conference, enrolling in a theology course, or joining a Bible study group. These activities will help you deepen your understanding of the faith and stay informed about The Church's teachings.

    - **Outcome:** Ongoing faith formation ensures that your knowledge of the faith continues to grow, equipping you to live out your beliefs more fully.

5. **Cultivate a Vision for the Future:**

    - ***Instructions:*** Spend time in prayer and reflection considering how you can contribute to the future of The Church. Identify specific ways you can use your talents and resources to support The Church's mission, whether through leadership, teaching, or charitable work. Write down your vision and set concrete goals to achieve it.

    - ***Outcome:*** Cultivating a vision for the future gives you a sense of purpose and direction, motivating you to take an active role in The Church's ongoing mission.

By adopting these spiritual practices, Catholics can not only strengthen their own faith but also contribute to the Church's renewal and growth. As The Church looks to the future, it is the commitment of individual believers to live out their faith with integrity and courage that will ensure its continued relevance and influence in the world. Together, Catholics can help The Church become a beacon of hope, guiding humanity toward a future marked by justice, peace, and the love of Christ.

Exercise: Visioning the Future of Catholicism

Objective: To help readers actively engage in envisioning and contributing to the future of the Catholic Church, focusing on how they can be agents of positive change within their communities and the broader world.

Instructions:

1. **Reflect on the Current State of the Church:**
   - *Duration:* 20 minutes.
   - *Instructions:* Begin by reflecting on your experiences with The Catholic Church today. Consider The Church's role in your life, the community, and the world. Write down your thoughts, focusing on both the strengths you see in the Church and areas where you believe there is room for growth or improvement.
   - *Outcome:* This reflection will help you understand your own perspective on The Church and identify areas where you feel passionate about making a difference.

2. **Identify Key Areas for Future Growth:**
   - *Duration:* 30 minutes.
   - *Instructions:* Based on your reflection, identify three key areas where you believe The Church can grow or improve in the future. These could include areas like social justice, youth engagement, digital evangelization, environmental stewardship, or ecumenical dialogue. Write down these areas and why you believe they are important.
   - *Outcome:* Identifying key areas for growth will help you focus your efforts and contribute meaningfully to the future of the Church.

3. **Develop a Personal Action Plan:**
   - ***Duration:*** 40 minutes.
   - ***Instructions:*** For each key area you identified, develop a specific action plan detailing how you can contribute to that area within your parish, community, or through broader Church initiatives. Include practical steps, such as volunteering, organizing events, or starting a discussion group. Set realistic goals and timelines for each action.
   - ***Outcome:*** A personal action plan will give you a clear, actionable path to contribute to The Church's future, ensuring that your efforts are focused and effective.

4. **Engage with Others:**
   - ***Duration:*** 1 hour.
   - ***Instructions:*** Share your reflections and action plan with a small group of fellow Catholics, such as a prayer group or Bible study group. Discuss each person's vision for the future of The Church and explore opportunities for collaboration. Consider forming a committee or task force within your parish to address one of the key areas collectively.
   - ***Outcome:*** Engaging with others fosters a sense of community and collective responsibility, allowing for a more significant impact through shared efforts.

5. **Implement Your Action Plan:**
    - *Duration:* Ongoing.
    - *Instructions:* Begin taking steps to implement your action plan. Start with small, manageable tasks, and gradually take on more significant initiatives as you gain confidence and experience. Document your progress and any challenges you encounter and adjust your plan as necessary to stay on track.
    - *Outcome:* Implementation of your action plan will allow you to actively participate in shaping the future of The Church, making a tangible difference in your community and beyond.

6. **Evaluate and Reflect:**
    - *Duration:* 30 minutes per month.
    - *Instructions:* At the end of each month, take time to evaluate your progress. Reflect on what you've accomplished, what challenges you've faced, and how your efforts are contributing to the broader vision for The Church's future. Adjust your action plan as needed and set new goals for the coming month.
    - *Outcome:* Regular evaluation ensures that your efforts remain effective and aligned with your overall vision, allowing for continuous growth and improvement.

7. **Celebrate and Share Successes:**

    - ***Duration:*** 1 hour.

    - ***Instructions:*** Periodically, gather with your group to celebrate the successes and milestones achieved through your collective efforts. Share stories, offer encouragement, and discuss new ideas for future initiatives. Consider documenting and sharing these successes with your broader parish community to inspire others to get involved.

    - ***Outcome:*** Celebrating successes helps to build momentum and encourages continued engagement, while also inspiring others to take action.

Outcome: By completing this exercise, you will actively engage in envisioning and contributing to the future of The Catholic Church. Through reflection, planning, collaboration, and action, you will help shape a Church that remains a powerful force for good in the world, grounded in the teachings of Christ and responsive to the needs of the modern world.

CONCLUSION

As we conclude this exploration of living a fulfilled and meaningful Catholic life in the modern world, the central theme is one of integration - how the profound truths of The Catholic Faith can be seamlessly woven into the fabric of daily life. The journey of faith is not a separate path from our everyday experiences; rather, it is the very lens through which we view and engage with the world. This conclusion aims to solidify the understanding that the teachings of Jesus, the awareness of The Christ Consciousness, and the relational love of The Holy Trinity are not just theological concepts but living realities that should guide and inspire every aspect of our lives.

At the heart of Catholic theology lies the mystery of The Holy Trinity - GOD as Father, Son, and Holy Spirit. This doctrine is not merely a complex theological construct, but a profound revelation of GOD's nature as a communion of love. The Father, Son, and Holy Spirit exist in a perfect relationship of mutual love and self-giving, which serves as a model for how we are called to live in relation to GOD and one another. This Trinitarian understanding of GOD invites us to see our lives as a reflection of this divine communion, where our relationships with others are grounded in love, respect, and a shared commitment to the common good .

The concept of Christ Consciousness further deepens this understanding by emphasizing the presence of Christ within us and around us. It is the awareness that we are called to embody the teachings of Jesus in our thoughts, actions, and interactions with others. Christ Consciousness is about recognizing the divine spark within every person and striving to live in a way that honors that divine presence. It is through this awareness that we are able to live out the commandment to love GOD and love our neighbor as ourselves, in all circumstances of life .

As we navigate the complexities of modern life, these theological insights offer us a framework for understanding our place in the world. They remind us that our faith is not just about personal salvation, but about participating in the ongoing work of GOD in the world - bringing about His kingdom of justice, peace, and love. In this way, our daily lives become a form of worship, where every action is an opportunity to glorify GOD and serve others.

For modern-day Catholics, the challenge lies in integrating these profound spiritual truths into the practical realities of everyday life. Balancing spiritual commitments with secular responsibilities is a common struggle, yet it is essential for living a life that is fully aligned with our faith.

One practical way to achieve this balance is through the practice of daily prayer and meditation. By setting aside time each day to connect with GOD, whether through formal prayers like The Rosary or through silent meditation, we anchor our lives in the divine. This daily practice helps us to maintain a sense of peace and purpose, even amidst the busyness of work and family life .

Another important tool is the use of The Examen, a form of prayerful reflection on the events of the day. By regularly examining our thoughts, actions, and interactions, we can become more aware of where we are aligning with the teachings of Christ and where we may be falling short. This awareness allows us to make conscious adjustments, ensuring that our daily lives are consistent with our spiritual values.

Real-life examples of successful integration of faith into daily life can be found in the stories of countless Catholics who live out their faith in the workplace, in their families, and in their communities. Consider the example of a Catholic business leader who makes ethical decisions based on the teachings of The Church, or a family that prioritizes attending Mass together despite a hectic schedule. These examples show that it is possible to live a fully integrated life, where faith is not compartmentalized but is the guiding force behind every decision and action.

Finally, the importance of community cannot be overstated. In a world that often values individualism, The Church offers a countercultural vision of communal life. Participation in parish life, involvement in small faith groups, and engagement in acts of service are all ways that Catholics can live out their faith in community. These communal practices not only strengthen individual faith but also build up the body of Christ, allowing the Church to be a beacon of hope and transformation in the world.

Moving Forward

As we move forward, the challenge for each of us is to continue deepening our understanding of the faith and finding new ways to integrate it into every aspect of our lives. The journey of faith is a lifelong process, one that requires constant reflection, prayer, and action. But it is also a journey that brings immense joy, peace, and fulfillment, as we draw closer to GOD and to one another.

In closing, the future of Catholicism lies not just in the hands of the clergy or theologians, but in the lives of everyday believers who choose to live their faith with authenticity and courage. By embracing the teachings of Jesus, cultivating The Christ Consciousness, and living in the love of The Holy Trinity, we can contribute to a future where The Church continues to be a powerful force for good in the world

FOOTNOTES

Part I: Basic Spiritual Tools

Chapter 01: Gifts from GOD – Free Will, Discernment, Wisdom

[1] Catechism of the Catholic Church, 2nd ed., (Vatican City: Libreria Editrice Vaticana, 1997), 1734.

[2] 1 Thessalonians 5:21 (NIV).

[3] Pope Francis, "The Spirit of Discernment: Speech at the General Audience," October 2018, Vatican.va.

[4] Proverbs 2:6 (NIV).

Chapter 02: Prayer and Meditation

[1] Matthew 6:6 (NIV).

[2] St. Teresa of Ávila, The Interior Castle, 1577.

[3] Catechism of the Catholic Church, 2nd ed., (Vatican City: Libreria Editrice Vaticana, 1997), 2714.

Chapter 03: Communing with Nature

[1] Psalm 19:1 (NIV).

[2] Matthew 13:31-32 (NIV); John 15:1-8 (NIV).

[3] Pope Francis, Laudato Si': On Care for Our Common Home, Vatican City: Vatican Press, 2015, Chapter 2, Section 84.

Chapter 04: Your Spiritual Companions – Guardian Angels, Spirit Guides, and Archangels

[1] Catechism of the Catholic Church, 2nd ed., (Vatican City: Libreria Editrice Vaticana, 1997), 336.

[2] Matthew 18:10 (NIV).

[3] Hebrews 12:1 (NIV).

Chapter 05: Sacred Catholic Texts

[1] John 1:14 (NIV).

[2] Catechism of the Catholic Church, 2nd ed., (Vatican City: Libreria Editrice Vaticana, 1997), 234.

[3] Genesis 1:2 (NIV).

[4] Matthew 28:19 (NIV).

[5] Matthew 5-7 (NIV).

Chapter 06: Sacred Music

[1] Psalm 95:1 (NIV).

[2] *Sacrosanctum Concilium* (Constitution on the Sacred Liturgy), Second Vatican Council, 1963, Chapter VI, Section 112.

Chapter 07: Spiritual Journaling

[1] Genesis 1:27, *New International Version.*

[2] Luke 5:16, *New International Version.*

[3] Thérèse of Lisieux, *The Story of a Soul*, Chapter 1.

Chapter 08: The Human Energy Field

[1] 1 Corinthians 6:19, New International Version.

[2] *Catechism of the Catholic Church, 2nd ed.* (Vatican City: Libreria Editrice Vaticana, 1997), no. 362.

[3] John Paul II, *Novo Millennio Ineunte* (Vatican City: Libreria Editrice Vaticana, 2001), no. 43.

Chapter 09: Energy Healing Basics and The Chakras

[1] 1 Corinthians 6:19, New International Version.

[2] John 13:34, New International Version.

[3] Philippians 4:13, New International Version.

[4] 1 Corinthians 13:4-7, New International Version.

Part II: Jesus the Boy, the Man, the Messiah

Chapter 10: The Early Years of Jesus

[1] John 1:14, *New International Version*.

[2] Matthew 3:16-17, *New International Version*.

[3] Luke 2:39-52, *New International Version*.

Chapter 11: The Lost Years of Jesus

[1] Luke 2:41-52, *New International Version*.

[2] *Catechism of the Catholic Church*, 2nd ed. (Vatican City: Libreria Editrice Vaticana, 1997), no. 531.

[3] John 1:14, *New International Version*.

Chapter 12: Books about Jesus:
- Aquarian Gospel of Jesus Christ
- The Nag Hammadi Scriptures
- The Unknown Life of Jesus Christ

[1] John 1:14, *New International Version (NIV)*.

[2] Dowling, Levi H., *The Aquarian Gospel of Jesus the Christ*.

[3] Nicolas Notovitch, *The Unknown Life of Jesus Christ*.

[4] Dionysius the Areopagite, *The Mystical Theology*.

Part III: Advanced Teachings of Jesus

Chapter 13: Becoming a Disciple of Jesus the Christ

[1] John 14:6, *Holy Bible, New Revised Standard Version*.

[2] Matthew 28:19-20, *Holy Bible, New Revised Standard Version*.

[3] Luke 5:16, *Holy Bible, New Revised Standard Version.*

[4] Acts 2:42-47, *Holy Bible, New Revised Standard Version.*

[5] Matthew 5:3-12, *Holy Bible, New Revised Standard Version.*

[6] Mark 10:45, *Holy Bible, New Revised Standard Version.*

Chapter 14: Jesus the Mystic and Mystical Teacher

[1] John 10:30, *Holy Bible, New Revised Standard Version.*

[2] John 14:20, *Holy Bible, New Revised Standard Version.*

[3] Luke 17:21, *Holy Bible, New Revised Standard Version.*

[4] Mark 1:35, *Holy Bible, New Revised Standard Version.*

Chapter 15: Jesus the Healer and You the Healer

[1] Matthew 9:35, *Holy Bible, New Revised Standard Version.*

[2] John 14:12, *Holy Bible, New Revised Standard Version.*

Chapter 16: Jesus and Teachings of "A Course in Miracles"

[1] Luke 17:21, *Holy Bible, New Revised Standard Version.*

[2] John 14:12, *Holy Bible, New Revised Standard Version.*

Part IV: Foundations of the Catholic Faith

Chapter 17: The Holy Trinity – GOD, Jesus and The Holy Spirit

[1] John 10:30, *Holy Bible, New Revised Standard Version.*

[2] John 14:26, *Holy Bible, New Revised Standard Version.*

Chapter 18: The Core Beliefs

[1] John 1:14, *Holy Bible, New Revised Standard Version.*

[2] *Catechism of the Catholic Church, 2nd Edition*, Libreria Editrice Vaticana, 1997.

Chapter 19: Understanding the Sacraments

[1] Luke 22:19, *Holy Bible, New Revised Standard Version.*

[2] John 20:23, *Holy Bible, New Revised Standard Version.*

Chapter 20: The Nicene Creed – the Profession of Faith

[1] John 1:1-3, *Holy Bible, New Revised Standard Version.*

[2] *Nicene Creed*, Council of Nicaea, AD 325, expanded at the Council of Constantinople, AD 381.

Chapter 21: Core Prayers of Catholic Devotional Practice

[1] Matthew 6:9-13, *Holy Bible, New Revised Standard Version.*

[2] John 6:35, *Holy Bible, New Revised Standard Version.*

[3] Luke 1:28, 42, *Holy Bible, New Revised Standard Version.*

Chapter 22: The Liturgical Calendar

[1] John 1:5, *Holy Bible, New Revised Standard Version.*

[2] Matthew 1:23, *Holy Bible, New Revised Standard Version.*

Part V: Being Catholic is More than Going to Church

Chapter 23: What Does it Means to Be Catholic?

[1] 1 Corinthians 12:27, *Holy Bible, New Revised Standard Version.*

[2] *Catechism of the Catholic Church (CCC)*, 460, 1131, 1324.

Chapter 24: Learning, Reading and Contemplating Sacred Texts (The Holy Bible, The New Testament, etc.)

[1] *Catechism of the Catholic Church (CCC)*, 105.

[2] St. Augustine, *Quaestiones in Heptateuchum*, 2, 73.

[3] John 1:1, *Holy Bible, New Revised Standard Version.*

Chapter 25: Going to Mass

[1] Luke 22:19, *Holy Bible, New Revised Standard Version.*

[2] *Catechism of the Catholic Church (CCC),* 1367.

[3] 1 Corinthians 10:17, *Holy Bible, New Revised Standard Version.*

Church 26: Volunteering at Church

[1] Matthew 20:28, *Holy Bible, New Revised Standard Version.*

[2] 1 Corinthians 12:27, *Holy Bible, New Revised Standard Version.*

[3] *Catechism of the Catholic Church (CCC),* 1397.

Chapter 27: Fellowship with Others – Locally, Nationally, Worldwide

[1] 1 Corinthians 12:12, *Holy Bible, New Revised Standard Version.*

[2] Matthew 22:39, *Holy Bible, New Revised Standard Version.*

Chapter 28: Service to Others – Elderly, Single Parents, Children, etc.

[1] Mark 10:45, *Holy Bible, New Revised Standard Version.*

[2] Matthew 25:40, *Holy Bible, New Revised Standard Version.*

Chapter 29: Church Ministries – Prayer Ministry, Sick Ministry, Youth Ministry, Food Pantry, etc.

[1] Mark 10:45, *Holy Bible, New Revised Standard Version.*

[2] Matthew 25:40, *Holy Bible, New Revised Standard Version.*

[3] *Catechism of the Catholic Church, 2nd Edition,* Libreria Editrice Vaticana, 1997, Paragraph 1267.

Part VI: Suggestions for Growth in The Catholic Faith

Chapter 30: Catholic Classes, Workshops and Seminars

[1] Matthew 28:19-20, *Holy Bible, New Revised Standard Version.*

[2] *Catechism of the Catholic Church, 2nd Edition,* Libreria Editrice Vaticana, 1997, Paragraph 1267.

Chapter 31: Catholic Spiritual Direction and Mentoring

[1] Genesis 1:27, *Holy Bible, New Revised Standard Version.*

[2] John 16:13, *Holy Bible, New Revised Standard Version.*

[3] 2 Timothy 2:2, *Holy Bible, New Revised Standard Version.*

Chapter 32: Catholic Church Elders

[1] Proverbs 16:31, *Holy Bible, New Revised Standard Version.*

[2] 1 Timothy 5:1-2, *Holy Bible, New Revised Standard Version.*

[3] John 16:13, *Holy Bible, New Revised Standard Version.*

Chapter 33: Catholicism and The Future

[1] Pope Francis, *Evangelii Gaudium (The Joy of the Gospel),* 2013.

NOTES:

BIBLIOGRAPHY

Part I: Basic Spiritual Tools

Chapter 01: Gifts from GOD – Free Will, Discernment, Wisdom

1. *Catechism of the Catholic Church*. 2nd ed., Vatican City: Libreria Editrice Vaticana, 1997.

2. *The Holy Bible*, New International Version. Colorado Springs: Biblica, 2011.

3. Pope Francis. "The Spirit of Discernment: Speech at the General Audience." Vatican.va, October 2018.

Chapter 02: Prayer and Meditation

1. *The Holy Bible*, New International Version. Colorado Springs: Biblica, 2011.

2. St. Teresa of Ávila. *The Interior Castle*. Translated by E. Allison Peers. London: Sheed & Ward, 1946.

3. *Catechism of the Catholic Church*. 2nd ed., Vatican City: Libreria Editrice Vaticana, 1997.

Chapter 03: Communing with Nature

1. *The Holy Bible*, New International Version. Colorado Springs: Biblica, 2011.

2. Pope Francis. *Laudato Si': On Care for Our Common Home*. Vatican City: Vatican Press, 2015.

3. *Catechism of the Catholic Church*. 2nd ed., Vatican City: Libreria Editrice Vaticana, 1997.

Chapter 04: Your Spiritual Companions – Guardian Angels, Spirit Guides, and Archangels

1. *Catechism of the Catholic Church*. 2nd ed., Vatican City: Libreria Editrice Vaticana, 1997.

2. *The Holy Bible*, New International Version. Colorado Springs: Biblica, 2011.

3. *The Book of Tobit*. New Revised Standard Version, Catholic Edition, 1989.

Chapter 05: Sacred Catholic Texts

1. *The Holy Bible*, New International Version. Colorado Springs: Biblica, 2011.

2. *Catechism of the Catholic Church*. 2nd ed., Vatican City: Libreria Editrice Vaticana, 1997.

3. *Liturgy of the Hours*. New York: Catholic Book Publishing Corp., 1975.

Chapter 06: Sacred Music

1. *The Holy Bible*, New International Version. Colorado Springs: Biblica, 2011.

2. *Sacrosanctum Concilium* (Constitution on the Sacred Liturgy). Second Vatican Council, 1963.

3. *Catechism of the Catholic Church*. 2nd ed., Vatican City: Libreria Editrice Vaticana, 1997.

Chapter 07: Spiritual Journaling

1. *Holy Bible, New International Version*. Grand Rapids, MI: Zondervan, 2011.

2. Thérèse of Lisieux. *The Story of a Soul*. Translated by John Clarke. Washington, DC: ICS Publications, 1996.

3. John Paul II. *Novo Millennio Ineunte*. Vatican City: Libreria Editrice Vaticana, 2001.

4. Barry, William A., and William J. Connolly. *The Practice of Spiritual Direction*. New York: HarperOne, 2009.

5. Keating, Thomas. *Intimacy with God: An Introduction to Centering Prayer*. New York: Crossroad Publishing Company, 2009.

6. Nouwen, Henri J. M. *The Way of the Heart: The Spirituality of the Desert Fathers and Mothers*. New York: HarperOne, 2003.

7. Pennington, M. Basil. Lectio Divina: *Renewing the Ancient Practice of Praying the Scriptures*. New York: Crossroad Publishing Company, 1998.

Chapter 08: The Human Energy Field

1. *Catechism of the Catholic Church, 2nd ed.* Vatican City: Libreria Editrice Vaticana, 1997.

2. John Paul II. *Novo Millennio Ineunte*. Vatican City: Libreria Editrice Vaticana, 2001.

3. Keating, Thomas. *Intimacy with God: An Introduction to Centering Prayer*. New York: Crossroad Publishing Company, 2009.

4. Nouwen, Henri J. M. *The Way of the Heart: The Spirituality of the Desert Fathers and Mothers*. New York: HarperOne, 2003.

5. Rohr, Richard. *The Universal Christ: How a Forgotten Reality Can Change Everything We See, Hope For, and Believe*. New York: Convergent Books, 2019.

6. Wilber, Ken. *The Spectrum of Consciousness*. Wheaton, IL: Quest Books, 1993.

7. *Holy Bible, New International Version*. Grand Rapids, MI: Zondervan, 2011.

Chapter 09: Energy Healing Basics and The Chakras

1. *Catechism of the Catholic Church, 2nd ed.* Vatican City: Libreria Editrice Vaticana, 1997.

2. *Holy Bible, New International Version*. Grand Rapids, MI: Zondervan, 2011.

3. John Paul II. *Novo Millennio Ineunte*. Vatican City: Libreria Editrice Vaticana, 2001.

4. Keating, Thomas. *Intimacy with God: An Introduction to Centering Prayer*. New York: Crossroad Publishing Company, 2009.

5. Nouwen, Henri J. M. *The Way of the Heart: The Spirituality of the Desert Fathers and Mothers*. New York: HarperOne, 2003.

6. Rohr, Richard. *The Universal Christ: How a Forgotten Reality Can Change Everything We See, Hope For, and Believe*. New York: Convergent Books, 2019.

7. Myss, Caroline. *Anatomy of the Spirit: The Seven Stages of Power and Healing*. New York: Harmony Books, 1996.

8. Judith, Anodea. *Eastern Body, Western Mind: Psychology and the Chakra System as a Path to the Self*. Berkeley, CA: Celestial Arts, 2004.

Part II: Jesus the Boy, the Man, the Messiah

Chapter 10: The Early Years of Jesus

1. *Catechism of the Catholic Church, 2nd ed*. Vatican City: Libreria Editrice Vaticana, 1997.

2. *Holy Bible, New International Version*. Grand Rapids, MI: Zondervan, 2011.

3. Brown, Raymond E. *The Birth of the Messiah: A Commentary on the Infancy Narratives in the Gospels of Matthew and Luke*. New York: Doubleday, 1993.

4. Rohr, Richard. *The Universal Christ: How a Forgotten Reality Can Change Everything We See, Hope For, and Believe*. New York: Convergent Books, 2019.

5. Gormley, Beatrice. *We Were There: The Young People in the Gospels*. Minneapolis: Augsburg Fortress, 2001.

6. Benedict XVI. *Jesus of Nazareth: The Infancy Narratives*. New York: Image Books, 2012.

7. Keating, Thomas. *The Human Condition: Contemplation and Transformation*. New York: Paulist Press, 1999.

Chapter 11: The Lost Years of Jesus

1. *Catechism of the Catholic Church, 2nd ed*. Vatican City: Libreria Editrice Vaticana, 1997.

2. *Holy Bible, New International Version*. Grand Rapids, MI: Zondervan, 2011.

3. Brown, Raymond E. *The Birth of the Messiah: A Commentary on the Infancy Narratives in the Gospels of Matthew and Luke*. New York: Doubleday, 1993.

4. Benedict XVI. *Jesus of Nazareth: The Infancy Narratives*. New York: Image Books, 2012.

5. Pitre, Brant. *Jesus and the Jewish Roots of Mary: Unveiling the Mother of the Messiah.* New York: Image Books, 2018.

6. Gormley, Beatrice. *We Were There: The Young People in the Gospels.* Minneapolis: Augsburg Fortress, 2001.

7. Keating, Thomas. *The Human Condition: Contemplation and Transformation.* New York: Paulist Press, 1999.

Chapter 12: Books about Jesus:
- **Aquarian Gospel of Jesus Christ**
- **The Nag Hammadi Scriptures**
- **The Unknown Life of Jesus Christ**

1. *The Gospel of Thomas. The Nag Hammadi Library in English.* Edited by James M. Robinson, HarperOne, 1990.

2. *The Bible. New International Version (NIV).* Zondervan, 2011.

3. Dowling, Levi H. *The Aquarian Gospel of Jesus the Christ.* 1908.

4. Pagels, Elaine. *The Gnostic Gospels.* Vintage Books, 1979.

5. Notovitch, Nicolas. *The Unknown Life of Jesus Christ.* Translated by J.H. Connelly and L. Landsberg, 1894.

6. *Pseudo-Dionysius the Areopagite. The Mystical Theology.* Translated by Colm Luibheid and Paul Rorem, Paulist Press, 1987.

7. *The Urantia Book.* Urantia Foundation, 1955.

Part III: Advanced Teachings of Jesus

Chapter 13: Becoming a Disciple of Jesus the Christ

1. *The Holy Bible, New Revised Standard Version.* Division of Christian Education of the National Council of the Churches of Christ in the United States of America, 1989.

2. *Catechism of the Catholic Church. 2nd Edition.* Libreria Editrice Vaticana, 1997.

3. Pope John Paul II, *Redemptor Hominis (The Redeemer of Man).* Libreria Editrice Vaticana, 1979.

4. Thomas à Kempis, *The Imitation of Christ*. Dover Publications, 2003.

5. Nouwen, Henri J.M. *In the Name of Jesus: Reflections on Christian Leadership*. Crossroad, 1993.

6. Rohr, Richard. *The Universal Christ: How a Forgotten Reality Can Change Everything We See, Hope For, and Believe*. Convergent Books, 2019.

7. Lewis, C.S. *Mere Christianity*. HarperOne, 2001.

8. Sheen, Fulton J. *Life of Christ*. Image Books, 1958.

9. Wright, N.T. *Simply Jesus: A New Vision of Who He Was, What He Did, and Why He Matters*. HarperOne, 2011.

10. Augustine of Hippo, *Confessions*. Oxford University Press, 1998.

11. Johnson, Elizabeth A. *Consider Jesus: Waves of Renewal in Christology*. Crossroad, 1990.

Chapter 14: Jesus the Mystic and Mystical Teacher

1. *The Holy Bible, New Revised Standard Version*. Division of Christian Education of the National Council of the Churches of Christ in the United States of America, 1989.

2. *Catechism of the Catholic Church. 2nd Edition*. Libreria Editrice Vaticana, 1997.

3. Keating, Thomas. *Open Mind, Open Heart: The Contemplative Dimension of the Gospel*. Bloomsbury Continuum, 2006.

4. Rohr, Richard. *The Universal Christ: How a Forgotten Reality Can Change Everything We See, Hope For, and Believe*. Convergent Books, 2019.

5. Merton, Thomas. *New Seeds of Contemplation*. New Directions, 1961.

6. Nouwen, Henri J.M. *The Way of the Heart: Desert Spirituality and Contemporary Ministry*. HarperOne, 2003.

7. Sheen, Fulton J. *Life of Christ*. Image Books, 1958.

8. Main, John. *The Way of Unknowing: Expanding the Practice of Christian Meditation*. Crossroad, 1991.

9. Teresa of Ávila, *The Interior Castle*. Dover Publications, 2007.

10. Wright, N.T. *Simply Jesus: A New Vision of Who He Was, What He Did, and Why He Matters*. HarperOne, 2011.

Chapter 15: Jesus the Healer and You the Healer

1. *The Holy Bible, New Revised Standard Version*. Division of Christian Education of the National Council of the Churches of Christ in the United States of America, 1989.

2. *Catechism of the Catholic Church. 2nd Edition*. Libreria Editrice Vaticana, 1997.

3, Nouwen, Henri J.M. *The Wounded Healer: Ministry in Contemporary Society*. Image Books, 1979.

4. Kelsey, Morton. *Healing and Christianity: A Classic Study*. Augsburg Fortress, 1995.

5. Hinn, Benny. *Good Morning, Holy Spirit*. Thomas Nelson, 1990.

6. Yancey, Philip. *The Jesus I Never Knew*. Zondervan, 1995.

7. Rohr, Richard. *Breathing Under Water: Spirituality and the Twelve Steps*. St. Anthony Messenger Press, 2011.

8. Sheen, Fulton J. *Life of Christ*. Image Books, 1958.

9. Teresa of Avila, *The Interior Castle*. Dover Publications, 2007.

10. MacNutt, Francis. *The Practice of Healing Prayer: A How-To Guide for Catholics*. Ave Maria Press, 2010.

Chapter 16: Jesus and Teachings of "A Course in Miracles"

1. *The Holy Bible, New Revised Standard Version*. Division of Christian Education of the National Council of the Churches of Christ in the United States of America, 1989.

2. Schucman, Helen. *A Course in Miracles*. Foundation for Inner Peace, 1976.

3. *Catechism of the Catholic Church. 2nd Edition*. Libreria Editrice Vaticana, 1997.

4. Wapnick, Kenneth. *The Meaning of A Course in Miracles: A Foundation for Inner Peace*. Foundation for A Course in Miracles, 1995.

5. Williamson, Marianne. *A Return to Love: Reflections on the Principles of A Course in Miracles.* HarperOne, 1992.

6. Nouwen, Henri J.M. *The Return of the Prodigal Son: A Story of Homecoming.* Image Books, 1992.

7. Rohr, Richard. *The Universal Christ: How a Forgotten Reality Can Change Everything We See, Hope For, and Believe.* Convergent Books, 2019.

8. Merton, Thomas. *New Seeds of Contemplation.* New Directions, 1961.

9. Wright, N.T. Simply *Jesus: A New Vision of Who He Was, What He Did, and Why He Matters.* HarperOne, 2011.

10. Teresa of Avila, *The Interior Castle.* Dover Publications, 2007.

Part IV: Foundations of the Catholic Faith

Chapter 17: The Holy Trinity – GOD, Jesus and The Holy Spirit

1. *The Holy Bible, New Revised Standard Version.* Division of Christian Education of the National Council of the Churches of Christ in the United States of America, 1989.

2. *Catechism of the Catholic Church. 2nd Edition.* Libreria Editrice Vaticana, 1997.

3. Augustine of Hippo. *On the Trinity.* New City Press, 1991.

4. Sheed, Frank. *Theology and Sanity.* Ignatius Press, 1993.

5. Aquinas, Thomas. *Summa Theologica.* Christian Classics, 1981.

6. Rahner, Karl. *The Trinity.* Herder & Herder, 1997.

7. Ratzinger, Joseph (Pope Benedict XVI). *Introduction to Christianity.* Ignatius Press, 2004.

8. Rohr, Richard. *The Divine Dance: The Trinity and Your Transformation.* Whitaker House, 2016.

9. LaCugna, Catherine Mowry. *God for Us: The Trinity and Christian Life.* HarperOne, 1993.

10. Moltmann, Jürgen. *The Trinity and the Kingdom: The Doctrine of God.* Fortress Press, 1993.

Chapter 18: The Core Beliefs

1. *The Holy Bible, New Revised Standard Version*. Division of Christian Education of the National Council of the Churches of Christ in the United States of America, 1989.

2. *Catechism of the Catholic Church. 2nd Edition*. Libreria Editrice Vaticana, 1997.

3. Augustine of Hippo. *Confessions*. Oxford University Press, 1998.

4. Aquinas, Thomas. *Summa Theologica*. Christian Classics, 1981.

5. Sheed, Frank. *Theology and Sanity*. Ignatius Press, 1993.

6. Rahner, Karl. *Foundations of Christian Faith: An Introduction to the Idea of Christianity*. Crossroad Publishing Company, 1982.

7. Ratzinger, Joseph (Pope Benedict XVI). *Introduction to Christianity*. Ignatius Press, 2004.

8. Hahn, Scott. *The Lamb's Supper: The Mass as Heaven on Earth*. Doubleday, 1999.

9. John Paul II, Pope. *Ecclesia de Eucharistia*. Libreria Editrice Vaticana, 2003.

10. Schillebeeckx, Edward. *Christ the Sacrament of the Encounter with God*. Sheed & Ward, 1963.

Chapter 19: Understanding the Sacraments

1. *The Holy Bible, New Revised Standard Version*. Division of Christian Education of the National Council of the Churches of Christ in the United States of America, 1989.

2. *Catechism of the Catholic Church. 2nd Edition*. Libreria Editrice Vaticana, 1997.

3. Aquinas, Thomas. *Summa Theologica*. Christian Classics, 1981.

4. Sheed, Frank. *Theology for Beginners*. Servant Books, 1981.

5. Schillebeeckx, Edward. *Christ the Sacrament of the Encounter with God*. Sheed & Ward, 1963.

6. Hahn, Scott. *The Lamb's Supper: The Mass as Heaven on Earth*. Doubleday, 1999.

7. Martos, Joseph. *Doors to the Sacred: A Historical Introduction to Sacraments in the Catholic Church*. Liguori Publications, 2001.

8. Rahner, Karl. *The Church and the Sacraments*. Herder & Herder, 1963.

9. John Paul II, Pope. *Ecclesia de Eucharistia*. Libreria Editrice Vaticana, 2003.

10. Ratzinger, Joseph (Pope Benedict XVI). *God Is Near Us: The Eucharist, the Heart of Life*. Ignatius Press, 2003.

Chapter 20: The Nicene Creed – The Profession of Faith

1. *The Holy Bible, New Revised Standard Version*. Division of Christian Education of the National Council of the Churches of Christ in the United States of America, 1989.

2. *Catechism of the Catholic Church. 2nd Edition*. Libreria Editrice Vaticana, 1997.

3. *Nicene Creed*, Council of Nicaea, AD 325, expanded at the Council of Constantinople, AD 381.

4. Augustine of Hippo. *The Trinity*. New City Press, 1991.

5. Sheed, Frank. *Theology for Beginners*. Servant Books, 1981.

6. Kelly, J.N.D. *Early Christian Creeds*. Longmans, Green and Co., 1972.

7. Rahner, Karl. *The Trinity*. Herder & Herder, 1997.

8. Ratzinger, Joseph (Pope Benedict XVI). *Introduction to Christianity*. Ignatius Press, 2004.

9. Newman, John Henry. *An Essay on the Development of Christian Doctrine*. Longmans, Green and Co., 1909.

10. Pelikan, Jaroslav. *The Christian Tradition: A History of the Development of Doctrine, Vol. 1: The Emergence of the Catholic Tradition (100-600)*. University of Chicago Press, 1971.

Chapter 21: Core Prayers of Catholic Devotional Practice

1. *The Holy Bible, New Revised Standard Version*. Division of Christian Education of the National Council of the Churches of Christ in the United States of America, 1989.

2. *Catechism of the Catholic Church. 2nd Edition*. Libreria Editrice Vaticana, 1997.

3. Sheen, Fulton J. *The World's First Love: Mary, Mother of God*. Ignatius Press, 1996.

4. John Paul II, Pope. *Rosarium Virginis Mariae (On the Most Holy Rosary)*. Libreria Editrice Vaticana, 2002.

5. Hahn, Scott. *Hail, Holy Queen: The Mother of God in the Word of God*. Doubleday, 2001.

6. Ratzinger, Joseph (Pope Benedict XVI). *Introduction to Christianity*. Ignatius Press, 2004.

7. Schreck, Alan. *Catholic and Christian: An Explanation of Commonly Misunderstood Catholic Beliefs*. Servant Books, 2004.

8. de Montfort, St. Louis. *True Devotion to Mary*. TAN Books, 2010.

9. Hardon, John A. *The Catholic Catechism: A Contemporary Catechism of the Teachings of the Catholic Church*. Image, 1975.

10. Brown, Raymond E. *The Birth of the Messiah: A Commentary on the Infancy Narratives in Matthew and Luke*. Yale University Press, 1999.

Chapter 22: The Liturgical Calendar

1. *The Holy Bible, New Revised Standard Version*. Division of Christian Education of the National Council of the Churches of Christ in the United States of America, 1989.

2. *Catechism of the Catholic Church. 2nd Edition*. Libreria Editrice Vaticana, 1997.

3. *General Norms for the Liturgical Year and the Calendar*. Libreria Editrice Vaticana, 1969.

4. Martimort, A.G., ed. *The Church at Prayer: An Introduction to the Liturgy. Vol. 4: The Liturgy and Time*. Liturgical Press, 1986.

5. Parsch, Pius. *The Church's Year of Grace*. The Liturgical Press, 1957.

6. Johnson, Maxwell E. *Between Memory and Hope: Readings on the Liturgical Year*. Liturgical Press, 2000.

7. Nocent, Adrian. *The Liturgical Year: Advent, Christmas, Epiphany*. Liturgical Press, 1977.

8. Foley, Leonard. *Saint of the Day: Lives, Lessons, and Feasts*. Franciscan Media, 2009.

9. Holweck, Frederick. *A Biographical Dictionary of the Saints: With a Calendar of Their Feasts*. B. Herder, 1924.

10. Wuerl, Donald W. *The Catholic Way: Faith for Living Today*. Doubleday, 2001.

Part V: Being Catholic is More than Going to Church

Chapter 23: What Does it Means to Be Catholic?

1. *The Holy Bible, New Revised Standard Version*. Division of Christian Education of the National Council of the Churches of Christ in the United States of America, 1989.

2. *Catechism of the Catholic Church. 2nd Edition*. Libreria Editrice Vaticana, 1997.

3. Sheed, Frank. *Theology for Beginners*. Servant Books, 1981.

4. Hahn, Scott. *The Lamb's Supper: The Mass as Heaven on Earth*. Doubleday, 1999.

5. Ratzinger, Joseph (Pope Benedict XVI*). Introduction to Christianity*. Ignatius Press, 2004.

6. John Paul II, Pope. Ecclesia de Eucharistia. Libreria Editrice Vaticana, 2003.

7. Hardon, John A. *The Catholic Catechism: A Contemporary Catechism of the Teachings of the Catholic Church*. Image, 1975.

8. Martos, Joseph. *Doors to the Sacred: A Historical Introduction to Sacraments in the Catholic Church*. Liguori Publications, 2001.

9. Schreck, Alan. Catholic and Christian: *An Explanation of Commonly Misunderstood Catholic Beliefs*. Servant Books, 2004.

10. Barron, Robert. *Catholicism: A Journey to the Heart of the Faith*. Image, 2011.

Chapter 24: Learning, Reading and Contemplating Sacred Texts (The Holy Bible, The New Testament, etc.)

1. *The Holy Bible, New Revised Standard Version.* Division of Christian Education of the National Council of the Churches of Christ in the United States of America, 1989.

2. *Catechism of the Catholic Church. 2nd Edition.* Libreria Editrice Vaticana, 1997.

3. Augustine of Hippo. *Confessions.* Oxford University Press, 1998.

4. Brown, Raymond E. *An Introduction to the New Testament.* Yale University Press, 1997.

5. Hahn, Scott. *A Father Who Keeps His Promises: God's Covenant Love in Scripture.* Servant Publications, 1998.

6. Keating, Karl. *Catholicism and Fundamentalism: The Attack on "Romanism" by "Bible Christians."* Ignatius Press, 1988.

7. Lewis, C.S. *Mere Christianity.* HarperOne, 2001.

8. Pitre, Brant. *Jesus and the Jewish Roots of the Eucharist: Unlocking the Secrets of the Last Supper.* Image Books, 2011.

9. Pope Benedict XVI (Ratzinger, Joseph). *Jesus of Nazareth: From the Baptism in the Jordan to the Transfiguration.* Doubleday, 2007.

10. Sheed, Frank. *Theology for Beginners.* Servant Books, 1981.

Chapter 25: Going to Mass

1. *The Holy Bible, New Revised Standard Version.* Division of Christian Education of the National Council of the Churches of Christ in the United States of America, 1989.

2. *Catechism of the Catholic Church. 2nd Edition.* Libreria Editrice Vaticana, 1997.

3. Hahn, Scott. *The Lamb's Supper: The Mass as Heaven on Earth.* Doubleday, 1999.

4. Martos, Joseph. *Doors to the Sacred: A Historical Introduction to Sacraments in the Catholic Church.* Liguori Publications, 2001.

5. Ratzinger, Joseph (Pope Benedict XVI*).* *The Spirit of the Liturgy.* Ignatius Press, 2000.

6. Sheen, Fulton J. *Life of Christ.* Image Books, 2008.

7. John Paul II, Pope. *Ecclesia de Eucharistia*. Libreria Editrice Vaticana, 2003.

8. Barron, Robert. *Eucharist*. Orbis Books, 2008.

9. Martimort, A.G., ed. *The Church at Prayer: An Introduction to the Liturgy*. Liturgical Press, 1987.

10. Hardon, John A. *The Catholic Catechism: A Contemporary Catechism of the Teachings of the Catholic Church*. Image, 1975.

Church 26: Volunteering at Church

1. *The Holy Bible, New Revised Standard Version*. Division of Christian Education of the National Council of the Churches of Christ in the United States of America, 1989.

2. *Catechism of the Catholic Church. 2nd Edition*. Libreria Editrice Vaticana, 1997.

3. John Paul II, Pope. *Christifideles Laici (The Lay Members of Christ's Faithful People)*. Libreria Editrice Vaticana, 1988.

4. Hahn, Scott. *Evangelizing Catholics: A Mission Manual for the New Evangelization*. Our Sunday Visitor, 2014.

5. Barron, Robert. *Catholicism: A Journey to the Heart of the Faith*. Image, 2011.

6. Nouwen, Henri J.M. *The Return of the Prodigal Son: A Story of Homecoming*. Image Books, 1992.

7. Keating, Karl. *Catholicism and Fundamentalism: The Attack on "Romanism" by "Bible Christians."* Ignatius Press, 1988.

8. Martos, Joseph. *Doors to the Sacred: A Historical Introduction to Sacraments in the Catholic Church*. Liguori Publications, 2001.

9. Sheed, Frank. *Theology for Beginners*. Servant Books, 1981.

10. Weddell, Sherry A. *Forming Intentional Disciples: The Path to Knowing and Following Jesus*. Our Sunday Visitor, 2012.

Chapter 27: Fellowship with Others – Locally, Nationally, Worldwide

1. *The Holy Bible, New Revised Standard Version*. Division of Christian Education of the National Council of the Churches of Christ in the United States of America, 1989.

2. *Catechism of the Catholic Church. 2nd Edition.* Libreria Editrice Vaticana, 1997.

3. John Paul II, Pope. *Christifideles Laici (The Lay Members of Christ's Faithful People).* Libreria Editrice Vaticana, 1988.

4. Benedict XVI, Pope. *Deus Caritas Est (God Is Love).* Libreria Editrice Vaticana, 2005.

5. Hahn, Scott. *Evangelizing Catholics: A Mission Manual for the New Evangelization.* Our Sunday Visitor, 2014.

6. Barron, Robert. *Catholicism: A Journey to the Heart of the Faith.* Image, 2011.

7. Nouwen, Henri J.M. *Community and Growth.* Paulist Press, 1979.

8. Weddell, Sherry A. *Forming Intentional Disciples: The Path to Knowing and Following Jesus.* Our Sunday Visitor, 2012.

9. Second Vatican Council. *Lumen Gentium (Dogmatic Constitution on the Church).* Libreria Editrice Vaticana, 1964.

10. Francis, Pope. *Fratelli Tutti (On Fraternity and Social Friendship).* Libreria Editrice Vaticana, 2020.

Chapter 28: Service to Others – Elderly, Single Parents, Children, etc.

1. *The Holy Bible, New Revised Standard Version.* Division of Christian Education of the National Council of the Churches of Christ in the United States of America, 1989.

2. *Catechism of the Catholic Church. 2nd Edition.* Libreria Editrice Vaticana, 1997.

3. John Paul II, Pope. *Evangelium Vitae (The Gospel of Life).* Libreria Editrice Vaticana, 1995.

4. Benedict XVI, Pope. *Deus Caritas Est (God Is Love)*. Libreria Editrice Vaticana, 2005.

5. Francis, Pope. *Fratelli Tutti (On Fraternity and Social Friendship)*. Libreria Editrice Vaticana, 2020.

6. Hahn, Scott. *The Corporal Works of Mommy (And Daddy Too): A Catholic Parent's Guide to Feeding, Clothing, and Sheltering Your Family*. Emmaus Road Publishing, 2015.

7. Nouwen, Henri J.M. *The Wounded Healer: Ministry in Contemporary Society*. Image Books, 1979.

8. Catholic Relief Services. *Catholic Social Teaching: Our Best Kept Secret*. Orbis Books, 2003.

9. United States Conference of Catholic Bishops. *Communities of Salt and Light: Reflections on the Social Mission of the Parish*. USCCB Publishing, 1994.

10. Weddell, Sherry A. *Forming Intentional Disciples: The Path to Knowing and Following Jesus*. Our Sunday Visitor, 2012.

Chapter 29: Church Ministries – Prayer Ministry, Sick Ministry, Youth Ministry, Food Pantry, etc.

1. *The Holy Bible, New Revised Standard Version*. Division of Christian Education of the National Council of the Churches of Christ in the United States of America, 1989.

2. *Catechism of the Catholic Church. 2nd Edition*. Libreria Editrice Vaticana, 1997.

3. John Paul II, Pope. *Christifideles Laici (The Lay Members of Christ's Faithful People)*. Libreria Editrice Vaticana, 1988.

4. Benedict XVI, Pope. *Deus Caritas Est (God Is Love)*. Libreria Editrice Vaticana, 2005.

5. Francis, Pope. *Evangelii Gaudium (The Joy of the Gospel)*. Libreria Editrice Vaticana, 2013.

6. United States Conference of Catholic Bishops. *Communities of Salt and Light: Reflections on the Social Mission of the Parish*. USCCB Publishing, 1994.

7. Hahn, Scott. *Evangelizing Catholics: A Mission Manual for the New Evangelization*. Our Sunday Visitor, 2014.

8. Weddell, Sherry A. *Forming Intentional Disciples: The Path to Knowing and Following Jesus*. Our Sunday Visitor, 2012.

9. Nouwen, Henri J.M. *The Wounded Healer: Ministry in Contemporary Society*. Image Books, 1979.

10. Catholic Relief Services. *Catholic Social Teaching: Our Best Kept Secret*. Orbis Books, 2003.

Part VI: Suggestions for Growth in The Catholic Faith

Chapter 30: Catholic Classes, Workshops and Seminars

1. *The Holy Bible, New Revised Standard Version*. Division of Christian Education of the National Council of the Churches of Christ in the United States of America, 1989.

2. *Catechism of the Catholic Church. 2nd Edition*. Libreria Editrice Vaticana, 1997.

3. John Paul II, Pope. *Catechesi Tradendae (On Catechesis in Our Time)*. Libreria Editrice Vaticana, 1979.

4. Benedict XVI, Pope. *Verbum Domini (The Word of the Lord)*. Libreria Editrice Vaticana, 2010.

5. Francis, Pope. *Evangelii Gaudium (The Joy of the Gospel)*. Libreria Editrice Vaticana, 2013.

6. United States Conference of Catholic Bishops. *Our Hearts Were Burning Within Us: A Pastoral Plan for Adult Faith Formation in the United States*. USCCB Publishing, 1999.

7. Weddell, Sherry A. *Forming Intentional Disciples: The Path to Knowing and Following Jesus*. Our Sunday Visitor, 2012.

8. Hahn, Scott. *Evangelizing Catholics: A Mission Manual for the New Evangelization*. Our Sunday Visitor, 2014.

9. Ratzinger, Joseph Cardinal (Pope Benedict XVI). *Introduction to Christianity*. Ignatius Press, 2004.

10. Kelly, Matthew. *Rediscover Catholicism: A Spiritual Guide to Living with Passion & Purpose*. Beacon Publishing, 2010.

Chapter 31: Catholic Spiritual Direction and Mentoring

1. *The Holy Bible, New Revised Standard Version*. Division of Christian Education of the National Council of the Churches of Christ in the United States of America, 1989.

2. *Catechism of the Catholic Church. 2nd Edition*. Libreria Editrice Vaticana, 1997.

3. Barry, William A., and William J. Connolly. *The Practice of Spiritual Direction*. HarperOne, 2009.

4. Benner, David G. *Sacred Companions: The Gift of Spiritual Friendship & Direction*. InterVarsity Press, 2002.

5. Francis, Pope. *Gaudete et Exsultate (Rejoice and Be Glad): On the Call to Holiness in Today's World*. Libreria Editrice Vaticana, 2018.

6. John Paul II, Pope. *Pastores Dabo Vobis (I Will Give You Shepherds): On the Formation of Priests in the Circumstances of the Present Day*. Libreria Editrice Vaticana, 1992.

7. Dubay, Thomas. *Seeking Spiritual Direction: How to Grow the Divine Life Within*. Servant Books, 1993.

8. Nouwen, Henri J.M. *The Wounded Healer: Ministry in Contemporary Society*. Image Books, 1979.

9. USCCB Committee on Clergy, Consecrated Life, and Vocations. *Spiritual Direction: A Guide for Sharing the Father's Love*. United States Conference of Catholic Bishops, 2014.

10. Weddell, Sherry A. *Forming Intentional Disciples: The Path to Knowing and Following Jesus*. Our Sunday Visitor, 2012.

Chapter 32: Catholic Church Elders

1. *The Holy Bible, New Revised Standard Version*. Division of Christian Education of the National Council of the Churches of Christ in the United States of America, 1989.

2. *Catechism of the Catholic Church. 2nd Edition*. Libreria Editrice Vaticana, 1997.

3. John Paul II, Pope. *Letter to the Elderly*. Libreria Editrice Vaticana, 1999.

4. Benedict XVI, Pope. *Spe Salvi (In Hope We Are Saved)*. Libreria Editrice Vaticana, 2007.

5. Francis, Pope. *Evangelii Gaudium (The Joy of the Gospel)*. Libreria Editrice Vaticana, 2013.

6. Francis, Pope. *Amoris Laetitia (The Joy of Love)*. Libreria Editrice Vaticana, 2016.

7. Nouwen, Henri J.M. Aging: *The Fulfillment of Life*. Image Books, 1974.

8. Havighurst, Robert J. *Successful Aging*. Simon & Schuster, 1963.

9. Butler, Robert N. *The Longevity Revolution: The Benefits and Challenges of Living a Long Life*. PublicAffairs, 2008.

10. Weddell, Sherry A. *Forming Intentional Disciples: The Path to Knowing and Following Jesus*. Our Sunday Visitor, 2012.

Chapter 33: Catholicism and The Future

1. *The Holy Bible, New Revised Standard Version*. Division of Christian Education of the National Council of the Churches of Christ in the United States of America, 1989.

2. *Catechism of the Catholic Church. 2nd Edition*. Libreria Editrice Vaticana, 1997.

3. Francis, Pope. *Evangelii Gaudium (The Joy of the Gospel)*. Libreria Editrice Vaticana, 2013.

4. Francis, Pope. *Laudato Si' (On Care for Our Common Home)*. Libreria Editrice Vaticana, 2015.

5. John Paul II, Pope. *Fides et Ratio (Faith and Reason)*. Libreria Editrice Vaticana, 1998.

6. Benedict XVI, Pope. *Caritas in Veritate (Charity in Truth)*. Libreria Editrice Vaticana, 2009.

7. Ratzinger, Joseph (Pope Benedict XVI). *Introduction to Christianity*. Ignatius Press, 2004.

8. Weddell, Sherry A. *Forming Intentional Disciples: The Path to Knowing and Following Jesus*. Our Sunday Visitor, 2012.

9. Martin, James. *The Jesuit Guide to (Almost) Everything: A Spirituality for Real Life*. HarperOne, 2010.

10. Barron, Robert. *Catholicism: A Journey to the Heart of the Faith*. Image Books, 2011.

GLOSSARY OF TERMS

A

- **Adoration:** Worship focused on Christ's real presence in the Eucharist.
- **Advent:** Liturgical season of preparation for Christ's coming, leading to Christmas.
- **Aquinas, Thomas:** Medieval theologian known for works like *Summa Theologica*.
- **Arianism:** Early Christian heresy denying Jesus' full divinity.
- **Archangels:** High-ranking angels like Michael, Gabriel, and Raphael.
- **Aquarian Gospel of Jesus the Christ:** New Age text claiming to document Jesus' life, including his "lost years."
- **Augustine of Hippo:** Early theologian known for *On the Trinity*, foundational in Christian theology.

B

- **Baptism:** First sacrament of initiation in the Catholic Church, cleansing original sin.
- **Beatitudes:** Teachings of Jesus in Matthew 5:3-12, describing those blessed in the Kingdom of GOD.
- **Biblical Meditation:** Spiritual practice of contemplation on GOD, scripture, or divine truths.
- **Body of Christ:** Term describing the Church, emphasizing the unity of believers with Christ as the head.

C

- **Catechism of the Catholic Church:** Official text outlining Catholic teachings and practices.
- **Catechesis:** Religious instruction and formation in the Christian faith.
- **Chakra:** Energy centers within the body influencing physical, emotional, and spiritual well-being.

- **Christ Consciousness:** Awareness of Christ's presence within, guiding thoughts and actions.
- **Christmas:** Liturgical season celebrating Jesus' birth, beginning December 25.
- **Communion:** Receiving the Body and Blood of Christ in the Eucharist.
- **Communion of Saints:** Spiritual union of all Christians, living and deceased.
- **Compassion:** Deep awareness and sympathy for another's suffering, with a desire to alleviate it.
- **Community:** Group sharing common beliefs, values, and practices, especially in the Church.
- **Consubstantial:** Term from the Nicene Creed describing Jesus' relationship with GOD the Father.
- **Consecration:** Moment in Mass when bread and wine become the Body and Blood of Christ.
- **Contemplatio:** Fourth step in Lectio Divina, resting in GOD's presence.
- **Contemplative Prayer:** Prayer focused on resting in GOD's presence.
- **Council of Constantinople:** 381 AD council expanding the Nicene Creed, affirming the Trinity.
- **Council of Nicaea:** 325 AD council formulating the Nicene Creed, affirming Jesus' divinity.
- **Creation:** The natural world as a reflection of GOD's glory.
- **Creed:** Formal statement of Christian beliefs, such as the Nicene Creed.

D

- **Discernment:** Seeking GOD's guidance in making decisions aligned with His will.
- **Discipleship:** Following and living according to Jesus' teachings.
- **Divine Incarnation:** Christian belief in GOD becoming human in Jesus Christ.

- **Divine Inspiration:** Belief that Bible authors were guided by the Holy Spirit.
- **Divine Office (Liturgy of the Hours):** Daily prayers marking hours of the day in the Catholic Church.
- **Doxology:** Hymn of praise to GOD, such as the "Glory Be."

E

- **Easter:** Liturgical season celebrating Jesus' resurrection, lasting 50 days.
- **Ecumenism:** Movement promoting unity among Christian denominations.
- **Ecumenical Dialogue:** Conversations promoting understanding among different Christian denominations.
- **Energy Field:** Concept of an invisible force surrounding the body, reflecting one's state.
- **Energy Healing:** Practice of balancing the body's energy for health.
- **Environmental Stewardship:** Responsibility to care for and protect the environment as GOD's creation.
- **Eucharist:** Sacrament of the Body and Blood of Christ in the Mass.
- **Examen:** Daily reflection on the day's events to discern GOD's presence.

F

- **Faith Formation:** Process of deepening understanding of the Catholic faith through education and prayer.
- **Faith Journaling:** Writing reflections and prayers to deepen spiritual growth.
- **Feast Days:** Days dedicated to celebrating significant events in Christ's life and the saints.
- **Fellowship:** Spiritual and social bond among Church members.
- **Forgiveness:** Spiritual practice of releasing grievances, recognizing the divine nature in others.
- **Free Will:** GOD-given ability to make independent choices, reflecting human dignity.

G

- **Glory Be:** Traditional prayer praising the Holy Trinity.
- **Gnostic:** Relating to early Christian texts emphasizing esoteric knowledge.
- **Gospel:** First four books of the New Testament recounting Jesus' life and teachings.
- **Gratitude Journaling:** Daily practice of recording things one is thankful for.
- **Gregorian Chant:** Ancient form of plainchant in the Catholic Church.
- **Guardian Angels:** Spiritual beings assigned by GOD to protect and guide individuals.
- **Great Commission:** Jesus' instruction to make disciples of all nations, found in Matthew 28:19-20.
- **Great Commandment:** Jesus' instruction to "love your neighbor as yourself."

H

- **Hail Mary:** Prayer asking for the intercession of the Blessed Virgin Mary.
- **Healing Meditation:** Visualizing GOD's healing light for restoration.
- **Heart Chakra:** Energy center associated with love and compassion.
- **Hidden Years:** Period in Jesus' life between childhood and public ministry.
- **Holy Family:** Jesus, Mary, and Joseph, serving as the model of family life.
- **Holy Orders:** Sacrament ordaining men as deacons, priests, or bishops.
- **Holy Spirit:** Third person of the Holy Trinity, guiding and empowering believers.
- **Holy Trinity:** Christian doctrine of one GOD in three persons: Father, Son, and Holy Spirit.
- **Holy Week:** Final week of Lent, leading up to Easter, including key liturgical events.

- **Homily:** Sermon explaining scriptures during Mass.
- **Hymn:** Religious song or poem of praise to GOD.

I

- **Imago Dei:** Concept that humans are created in GOD's image.
- **Incarnation:** Belief in GOD becoming human in Jesus Christ.
- **Intercessory Prayer:** Praying on behalf of others for GOD's assistance.
- **Invocation:** Prayer calling upon a spiritual being for guidance or protection.

J

- **Jesus Prayer:** Simple prayer focusing on Christ: "Lord Jesus Christ, Son of GOD, have mercy on me, a sinner."
- **John 10:30:** Passage where Jesus declares, "I and the Father are one."
- **John 14:26:** Passage describing the Holy Spirit as the Advocate who teaches and reminds believers.
- **Joyful Mysteries:** Events in the life of Jesus and Mary meditated upon in the Rosary.
- **Judgment:** Concept of divine assessment of souls after death.

K

- **Kingdom of GOD:** Central concept in Jesus' teachings, referring to GOD's reign manifested in believers' lives.

L

- **Laying on of Hands:** Christian practice invoking GOD's healing power through physical touch.
- **Lector:** Person who reads scripture passages during Mass.
- **Lectio Divina:** Traditional practice of scripture reading, meditation, and prayer.
- **Lent:** 40-day liturgical season of penance leading up to Easter.
- **Liturgical Calendar:** Cycle of seasons and feasts structuring Church worship.

- **Liturgy:** Official public worship of the Church, especially the Mass.
- **Logos:** Greek term meaning "Word," used in the Gospel of John to describe Jesus.
- **Luke 2:41-52:** Passage recounting Jesus in the Temple at age twelve.

M

- **Mass:** Central act of Catholic worship, including the Liturgy of the Word and Eucharist.
- **Meditation:** Spiritual practice of focused reflection on scripture or GOD's presence.
- **Messiah:** The anointed one promised in the Old Testament, fulfilled in Jesus Christ.
- **Ministry:** Service or role within the Church, often involving volunteer work.
- **Mindful Movement:** Physical activities performed with awareness and intention.
- **Mindful Presence:** Practice of being fully present and attentive in each moment.
- **Mindful Walking:** Meditative practice of walking with full awareness.
- **Mystical Theology:** Spiritual tradition emphasizing direct experience of GOD.
- **Mysticism:** Tradition of seeking direct knowledge of GOD through prayer and contemplation.

N

- **Nag Hammadi Scriptures:** Collection of early Christian and Gnostic texts discovered in 1945.
- **Nativity:** Birth of Jesus Christ, celebrated on December 25th.
- **New Testament:** Second part of the Christian Bible, focusing on Jesus' life and teachings.
- **Nicene Creed:** Profession of faith formulated by the Councils of Nicaea and Constantinople.

- **Novena:** Nine-day period of prayer for specific intentions or devotions.

O

- **Old Testament:** First part of the Christian Bible, detailing GOD's covenant with Israel.
- **Oratio:** Third step in Lectio Divina, responding to GOD in prayer after meditation.
- **Orthodoxy:** Adherence to traditional teachings of the Church, particularly in doctrine.
- **Our Father:** Central prayer taught by Jesus, also known as the Lord's Prayer.

P

- **Parish:** Local church community under the care of a pastor.
- **Paschal Triduum:** Three-day period commemorating Jesus' Passion, Death, and Resurrection.
- **Patience:** Capacity to accept delay or suffering without anger, modeled by Jesus.
- **Pentecost:** Feast celebrating the descent of the Holy Spirit and the birth of the Church.
- **Prayer:** Communication with GOD involving praise, confession, and requests.
- **Prayer Journaling:** Writing down prayers to reflect on spiritual growth.
- **Preferential Option for the Poor:** Catholic teaching prioritizing the needs of the poor and vulnerable.
- **Proverbs 16:31:** Scripture highlighting the value of wisdom and righteousness in old age.

R

- **Real Presence:** Catholic doctrine of Jesus' true presence in the Eucharist.
- **Reconciliation:** Sacrament of confessing sins and receiving absolution, also known as Confession.

- **Reflection:** Spiritual practice of contemplating experiences in relation to faith.
- **Root Chakra:** Energy center associated with stability and grounding.
- **Rosary:** Prayer involving the repetition of Hail Marys while meditating on Christ's life.

S

- **Sacraments:** Sacred rites instituted by Christ, essential for spiritual growth.
- **Sacred Liturgy:** Formal public worship, especially the Eucharist.
- **Sacred Music:** Music composed for religious worship.
- **Sacred Space:** Area designated for prayer and meditation.
- **Sacred Texts:** Writings considered holy and authoritative, such as the Bible.
- **Sacrosanctum Concilium:** Vatican II document on liturgical reform and music.
- **Saints' Days:** Liturgical days honoring holy men and women.
- **Salvation:** Deliverance from sin and its consequences, leading to eternal life with GOD.
- **Scripture:** Sacred writings in the Bible, inspired by GOD.
- **Second Vatican Council:** 1962-1965 council addressing Church reforms and relations with the modern world.
- **Sermon on the Mount:** Collection of Jesus' teachings in Matthew 5-7, emphasizing spiritual and ethical living.
- **Service:** Acts of helping others, expressing faith in practical ways.
- **Sign of the Cross:** Gesture and prayer invoking the Holy Trinity.
- **Single Parents:** Individuals raising children alone, often requiring community support.
- **Social Justice:** Catholic teaching emphasizing fairness, equality, and respect for all.
- **Solar Plexus Chakra:** Energy center associated with personal power and self-esteem.

- **Solidarity:** Unity and mutual support within a group, especially for the marginalized.
- **Spiritual Awakening:** Becoming more aware of one's spiritual nature and connection to GOD.
- **Spiritual Companions:** Beings like Guardian Angels and Spirit Guides offering guidance.
- **Spiritual Direction:** Guidance in one's spiritual journey to discern GOD's will.
- **Spiritual Fatigue:** State of exhaustion or disconnection from spiritual life.
- **Spiritual Gifts:** Special abilities given by the Holy Spirit for service.
- **Spiritual Growth:** Developing a deeper relationship with GOD and aligning with His will.
- **Spiritual Healing:** Seeking wholeness through prayer and spiritual practices.
- **Spiritual Journal:** Diary for recording spiritual reflections and prayers.
- **Spiritual Learning Plan:** Personalized plan for deepening knowledge of Catholic faith.
- **Spiritual Retreat:** Time dedicated to prayer and reflection, often away from distractions.
- **Spiritual Tools:** Practices like prayer and meditation for deepening faith.
- **Spirit Guides:** Beings believed to assist in one's spiritual journey.
- **Service:** Acts of helping or supporting others, especially in a Christian context.

T

- **Temple:** Holy place in Jerusalem where Jews worshipped GOD, significant in Jesus' life.
- **Throat Chakra:** Energy center associated with communication and truth.
- **Trinity:** Christian doctrine of one GOD in three persons: Father, Son, and Holy Spirit.

- **Trinitarian Model:** Concept of Church relationships reflecting the unity within the Holy Trinity.
- **Transubstantiation:** Belief that bread and wine become Christ's Body and Blood during Mass.

U

- **Union with GOD:** Ultimate goal of mysticism, experiencing deep connection with the divine.
- **Universal Call to Holiness:** Belief that all Christians are called to live holy lives.
- **Universal Church:** Entirety of the Catholic Church, encompassing all believers.

V

- **Vatican II:** Ecumenical council (1962-1965) that brought significant changes to the Church.
- **Vestments:** Garments worn by clergy during liturgy, varying by season and occasion.
- **Virtue:** Morally good trait, exemplified by Jesus.
- **Visualization:** Meditation technique imagining a scene or divine presence.
- **Vocation:** Calling from GOD to a particular way of life, such as marriage or priesthood.
- **Vocal Prayer:** Prayer spoken aloud or silently, like the Our Father.
- **Volunteer:** Person who freely offers time and talents to help others.
- **Volunteering:** Offering time and talents in service to others.

W

- **Waiting on GOD:** Trusting in GOD's timing during periods of delay.
- **Wisdom:** Divine gift for making sound judgments and decisions.
- **Wisdom Journal:** Journal for recording insights and advice, often from elders.

Y

- **Youth Ministry:** Ministry supporting the spiritual growth of young people.

NOTES:

PRAYERS AND OTHER RESOURSES

Prayers

1. The Sign of the Cross

- *In the name of the Father, and of the Son, and of the Holy Spirit. Amen.*

2. The Lord's Prayer (Our Father)

- *Our Father, who art in heaven, hallowed be thy name;
Thy kingdom come;
Thy will be done on earth as it is in heaven.
Give us this day our daily bread;
And forgive us our trespasses, as we forgive those who trespass against us;
And lead us not into temptation but deliver us from evil.
Amen.*

3. Hail Mary

- *Hail Mary, full of grace, the Lord is with thee;
Blessed art thou among women, and blessed is the fruit of thy womb, Jesus.
Holy Mary, Mother of GOD, pray for us sinners, now and at the hour of our death. Amen.*

4. Glory Be (Doxology)

- *Glory be to the Father, and to the Son, and to the Holy Spirit;
As it was in the beginning, is now, and ever shall be, world without end. Amen.*

5. Apostles' Creed

- *I believe in GOD, the Father almighty, Creator of heaven and earth,
and in Jesus Christ, His only Son, our Lord,
who was conceived by the Holy Spirit, born of the Virgin Mary,*

suffered under Pontius Pilate, was crucified, died and was buried;
He descended into hell; on the third day He rose again from the dead;
He ascended into heaven, and is seated at the right hand of GOD the Father almighty;
from there He will come to judge the living and the dead.
I believe in the Holy Spirit, the holy catholic Church, the communion of saints,
the forgiveness of sins, the resurrection of the body, and life everlasting. Amen.

6. Nicene Creed

- I believe in one GOD, the Father almighty,
  maker of heaven and earth, of all things visible and invisible.
  I believe in one Lord Jesus Christ, the Only Begotten Son of GOD,
  born of the Father before all ages.
  GOD from GOD, Light from Light, true GOD from true GOD,
  begotten, not made, consubstantial with the Father;
  through Him all things were made.
  For us men and for our salvation He came down from heaven,
  and by the Holy Spirit was incarnate of the Virgin Mary, and became man.
  For our sake He was crucified under Pontius Pilate,
  He suffered death and was buried, and rose again on the third day
  in accordance with the Scriptures.
  He ascended into heaven and is seated at the right hand of the Father.
  He will come again in glory to judge the living and the dead
  and His kingdom will have no end.
  I believe in the Holy Spirit, the Lord, the giver of life,
  who proceeds from the Father and the Son,
  who with the Father and the Son is adored and glorified,
  who has spoken through the prophets.

I believe in one, holy, catholic and apostolic Church.
I confess one Baptism for the forgiveness of sins
and I look forward to the resurrection of the dead
and the life of the world to come. Amen.

7. Hail Holy Queen (Salve Regina)

- Hail, holy Queen, Mother of mercy,
  our life, our sweetness, and our hope.
  To thee do we cry, poor banished children of Eve;
  to thee do we send up our sighs,
  mourning and weeping in this valley of tears.
  Turn then, most gracious advocate,
  thine eyes of mercy toward us;
  and after this our exile
  show unto us the blessed fruit of thy womb, Jesus.
  O clement, O loving, O sweet Virgin Mary.
  Pray for us, O holy Mother of GOD,
  that we may be made worthy of the promises of Christ.
  Amen.

8. Memorare

- Remember, O most gracious Virgin Mary,
  that never was it known
  that anyone who fled to thy protection,
  implored thy help,
  or sought thy intercession was left unaided.
  Inspired by this confidence,
  I fly unto thee,
  O Virgin of virgins, my Mother;
  to thee do I come,
  before thee I stand, sinful and sorrowful.
  O Mother of the Word Incarnate,
  despise not my petitions,
  but in thy mercy hear and answer me. Amen.

9. Act of Contrition

- O my GOD, I am heartily sorry for having offended You,
  and I detest all my sins, because I dread the loss of heaven
  and the pains of hell; but most of all because they offend

You,
my GOD, who are all good and deserving of all my love.
I firmly resolve, with the help of Your grace,
to confess my sins, to do penance, and to amend my life.
Amen.

10. The Angelus

- *The Angel of the Lord declared to Mary:
And she conceived of the Holy Spirit.
Hail Mary, full of grace... (Hail Mary)
Behold the handmaid of the Lord:
Be it done unto me according to Thy word.
Hail Mary, full of grace... (Hail Mary)
And the Word was made Flesh:
And dwelt among us.
Hail Mary, full of grace... (Hail Mary)
Pray for us, O Holy Mother of GOD,
that we may be made worthy of the promises of Christ.
Let us pray: Pour forth, we beseech Thee, O Lord,
Thy grace into our hearts,
that we, to whom the Incarnation of Christ, Thy Son,
was made known by the message of an angel,
may by His Passion and Cross
be brought to the glory of His Resurrection,
through the same Christ Our Lord. Amen.*

11. The Magnificat

- *My soul proclaims the greatness of the Lord;
my spirit rejoices in GOD my Savior
for He has looked with favor on His lowly servant.
From this day all generations will call me blessed:
the Almighty has done great things for me,
and holy is His Name.
He has mercy on those who fear Him
in every generation.
He has shown the strength of His arm,
He has scattered the proud in their conceit.
He has cast down the mighty from their thrones,
and has lifted up the lowly.*

*He has filled the hungry with good things,
and the rich He has sent away empty.
He has come to the help of His servant Israel
for He has remembered His promise of mercy,
the promise He made to our fathers,
to Abraham and his children forever.*

12. The Rosary

- *A prayer that includes the recitation of the Our Father, Hail Mary, and Glory Be, while meditating on the Mysteries of the life of Christ and the Virgin Mary.*

13. The Fatima Prayer

- *O my Jesus, forgive us our sins,
  save us from the fires of hell,
  lead all souls to Heaven,
  especially those in most need of Thy mercy. Amen.*

14. The Divine Mercy Chaplet

- *Eternal Father, I offer you the Body and Blood,
  Soul and Divinity of Your dearly beloved Son,
  Our Lord Jesus Christ,
  in atonement for our sins and those of the whole world.
  For the sake of His sorrowful Passion,
  have mercy on us and on the whole world.*

15. St. Michael the Archangel Prayer

- *St. Michael the Archangel, defend us in battle,
  be our defense against the wickedness and snares of the devil;
  may GOD rebuke him, we humbly pray;
  and do thou, O Prince of the heavenly host,
  by the power of GOD, thrust into hell Satan
  and all the evil spirits who prowl about the world
  seeking the ruin of souls. Amen.*

16. Act of Faith

- *O my GOD, I firmly believe
  that You are one GOD in three Divine Persons:
  Father, Son, and Holy Spirit.
  I believe that Your Divine Son became man
  and died for our sins,
  and that He will come to judge the living and the dead.
  I believe these and all the truths
  which the Holy Catholic Church teaches,
  because You have revealed them,
  who can neither deceive nor be deceived. Amen.*

17. Act of Hope

- *O my GOD,
  relying on Your infinite goodness and promises,
  I hope to obtain pardon of my sins,
  the help of Your grace, and life everlasting,
  through the merits of Jesus Christ,
  my Lord and Redeemer. Amen.*

18. Act of Charity (Love)

- *O my GOD,
  I love You above all things,
  with my whole heart and soul,
  because You are all good and worthy of all my love.
  I love my neighbor as myself for the love of You.
  I forgive all who have injured me
  and ask pardon of all whom I have injured. Amen.*

19. Prayer to the Holy Spirit (Come, Holy Spirit)

- *Come, Holy Spirit,
  fill the hearts of Your faithful
  and kindle in them the fire of Your love.
  Send forth Your Spirit and they shall be created,
  and You shall renew the face of the earth.
  Let us pray.
  O GOD, who by the light of the Holy Spirit,
  did instruct the hearts of the faithful,
  grant that by the same Holy Spirit*

we may be truly wise and ever enjoy His consolations,
through Christ Our Lord. Amen.

20. Morning Offering

- O Jesus, through the Immaculate Heart of Mary,
  I offer You my prayers, works, joys, and sufferings of this day
  for all the intentions of Your Sacred Heart,
  in union with the Holy Sacrifice of the Mass throughout the world,
  for the salvation of souls,
  the reparation of sins,
  the reunion of all Christians,
  and in particular for the intentions of the Holy Father this month. Amen.

21. Guardian Angel Prayer

- Angel of GOD, my guardian dear,
  to whom GOD's love commits me here,
  ever this day be at my side,
  to light and guard, to rule and guide. Amen.

22. Anima Christi

- Soul of Christ, sanctify me.
  Body of Christ, save me.
  Blood of Christ, inebriate me.
  Water from the side of Christ, wash me.
  Passion of Christ, strengthen me.
  O good Jesus, hear me.
  Within Your wounds hide me.
  Permit me not to be separated from You.
  From the wicked foe, defend me.
  At the hour of my death, call me
  and bid me come to You,
  that with Your saints I may praise You
  forever and ever. Amen.

23. Litany of the Saints

- Lord, have mercy.
  Christ, have mercy.
  Lord, have mercy.
  Christ, hear us.
  Christ, graciously hear us.
  GOD the Father of Heaven, have mercy on us.
  GOD the Son, Redeemer of the world, have mercy on us.
  GOD the Holy Spirit, have mercy on us.
  Holy Trinity, One GOD, have mercy on us.
  Holy Mary, pray for us.
  Holy Mother of GOD, pray for us.
  Holy Virgin of virgins, pray for us.
  [Here follows the invocation of specific saints]
  All you holy men and women, Saints of GOD, intercede for us.
  Lamb of GOD, who takes away the sins of the world, spare us, O Lord.
  Lamb of GOD, who takes away the sins of the world, graciously hear us, O Lord.
  Lamb of GOD, who takes away the sins of the world, have mercy on us. Amen.

24. Prayer of St. Francis (Make Me an Instrument of Your Peace)

- Lord, make me an instrument of your peace: where there is hatred, let me sow love; where there is injury, pardon; where there is doubt, faith; where there is despair, hope; where there is darkness, light; where there is sadness, joy.

25. Benedictus (The Canticle of Zechariah)

- Blessed be the Lord, the GOD of Israel;
  He has come to His people and set them free.
  He has raised up for us a mighty savior,
  born of the house of His servant David.
  Through His holy prophets, He promised of old
  that He would save us from our enemies,
  from the hands of all who hate us.
  He promised to show mercy to our fathers

and to remember His holy covenant.
This was the oath He swore to our father Abraham:
to set us free from the hands of our enemies,
free to worship Him without fear,
holy and righteous in His sight all the days of our life.
You, my child, shall be called the prophet of the Most High,
for you will go before the Lord to prepare His way,
to give His people knowledge of salvation
by the forgiveness of their sins.
In the tender compassion of our GOD
the dawn from on high shall break upon us,
to shine on those who dwell in darkness and the shadow of death,
and to guide our feet into the way of peace.

Sacred Texts

1. The Holy Bible

- The most important sacred text in Christianity, comprising the Old and New Testaments, and considered the inspired Word of GOD.

2. The Catechism of the Catholic Church

- A comprehensive summary of Catholic doctrine, covering faith, sacraments, morality, and prayer, providing authoritative teaching for Catholics.

3. The Roman Missal

- The official liturgical book containing the prayers, chants, and instructions for the celebration of the Mass.

4. The Liturgy of the Hours (Divine Office)

- The official set of daily prayers marking the hours of each day, recited by clergy, religious, and laity to sanctify the day.

5. The Summa Theologica by St. Thomas Aquinas

- A monumental theological text that systematically presents Catholic teachings on a wide range of theological topics.

6. The Documents of Vatican II

- A collection of key texts from the Second Vatican Council (1962-1965) that address Church doctrine, liturgy, ecumenism, and the modern world.

7. The Rule of St. Benedict

- The foundational text for Western monasticism, outlining the principles of monastic life that emphasize prayer, work, and community.

8. The Spiritual Exercises by St. Ignatius of Loyola

- A guide for spiritual retreat and discernment, focusing on meditations, prayers, and contemplative practices.

9. The Imitation of Christ by Thomas à Kempis

- A spiritual classic that emphasizes the interior life and the imitation of Christ's humility and obedience.

10. The Enchiridion of Indulgences

- A manual listing prayers, devotions, and practices that are granted indulgences by the Catholic Church.

11. The Roman Ritual

- The liturgical book containing the rites for the administration of the sacraments and other sacred acts.

12. The Douay-Rheims Bible

- The English translation of the Bible traditionally used by Catholics before the 20th century, known for its fidelity to the Latin Vulgate.

13. The Glories of Mary by St. Alphonsus Liguori

- A devotional text that extols the virtues and intercessory power of the Blessed Virgin Mary.

14. The Breviary

- The book containing the Divine Office, used for the daily recitation of the Liturgy of the Hours.

15. True Devotion to Mary by St. Louis de Montfort

- A treatise promoting total consecration to Jesus through Mary, highly influential in Marian devotion.

16. The Baltimore Catechism

- A concise summary of Catholic doctrine in question-and-answer format, widely used in Catholic education in the United States.

17. The Little Office of the Blessed Virgin Mary

- A liturgical prayer book traditionally prayed by the laity as a form of daily devotion to the Virgin Mary.

18. The Confessions by St. Augustine

- An autobiographical work that explores Augustine's conversion to Christianity and his reflections on GOD's grace.

19. The Rule of the Secular Franciscan Order

- The guiding document for members of the Secular Franciscan Order, focusing on living the Gospel in the spirit of St. Francis.

20. The Letters of St. Paul

- A collection of epistles in the New Testament that form a significant part of Christian theology and pastoral instruction.

21. The Catechism of the Council of Trent

- A doctrinal manual produced after the Council of Trent to educate clergy and laity on Catholic teachings in response to the Protestant Reformation.

22. The Roman Pontifical

- The liturgical book used by bishops for the administration of sacraments such as confirmation, ordination, and the consecration of churches.

23. The Eastern Catholic Divine Liturgy

- The liturgical texts used in the Divine Liturgy of Eastern Catholic Churches, rich in tradition and theology, often associated with St. John Chrysostom and St. Basil the Great.

24. The Spiritual Canticle by St. John of the Cross

- A mystical poem and commentary that explores the soul's journey toward union with GOD.

25. The Lives of the Saints (Butler's Lives of the Saints)

- A collection of hagiographies that provide spiritual inspiration and examples of holy living through the lives of saints.

Sacred Music

1. Gregorian Chant

- The traditional plainchant of the Roman Catholic Church, characterized by monophonic, unaccompanied vocal music. Examples include the "Kyrie," "Sanctus," and "Agnus Dei."

2. Missa Papae Marcelli by Giovanni Pierluigi da Palestrina

- One of the most famous Mass settings in polyphonic style, composed to demonstrate the clarity of sacred texts in choral music.

3. Ave Maria by Franz Schubert

- A beautiful setting of the traditional Latin prayer, widely performed in both liturgical and concert settings.

4. Ave Verum Corpus by Wolfgang Amadeus Mozart

- A short Eucharistic hymn composed for the Feast of Corpus Christi, renowned for its serenity and beauty.

5. Requiem by Wolfgang Amadeus Mozart

- A powerful and moving setting of the Requiem Mass, completed posthumously, and considered one of the greatest works in the sacred music repertoire.

6. Magnificat by Johann Sebastian Bach

- A vibrant and intricate musical setting of the Magnificat, the Canticle of Mary, performed during Vespers.

7. Stabat Mater by Giovanni Battista Pergolesi

- A poignant setting of the Stabat Mater, a hymn that reflects on the sorrows of the Virgin Mary at the foot of the Cross.

8. Miserere by Gregorio Allegri

- A famous setting of Psalm 51, traditionally sung during the Tenebrae service of Holy Week at the Sistine Chapel.

9. Panis Angelicus by César Franck

- A well-loved Eucharistic hymn that meditates on the mystery of the bread of angels, often sung during Communion.

10. Requiem by Gabriel Fauré

- A more serene and comforting setting of the Requiem Mass, emphasizing themes of rest and eternal peace.

11. Te Deum by Marc-Antoine Charpentier

- A grand and festive setting of the ancient hymn of praise, often performed at major Church celebrations.

12. Dies Irae

- A medieval Latin hymn describing the Last Judgment, traditionally part of the Requiem Mass and set to music by many composers.

13. O Magnum Mysterium by Tomás Luis de Victoria

- A motet for the Christmas season, reflecting on the mystery of the Incarnation with profound simplicity and beauty.

14. Salve Regina

- A Marian antiphon sung at the conclusion of Compline, expressing devotion and petition to the Blessed Virgin Mary.

15. Tantum Ergo by Thomas Aquinas (set by various composers)

- The last two verses of the hymn "Pange Lingua," often sung during Benediction of the Blessed Sacrament.

16. Pange Lingua Gloriosi by Thomas Aquinas (set by various composers)

- A hymn that honors the mystery of the Eucharist, traditionally sung during the procession on Holy Thursday.

17. Gloria from "Missa Solemnis" by Ludwig van Beethoven

- A powerful and joyful setting of the "Gloria" from the Mass, expressing the glory of GOD.

18. Veni Creator Spiritus

- A hymn invoking the Holy Spirit, traditionally sung at Pentecost and during the ordination of priests.

19. O Sacred Head, Now Wounded by J.S. Bach

- A Passion hymn meditating on the suffering of Christ, part of Bach's "St. Matthew Passion."

20. Jesu, Joy of Man's Desiring by Johann Sebastian Bach

- A beloved chorale, often performed during weddings and other sacred occasions, expressing devotion to Christ.

21. Lauda Sion by St. Thomas Aquinas (set by various composers)

- A sequence hymn for the Feast of Corpus Christi, praising the Eucharist.

22. Hodie Christus Natus Est by Giovanni Gabrieli

- A joyful motet celebrating the birth of Christ, often performed at Christmas.

23. Puer Natus Est Nobis

- An ancient Gregorian chant introit for Christmas Day, celebrating the birth of the Savior.

24. Ave Maris Stella

- A Marian hymn, traditionally sung during Vespers, invoking the intercession of the "Star of the Sea."

25. Lamentations of Jeremiah by Thomas Tallis

- A setting of the biblical Lamentations, traditionally sung during Holy Week, known for its deep emotional and spiritual intensity.

SUGGESTED READING LIST

1. The Holy Bible (New Revised Standard Version)
- The foundation of Christian faith and practice, containing the Old and New Testaments.

2. Catechism of the Catholic Church
- A comprehensive summary of Catholic doctrine, covering faith, morals, and the sacraments.

3. Confessions by Augustine of Hippo
- A spiritual autobiography of one of the Church's greatest theologians, offering profound insights into sin, grace, and conversion.

4. Summa Theologica by Thomas Aquinas
- A monumental work of theology and philosophy, systematically exploring the nature of God, ethics, and the sacraments.

5. The Imitation of Christ by Thomas à Kempis
- A classic of Christian spirituality, emphasizing humility, devotion, and the imitation of Christ's life.

6. The Interior Castle by Teresa of Ávila
- A mystical text that describes the soul's journey through various stages of spiritual development, leading to union with God.

7. The Dark Night of the Soul by John of the Cross
- A profound exploration of spiritual desolation and the soul's path to divine union.

8. City of God by Augustine of Hippo

- A theological and philosophical defense of Christianity, addressing the relationship between the Church and the secular world.

9. Mere Christianity by C.S. Lewis

- A clear and accessible explanation of Christian beliefs, written by one of the most influential Christian apologists of the 20th century.

10. The Divine Comedy by Dante Alighieri

- An epic poem that explores the themes of sin, redemption, and the afterlife, offering a rich allegorical journey through Hell, Purgatory, and Heaven.

11. The Story of a Soul by Thérèse of Lisieux

- The autobiography of St. Thérèse of Lisieux, which introduced her "little way" of spiritual childhood and trust in God.

12. The Rule of St. Benedict

- The foundational text of Western monasticism, outlining the principles of communal living, prayer, and work.

13. The Confessions of St. Patrick

- The spiritual memoir of Ireland's patron saint, recounting his life and missionary work.

14. The Spiritual Exercises by Ignatius of Loyola

- A manual for spiritual retreat and meditation, used widely in Jesuit formation and Catholic spiritual practice.

15. The Life of St. Francis of Assisi by St. Bonaventure

- A hagiographical account of the life of St. Francis, emphasizing his radical commitment to poverty.

16. On the Trinity by Augustine of Hippo

- A theological treatise exploring the nature of the Holy Trinity, one of the most challenging and central doctrines of the Catholic faith.

17. Introduction to the Devout Life by Francis de Sales

- A guide to living a holy life in the midst of the world, emphasizing the possibility of sanctity for all, not just for clergy or religious.

18. The City of God by Augustine of Hippo

- A seminal work that defends Christianity against paganism and outlines a vision of human history as a conflict between the City of God and the City of Man.

19. The Divine Office (Liturgy of the Hours)

- The official set of prayers marking the hours of each day, sanctifying the day with prayer and scripture.

20. The Lamb's Supper: The Mass as Heaven on Earth by Scott Hahn

- A theological exploration of the Mass, drawing connections between the Eucharist and the Book of Revelation.

21. The Mystical Theology by Pseudo-Dionysius the Areopagite

- An influential text in Christian mysticism, focusing on the ineffable nature of God and the journey toward divine union.

22. Orthodoxy by G.K. Chesterton

- A defense of Christian orthodoxy and a witty exploration of faith, reason, and paradox.

23. Introduction to Christianity by Joseph Ratzinger (Pope Benedict XVI)

- A profound and accessible introduction to the central beliefs of the Christian faith, written by one of the most important theologians of the 20th century.

24. The Confessions of St. Augustine

- Another essential work by Augustine, offering a personal reflection on his life, his conversion, and his understanding of God.

25. The Wounded Healer by Henri J.M. Nouwen

- A reflection on ministry and spiritual life, emphasizing the role of vulnerability and suffering in the process of healing.